perfect
party cakes
made easy

perfect
party cakes
made easy

Carol Deacon

NH
NEW
HOLLAND

Contents

Introduction

The trouble with birthdays, anniversaries and Christmas is that they keep on coming. Just when you think you've made the ultimate cake for a celebration, another occasion appears on the horizon and you're back to square one, thinking 'What on earth shall I make for them this year?'

Hopefully, this book will inspire you with enough suggestions and ideas to keep all your family and friends in cakes for a long time to come, with the minimum of fuss or purchase of expensive cake decorating equipment on your part.

Feel free to alter and adapt the designs or invent shortcuts wherever you wish. For instance, if you are in a hurry and don't wish to cover a cake board, then simply leave it plain. If you don't have time to make lots of characters, then just make one. If you have another technique you are more familiar with, perhaps for making roses, use that instead of the one I suggest. There is no ultimate 'right' way of doing things – just use the method you feel happiest with and make your own unique creation.

Above all, don't be scared of having a go!

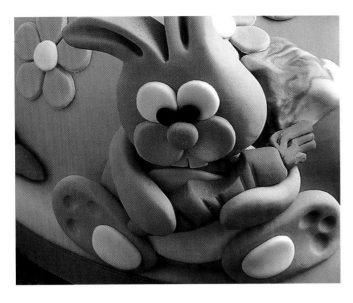

Techniques and materials

Most of the cakes featured in this book can be assembled from shop-bought cakes and, if you're really pressed for time, that's a perfectly satisfactory alternative to baking your own. However, many cake decorating enthusiasts enjoy baking, and on the following pages I have provided everything you need to know to make a successful cake, whether it be chocolate, sponge or fruit, and in a variety of shapes and sizes. There are also recipes for different icings and tips to save you time and money. Finally, I have explained - with clear step-by-step photographs - the basic techniques that will enable you to put together a party cake in no time at all!

Basic recipes

If you are going to spend time making the outside of a cake look spectacular, it is worth making the same effort to ensure that the inside tastes wonderful too. These recipes have been tried and tested on friends and family on numerous occasions and get the thumbs up every time. Both the madeira and the chocolate cake will freeze well (undecorated) for up to three months.

Madeira sponge cake

This is one of my favourite recipes as it is so quick and easy to do – you just throw everything in the bowl together and mix. The cake it produces has a firm yet moist texture and is excellent for carving into irregular shapes.

Square tin		15 cm (6 in)*	18 cm (7 in)	20 cm (8 in)
Round tin	15 cm (6 in)	18 cm (7 in)	20 cm (8 in)	23 cm (9 in)
Self-raising flour	170 g (6 oz/1½ cups)	230 g (8 oz/2 cups)	350 g (12 oz/2½ cups)	450 g (1 lb/4 cups)
Caster sugar	115 g (4 oz/½ cup)	170 g (6 oz/¾ cup)	285 g (10 oz/1½ cups)	400 g (14 oz/1½ cups)
Soft margarine	115 g (4 oz/½ cups)	170 g (6 oz/¾ cups)	285 g (10 oz/1¼ cups)	400 g (14 oz/1¾ cups)
Eggs (medium)	2	3	5	7
Milk	15 ml (1 tbsp)	30 ml (2 tbsp)	45 ml (3 tbsp)	52 ml (3½ tbsp)
Baking time (approx)	1–1¼ hrs	1¼–1½ hrs	1½–1¾ hrs	1¾–2 hrs

* **Pudding bowl and loaf tin cakes** – if you are baking a cake in a 1 litre (1¾ pint) pudding bowl or 900 g (2 lb) loaf tin for cakes such as the Twitcher (page 146) or Sports Car (page 154), follow the recipe amounts for the 15 cm (6 in) **square** cake and grease and line the bowl/tin as usual.

Method
1 Grease and line the relevant cake tin or bowl and pre-heat the oven to 150°C/300°F/Gas 2.
2 Sift the flour into a mixing bowl and add all the other ingredients. Bind all the ingredients together, carefully, using a slow setting on your mixer, then once the ingredients have combined, increase the speed and beat for one minute.

3 Spoon the mixture into the prepared baking tin and smooth the top.
4 Cook in the centre of the oven for the specified time. Test the cake by lightly pressing the centre. It should spring back and the top should be golden brown. To be extra sure, insert a skewer. If it comes out clean, the cake is cooked. Leave in the tin for five minutes, then turn out to cool on a wire tray.

Variations
It's easy to vary the flavour of the cake. Add the zest of a lemon or orange to the mix before cooking for a citrus touch. Alternatively, a teaspoon of almond essence or 60 g (2 oz) of desiccated coconut can add a hint of something from the Caribbean.

Chocolate sponge cake

The secret of a good, strong chocolate cake is to use good, strong chocolate in the baking. Use chocolate with a high percentage of cocoa solids (preferably 70 per cent). This recipe is superb because the cake it produces has a soft, velvety texture yet is strong enough to withstand being carved into shapes. A crust will form on the top as it cooks. Slice this off and discard, or sell to the highest bidder before decorating!

Square tin		15 cm (6 in)	18 cm (7 in)	20 cm (8 in)
Round tin	15 cm (6 in)	18 cm (7 in)	20 cm (8 in)	23 cm (9 in)
Butter	90 g (3 oz/6 tbsp)	115 g (4 oz/½ cup)	170 g (6 oz/¾ cup)	230 g (8 oz/1 cup)
Caster sugar	40 g (1¾ oz/3½ tbsp)	75 g (2½ oz/5½ tbsp)	115 g (4 oz/½ cup)	150 g (5 oz/¾ cup)
Eggs (medium), separated	3	4	6	8
Plain chocolate	150 g (5 oz)	170 g (6 oz)	230 g (8 oz)	285 g (10 oz)
Self-raising flour	90 g (3 oz/¾ cup)	115 g (4 oz/1 cup)	170 g (6 oz/1½ cup)	230 g (8 oz/2 cups)
Icing sugar	30 g (1 oz/¼ cup)	30 g (1 oz/¼ cup)	60 g (2 oz/⅓ cup)	90 g (3 oz/¾ cup)
Baking time (approx)	40–55 mins	45 mins–1 hr	1–1¼ hrs	1–1¼ hrs

Method

1 Pre-heat the oven to 180°C/350°F/Gas 4. Grease and line the relevant tin and separate the eggs.
2 Melt the chocolate either in a small bowl over a saucepan of boiling water or in a heat-proof bowl in the microwave.
3 Cream the butter and caster sugar together until light and fluffy.
4 Beat in the egg yolks and, once they are mixed in smoothly, add the melted chocolate.
5 Set the mixer to a slow speed and carefully add the flour.
6 Scrape the chocolate mixture into a spare bowl and quickly wash and dry the mixing bowl. It is important to get rid of any grease. (If you have a spare bowl for your mixer, just swap them over.)
7 Attach the whisk attachment to your mixer and whisk the egg whites into stiff peaks. Whisk in the icing sugar.
8 Re-attach the beater to the mixer and slowly mix the chocolate mixture into the egg whites. Pour the mixture into the baking tin and bake for the required time.
9 Due to the crust, it may be difficult to tell if the cake has baked from touch alone so insert a skewer or knife. If it comes out clean, the cake should be cooked. Turn out and cool on a wire tray.

Fruit cake

Although it's tempting to buy a shop-bought fruit cake, especially at Christmas, it means you miss out on two wonderful benefits. Firstly, the sumptuous cooking smells of cinnamon and spices filling the house and secondly, the chance to stir the mixture and make a wish!

Don't try to skip double-lining the side and base of the tin with greaseproof paper or wrapping a double layer of brown paper secured with string around the outside – it really does protect the outside of the cake as it cooks.

Square tin	15 cm (6 in)	18 cm (7 in)	20 cm (8 in)
Round tin	18 cm (7 in)	20 cm (8 in)	23 cm (9 in)
Currants	150 g (5 oz/1 cup)	175 g (6 oz/1 heaped cup)	200 g (7 oz/1½ cups)
Sultanas	150 g (5 oz/1 cup)	175 g (6 oz/1 heaped cup)	200 g (7 oz/1½ cups)
Raisins	150 g (5 oz/1 cup)	175 g (6 oz/1 heaped cup)	200 g (7 oz/1½ cups)
Mixed peel	30 g (1 oz/¼ cup)	40 g (1½ oz/3 tbsp)	60 g (2 oz/½ cup)
Halved glacé cherries	60 g (2 oz/⅓ cup)	70 g (2½ oz/½ cup)	90 g (3 oz/¾ cup)
Brandy	60 ml (4 tbsp)	90 ml (6 tbsp)	120 ml (8 tbsp)
Butter	150 g (5 oz/½ cup)	175 g (6 oz/¾ cup)	200 g (7 oz/¾ cup)
Soft dark brown sugar	150 g (5 oz/1 packed cup)	175 g (6 oz/1 heaped cup)	200 g (7 oz/1½ cups)
Eggs (medium)	3	4	6
Plain flour	175 g (6 oz/1½ cups)	200 g (7 oz/1¾ cups)	230 g (8 oz/2 cups)
Mixed spice	2 tsp	1 tbsp	1 tbsp
Lemons (zest only)	1	1	1
Ground almonds	20 g (¾ oz/¼ cup)	30 g (1 oz/⅓ cup)	40 g (1½ oz/½ cup)
Flaked almonds	20 g (¾ oz/¼ cup)	30 g (1 oz/⅓ cup)	40 g (1½ oz/½ cup)
Cinnamon	1 tsp	1 tsp	1½ tsp
Baking time (approx)	1½–2 hrs	2–2¼ hrs	2 ¼–2½ hrs

Method

1 Place all the dried fruits in a mixing bowl. Pour over the brandy. Stir and cover, and leave to stand overnight.

2 Grease the cake tin. Double line the inside of the tin with greaseproof paper. Tie two strips of brown paper around the outside of the tin and secure with string. Pre-heat the oven to 150°C/300°F/Gas 2.

3 Cream together the butter and sugar, then beat in the eggs. Mix in the sifted flour, spices and ground almonds.

4 Stir in the soaked fruits, lemon zest and flaked almonds.

5 Spoon into the tin, level the surface and bake. Check the cake about 15 minutes before the cooking time is up. If the top seems to be browning too much, place some greaseproof paper over the top. To test the cake when its cooking time is up, insert a skewer. If it comes out clean, the cake is baked. If not, place the cake back in the oven and test again at 15-minute intervals.

6 Allow the cake to cool completely in the tin before turning out and removing the paper.

7 To store the cake, pierce the top of the cake with a cocktail stick a number of times and drizzle a little brandy into the holes. Double wrap the cake in greaseproof paper and then in aluminium foil. Store in a box or tin (never a plastic storage box) and 'feed' about once a week with a little brandy. Maximum storage time is about three months.

Microwave cakes

Although personally I don't think you can beat the real thing, microwave cakes do have their place. Well, with only four minutes' cooking time you can't really go wrong! They do have a slightly different texture to a cake baked in a conventional way and because they don't brown on top like ordinary cakes, they look a bit anaemic when they first come out. But by the time you have smoothed some

icing over them or a thick covering of buttercream, I don't think you'll find anyone complaining. It's also fascinating watching them rise through the window of the microwave – a bit like television! These amounts are for an 18 cm (7 in) round microwave cake tin or a 1 litre (1¾ pint) heat-proof pudding bowl. **Never** use a metal cake tin in the microwave oven.

Vanilla cake

Ingredients
120 g (4 oz/½ cup) butter
120 g (4 oz/½ cup) caster sugar
2 large eggs
1 tsp vanilla essence
120 g (4 oz/1 cup) self-raising flour
½ tsp baking powder

1 Grease and line the microwave dish.
2 Cream the butter and sugar together until light and fluffy.
3 Beat in the eggs and vanilla essence.
4 Stir in the flour and baking powder.
5 Spoon into the prepared dish and cook on full power for four minutes. Leave to stand for about ten minutes before turning out.

Chocolate cake

Ingredients
120 g (4 oz/½ cup) butter
120 g (4 oz/½ cup) caster sugar
2 large eggs
90 g (3 oz/¾ cup) self-raising flour and 1 tsp baking powder
30 g (1 oz/¼ cup) unsweetened cocoa powder

1 Follow steps 1–3 as for the vanilla cake above (omitting the vanilla essence in step 3).
2 Stir in the flour, cocoa and baking powder.
3 Cook on full power for four minutes and leave to stand for ten minutes before turning out.

Stock syrup

This is the baker's secret! If you have to decorate a sponge cake a few days in advance of when it will be eaten, you can use a little stock syrup to ensure that the cake will still be wonderfully moist.

Ingredients
100 g (4 oz/½ cup) caster sugar
150 ml (⅛ pint/⅔ cup) water

1 Put the sugar and water in a saucepan and stir together.
2 Heat and bring to the boil.
3 Simmer gently for 2 - 3 minutes until the sugar has completely dissolved, then allow to cool.

To use, slice the cake in half as normal but before spreading it with buttercream, 'paint' the top side of each layer with the syrup, using a pastry brush. Allow it to soak in slightly but don't saturate the cake. Then spread with buttercream, reassemble the cake and decorate as usual. For an extra special cake, flavour the syrup with a spirit or liqueur (a dash of rum works especially well with chocolate cake!).

Stock syrup can be stored in the fridge in a screw-top jar for up to two weeks. This quantity should be enough for two cakes, but it really depends on the sizes of the cakes, the number of layers you divide them into and how liberally you apply the syrup.

Icing recipes

Buttercream

As you will notice, I tend to use buttercream a lot on my cakes, the main reason being its versatility. As well as being used to fill and provide a covering for cakes before they are decorated, it can also be coloured, stippled or piped. I find it makes the best base for covering a cake because as you spread it, it fills in any little holes in the sponge, leaving a perfectly smooth surface. However, feel free to substitute other fillings, such as jam, if you prefer.

After you have coated the cake in buttercream, if you have time, place the cake in the fridge for an hour so the cake can 'set up'. This will help to prevent the cake moving about or collapsing as you cover it and will also stop the buttercream from oozing out of the sides. When you take the cake out of the fridge, spread another thin layer of buttercream over the top and sides of the cake to give the sugarpaste a good surface to adhere to.

Buttercream can be frozen in an airtight plastic container in the freezer for up to three months.

Ingredients
250 g (9 oz/2 cups) unsalted butter (softened)
500 g (1 lb 2 oz/4½ cups) icing sugar (sieved)
½ tsp vanilla extract
1 tbsp hot water

1 Place the butter in a bowl and mix until light and fluffy.
2 Carefully mix in the sugar, vanilla and water and beat well. If you beat it on quite a fast speed for about 5 minutes, it should turn virtually white which is extremely useful if you are going to use it to make waves on cakes such as the Deep Sea Fishing cake on page 178.

Variations

For chocolate buttercream, flavour the icing with either 100 g (3½ oz) melted plain chocolate or 1 tablespoon of cocoa mixed into 2 tablespoons of hot water. For coffee, mix 1 tablespoon of instant coffee into a paste with 1 tablespoon of water and add to the buttercream. Alternatively, instead of the vanilla, substitute a different flavoured essence such as peppermint, lemon or almond instead.

Sugarpaste

Ready-made sugarpaste (or rolled fondant icing) is a great time saver and can usually be found in the supermarket. It may be called something like 'ready-to-roll' icing. There are a number of brands available and it's worth experimenting to see which one you find easiest to work with. Alternatively, your local cake decoration equipment shop should stock sugarpaste in various colours or you could try a specialist mail order company.

In case you have problems obtaining sugarpaste, here is a simple home-made version that works just as well as the commercial brands. See page 19 for instructions on colouring sugarpaste.

Sugarpaste using real egg white should be used as soon as possible. If made with dried egg albumen, use the sugarpaste within a week.

Ingredients
500 g (1 lb 2 oz/4½ cups) icing sugar
1 egg white (or preferably, the equivalent amount of dried egg white mixed with water)
30 ml (2 tbsp) liquid glucose (available from chemists, drug stores, cake decorating equipment shops and some supermarkets)

1 Place the icing sugar in a bowl and make a well in the centre.
2 Tip the egg white and glucose into the well and stir in with a wooden spoon.
3 Finish binding the icing together with your hands, kneading until all the sugar is incorporated. The sugarpaste should feel silky and smooth.
4 Store immediately in a plastic bag.

Colouring sugar or desiccated coconut

If you are pressed for time, this is a quicker way to cover a cake board than using rolled out sugarpaste. If coloured green, the sugar or coconut makes realistic-looking grass. For a watery look, use blue food colour. Place the sugar or coconut into a small bowl and add a small amount of food colour (use paste, not liquid). Mix in the colour, adding more if necessary until you achieve the required shade.

Royal icing

Traditionally, royal icing is always made with egg whites. However, because of the slight risk of salmonella poisoning, I try to avoid using real eggs wherever possible. Most supermarkets and all cake decorating shops sell dried egg white (it may be called dried egg albumen, easy egg or even meringue powder) which produces icing just as good as the real thing. Read the instructions on the packet in case the amounts differ slightly from the ones I've given here.

Ingredients

20 g (½ oz/1 tbsp) dried egg white
90 ml (2½ fl oz/5 tbsp) cold water
500 g (1 lb 2 oz/4½ cups) icing sugar

1 Mix the egg white and water together until smooth.
2 Sieve the icing sugar into a grease-free bowl.
3 Tip in the egg mixture and, if using an electric mixer, beat on a slow speed for five minutes until the icing stands up in peaks.
4 Place the icing into a bowl and lay a piece of plastic cling film directly on top of the icing. Place an airtight lid on the bowl and keep covered at all times when not in use.

Gelatin icing

Gelatin icing is an extremely useful icing to have in your repertoire because it sets very hard. It can be used to make things that you want to stand proud from the cake (from delicate flowers and leaves to flags, sails or even turrets as in the Fairy-tale Castle cake on page 100). It can also be moulded over objects and left to take on their shape. It can be coloured in the same way as sugarpaste and also has the added benefit of being usable straight away.

TIP: If, when you come to use it, you find that either the gelatin or modelling icing has become too hard, you can soften it by microwaving it on full power for just 4–5 seconds.

Ingredients

60 ml (4 tbsp) water
1 sachet (approx 12 g /1 oz or enough to set 600 ml/1 pint) gelatin powder
10 ml (2 tsp) liquid glucose
500 g (1 lb 2 oz/4½ cups) icing sugar
1–4 tbsp cornflour

1 Place the water in a small, heat-proof bowl. Sprinkle the gelatin over the top and leave it to soak for about two minutes. Sieve the icing sugar into a mixing bowl and make a well in the centre.
2 Put about 1 cm (⅜ in) of water into a saucepan. Stand the bowl in the water and heat gently until the gelatin dissolves.
3 Remove the bowl from the water and stir in the liquid glucose. Allow to cool for a minute.
4 Tip the gelatin mixture into the centre of the icing sugar. Using a knife, begin to stir it in. When it has bound together, knead it into a bread-dough consistency adding cornflour as required. Store in small plastic bags until required.

Modelling icing

There is a vegetarian equivalent of gelatin available but even though I have tried three times, I cannot manage to make a modelling paste of useable quality. Therefore, I have included this recipe which uses gum traganth (a powder that comes from a tree). The only slight disadvantage is that at present you can only obtain the gum from specialist cake decorating shops (find your nearest in the phone book or see the suppliers list on page 188 for mail order). Also, in theory, after you have made up the paste you should leave it tightly wrapped in two plastic bags for at least eight hours. This gives the gum time to work and makes the paste more stretchy and pliable. However, as I never seem to have a spare eight hours, I have used it straight away with perfectly acceptable results. Keep it tightly wrapped when not in use as it hardens very quickly.

Ingredients

500 g (1 lb 2 oz/4½ cups) icing sugar
30 ml (2 tbsp) gum traganth
10 ml (2 tsp) liquid glucose
60 ml (4 tbsp) cold water
Cornflour
(You may find it easier to halve the above quantities and make it in two lots. For the turrets on the Fairy-tale Castle Cake on page 100, you will need to make the full amount.)

1 Mix the icing sugar and gum together in a mixing bowl and make a well in the centre.
2 Pour in the glucose and water and mix together. Knead to a bread-like consistency on a surface dusted with cornflour. Place inside two plastic bags and, if you have time, leave for eight hours before use.

Basic techniques

From dealing with air bubbles to getting rid of dusty icing sugar marks, this section should help you to achieve a really professional finish.

Covering a cake

When using sugarpaste to cover a cake, always roll it out on a surface dusted with icing sugar to prevent it sticking to your worksurface. Never use flour or cornflour. Roll it out approximately 15 cm (6 in) larger than the top of the cake to allow enough icing to cover the sides as well. It should be 5–8 mm (⅛–¼ in) thick. You can either lift and place the icing over the top of the cake – as you would pastry – using a rolling pin, or slide your hands, palms uppermost, underneath the icing and lift it, keeping your hands flat. Smooth over the top and sides using the palm of your hand and trim away the excess from the base with a sharp knife (fig 1). For a really professional finish, use a pair of cake smoothers. Starting at the top, run them over the surface of the cake to expel any air and iron out any lumps and bumps (fig 2).

If a large, unsightly air bubble develops, prick it with a clean dressmaker's needle or cocktail stick held at an angle, then carefully press out the air.

Covering the cake board

All-in-one

This is the easiest way to cover a cake board with the cake placed on top afterwards. Moisten the entire board with water and begin to roll out a ball of sugarpaste on your worksurface. Lift and place the icing on to the board and continue to roll it out just over the edge of the board (fig 3). Run a cake smoother over the surface and trim and neaten the edges.

The bandage method

This is done after the cake itself has been covered. Run a tape measure around the side of the cake and cut a strip of icing that length and slightly wider than the exposed cake board. Roll the icing up like a bandage and moisten the cake board with water. Starting from the back of the cake, slowly unwind the 'bandage' over the board (fig 4). Run a cake smoother over the icing and trim and neaten the edges.

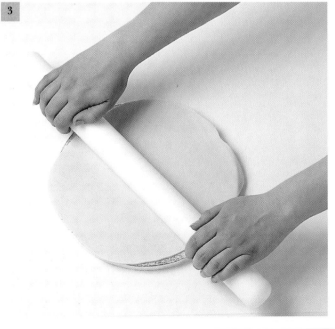

4

Covering the board around an awkward-shaped cake

Although covering a board after the cake is in position might look more difficult than covering it all-in-one and placing the cake on top afterwards, it is easier than it looks and has one distinct advantage. Because you slide the sugarpaste (rolled fondant icing) up against the edge of the cake, it makes a neater join at the base of the cake.

Moisten the cake board with a little water. Thinly roll out the sugarpaste and cover the exposed board in sections *(fig 6)*. Run a cake smoother over the surface to flatten any lumps and trim away the excess from the edges using a sharp knife.

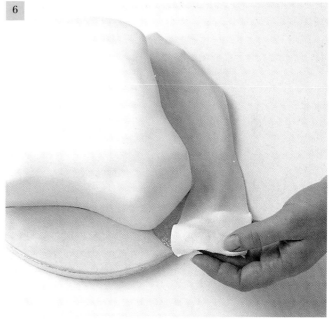

6

The fabric effect

This is also done after the cake itself has been covered. Measure around the cake and cut a strip of icing about 10 cm (4 in) longer than that length and about 4 cm (1 ½ in) wider than the exposed board. Moisten the cake board and roll up the icing like a bandage. Unwind it allowing the icing to fall into folds around the cake as you go *(fig 5)*. Press down the icing at the edges and trim away any excess.

Edging the cake board

You can neaten the outer edge of the cake board by sticking small strips of double-sided tape around the board and attaching a length of ribbon to it.

Painting on Sugarpaste

Always use food colour to paint with on your cake. The paste colours work best. Also, if possible, leave the covered cake overnight to harden. This will stop you denting the cake if you lean on it.

First brush the area to be painted using a large brush or pastry brush to get rid of any excess icing sugar which could cause the colours to bleed.

Place a few dabs of paste food colour on to a saucer and 'let down' slightly with a little water. If you wish, paint a very light and pale outline of the image onto the cake first to use as a guide. Then fill it in.

Paint onto the cake as you would watercolour, mixing the colours to achieve different shades. If painting a heavy black food colour outline around your images, do this after you have painted the middles. (If you do it first it will bleed into the central colour.)

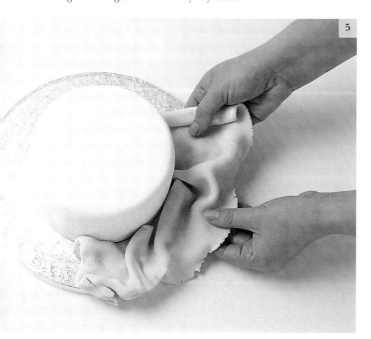

5

1 Cut some greaseproof (waxed) paper into a triangle.

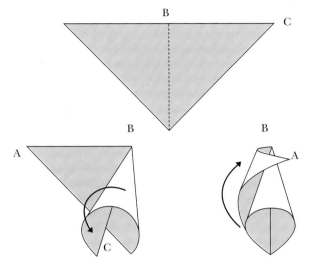

2 Pick up corner 'C' and fold over, so that 'B' forms a sharp cone in the centre.

3 Wrap corner 'A' around the cone.

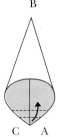 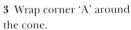 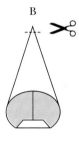

4 Make sure that both 'A' and 'C' are at the back and that the point of the cone is sharp.

5 Fold points 'A' and 'C' inside the top edge of the bag to hold it securely. Snip off the end and insert a piping nozzle.

To remove mistakes, gently rub and break up the painted error using a soft paintbrush dipped into clean water. Then wipe away with a clean, damp cloth.

Making a piping bag

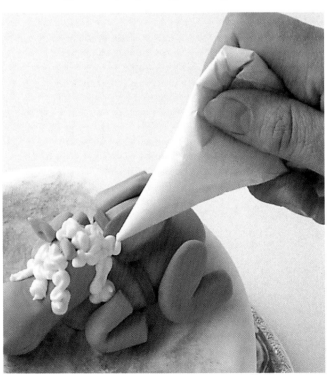

Hints and tips

● A lot of the hard work can be taken out of kneading marzipan (almond paste) by heating it for a few seconds in a microwave. However, don't overdo it or the oil in the centre of the marzipan will get very hot and can give you a nasty burn.

● After you've painstakingly covered your cake with sugarpaste (rolled fondant icing), you might find that an unsightly air bubble has appeared on the surface. Simply prick the bulge with a clean dressmaker's pin and gently press the area flat.

● Get rid of any dusty icing sugar marks after you have finished by wiping away with either a clean damp cloth or paintbrush. Be careful when cleaning dark colours such as red, black or dark green as they bleed easily.

● Clingfilm (plastic wrap) can not only be used to wrap the sugarpaste but, scrunched up into a ball, it can act as a support for things that are drying.

Modelling sugarpaste

Colouring

When colouring sugarpaste, always try to use paste food colours. Liquid colour tends to make the sugarpaste soggy, especially if you are trying to achieve a deep colour. Apply the colour with a knife or cocktail stick and knead in. Most of the colours wash off easily but to protect your hands and especially nails from staining, you could wear rubber or plastic gloves when colouring the icing.

It is also possible to colour white sugarpaste by mixing it with coloured sugarpaste. For instance, knead a small lump of black icing into a large chunk of white to produce grey.

To achieve a flesh tone for modelling people, the best colour I have found for white tones is paprika food colour paste. This can be found in all cake decorating equipment shops, but if you cannot find it, knead a little pink and yellow sugarpaste into some white. For darker skin tones, colour the icing with dark brown food colour paste or knead white and brown sugarpaste together. For Asian tones, I use autumn leaf food colour paste mixed with a little paprika.

It is best to make up all your colours before you start on a cake and to store them in small plastic food bags when not in use. When you have finished your cake, keep it out of direct sunlight or you may find some of the colours fade before the party.

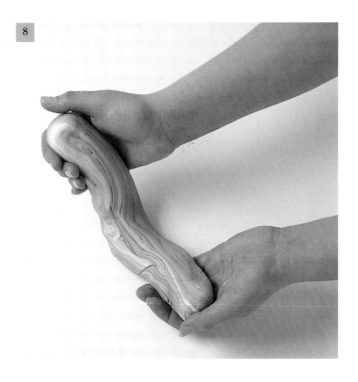

8

Woodgrain effect

Woodgrain is an easy effect to achieve and can be done in two ways. One way is to roll a lump of white sugarpaste into a sausage and apply dashes of brown food colour with a knife *(fig 7)*. Alternatively, roll a couple of lumps of brown and white sugarpaste together into a sausage. Then fold the sugarpaste in half and roll it into a sausage again. Repeat until you see a streaky, wood effect appearing *(fig 8)*, then roll it out and use as usual.

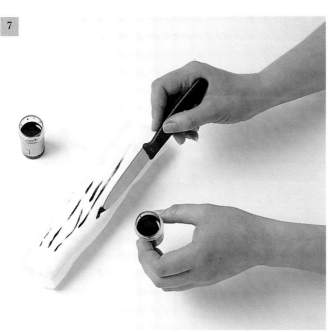

7

Marbling

Like all the best tricks, this looks stunning but is in fact extremely easy to do. Simply take a ball of white sugarpaste and partially knead in a small ball of coloured sugarpaste or a few streaks of food colour *(fig 9)*. Then

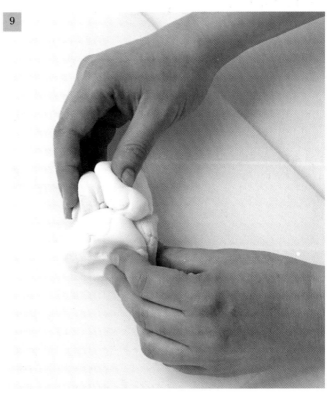

9

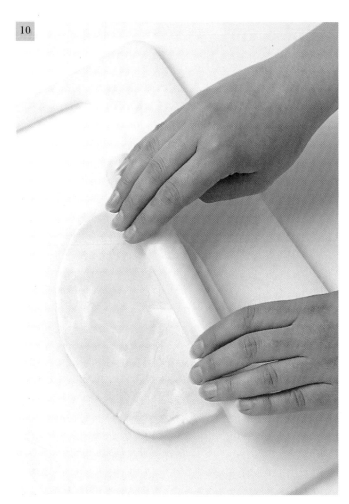

simply roll out the icing as usual *(fig 10)*. If you go too far and the icing turns into a solid colour, simply reverse the process by partially kneading some white sugarpaste back in and rolling out again.

Cleaning and rectifying mistakes on sugarpaste

To clean any mistakes made when painting with food colour, gently rub the error with a paintbrush dipped in clean water to dissipate the colour. Then wipe away with a clean, damp cloth.

To remove dusty icing sugar marks from the finished cake, simply wipe them away with a soft, damp paintbrush.

Making figures

Although they may initially look complicated, if you take the figures apart *(figs 11 and 12)* you will see that in fact they are comprised of very simple shapes – usually just a head, body, legs and arms. Once you have mastered the basic components you can place them in any position you wish, although it is much easier to make a sitting or lying down figure rather than a standing one. Sit them on top of the cake itself surrounded by other 'props', such as on the Handyman Cake on page 106 or in an armchair. Another fun way to present figures is to stick them around the sides of the cake. You can then use the sides of the cake for additional support.

Stick the figures together using water. The secret is not to use too much, especially for small items such as ears, otherwise they will just slide off the head.

When it comes to the clothes, you can paint patterns with food colour or add fine details such as buttons made out of flattened dots of sugarpaste or circles pressed into the icing with an implement like a drinking straw.

To check whether the proportions of a figure are anywhere near accurate, try to imagine how the character would move with the limbs that you've given him. If he stood up, would his legs be too short? Can he scratch his nose with his hands?

When it comes to the facial details, there are many ways to give your figure expression *(fig 13)*. The eyes can be comprised of just the most minimal dots and lines, or they could be painted with food colour or built up from small discs of coloured sugarpaste. Usually, the ears and

top of the nose should be level with the eyes. Think about it – it would be impossible to wear glasses if they weren't!

For maximum cuteness, children and cuddly animal types usually have bigger eyes than adults.

The mouth can be painted or made by pressing something small and circular, such as a drinking straw, into the icing to make a smile or a frown. Make a small hole with the end of a paintbrush and your figure will look instantly surprised.

To ring the changes, I have tried to use different methods of making faces on different cakes. Don't be scared of taking an element from one cake and using it on another.

To achieve a certain expression, it is sometimes easier to draw it out on a piece of paper first. You may also find it helpful to use a mirror to see what your own features do if you pull your face a certain way.

When it comes to the hair, again there are many ways of making this. It could be piped or smeared on in royal icing or buttercream. It could be cut out of strips of sugarpaste. Base the hairstyle on that of the recipient and use the method most apt.

Add any distinguishing features such as glasses, beards or moustaches and as any great cartoonist does, exaggerate (without being too cruel, obviously!).

Making animals

As with the figures, if you actually take a model of an animal apart, you will see that it comprises extremely simple-to-make shapes. For instance,

the dog (*fig 14*) is made from a couple of conical shapes stuck on top of each other and decorated with two oval ears and a few spots. The cat is even simpler, made from a sausage of sugarpaste curled up to look as though the cat is sound asleep, with just a pair of ears pinched out of one end.

If you are making a whole cake in the shape of an animal, it is worthwhile making a small model out of sugarpaste first. This allows you to experiment with proportions and colours without wasting vast amounts of materials. Making a small model will also often give you an idea of how the final full-sized cake could be improved.

14

Basic Equipment

SIEVE (STRAINER) Vital for sifting flour and icing sugar. Also a useful tool for making bushes or hair by simply pushing a lump of sugarpaste through the mesh.

MIXING BOWLS Even the simplest cake uses more than one bowl, so a good selection of bowls is useful.

CAKE SMOOTHERS By using a smoother like an iron, and running it over the surface of a covered cake, small bumps and lumps can literally be ironed out. Essential for achieving a smooth professional finish.

MEASURING SPOONS A set of standard spoons ensures that you use the same quantities each time you re-make a recipe.

DRINKING STRAWS These can be used as tiny circle cutters and are ideal for making eyes. Held at an angle and pressed into sugarpaste, they can also be used for making the scales on dragons or snakes.

PIPING NOZZLES OR TUBES A varied selection is always useful and they can always double up as small circle cutters. Metal nozzles are more expensive than plastic but are sharper and more accurate.

COCKTAIL STICKS They can be used as hidden supports inside models, for adding food colour to sugarpaste, and for making frills and dotty patterns.

TURNTABLE Although not strictly speaking essential, once you've used one, you'll wonder what you ever did without it. Cheaper versions are available in plastic.

RULER Not just for measuring, a ruler can also be useful for pressing lines and patterns into sugarpaste.

SCISSORS A decent pair of sharp scissors is essential for shaping ribbons, snipping the ends off piping bags, cutting linings for tins, and sometimes sugarpaste.

TAPE MEASURE Handy for measuring cakes and boards to ensure that you have rolled out enough sugarpaste to go around.

COOLING RACK Available in all shapes and sizes, and used for cooling cakes.

SMALL DISHES Useful for holding water when modelling, icing sugar when rolling out sugarpaste. Also ideal when mixing food colour into small quantities of royal icing.

BAKING TINS A good assortment of shapes and sizes is useful.

ROLLING PIN A long rolling pin like the one shown will not leave handle dents behind in the sugarpaste. Tiny ones are also available and are handy for rolling out small quantities of sugarpaste when modelling. If you don't possess a small rolling pin, a paintbrush handle will often do the job just as well.

CUTTERS A vast range is available in both plastic and metal.

SOFT PASTRY BRUSH It is useful to have two – one for dampening or cleaning large areas, the other for brushing away dusty fingerprints or specks of dried sugarpaste.

PAINTBRUSHES A selection of various sizes is useful. A medium brush is good for sticking things with water when modelling, and a fine brush for adding delicate detail. Although more expensive, sable brushes are the best.

SCALPEL Invaluable when sharp, careful cutting is required such as when scribing around a template.

GREASEPROOF PAPER Used for lining tins, making piping bags, storing fruit cakes, and instead of tracing paper.

WOODEN SPOON As well as mixing, the handle can be used as a modelling tool for making folds in sugarpaste.

PALETTE KNIFE (METAL SPATULA) For spreading jam or buttercream, mixing colour into larger quantities of royal icing, and lifting small bits of sugarpaste.

BREAD KNIFE A long, sharp serrated knife is essential for shaping and slicing cakes.

SMALL SHARP KNIFE A small kitchen knife with a sharp, straight blade will become one of your most important bits of equipment.

BOARD Useful when modelling small items. Non-stick ones are also available.

RULER

MEASURING SPOONS

SIEVE

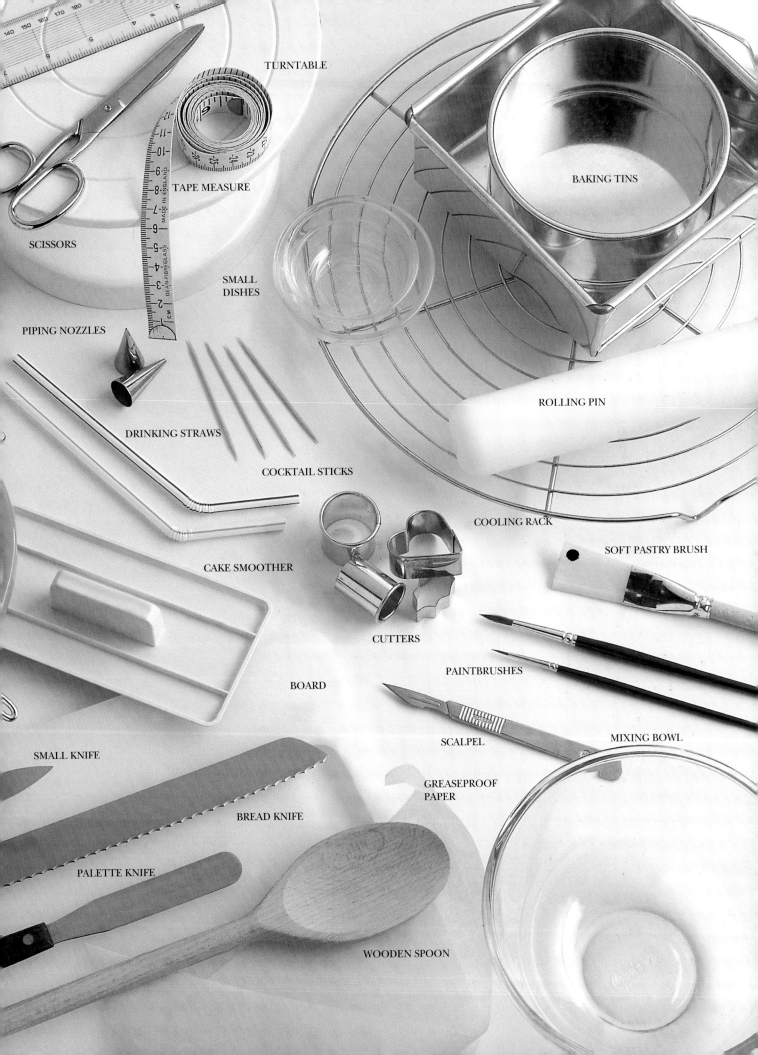

TURNTABLE

TAPE MEASURE

SCISSORS

SMALL
DISHES

BAKING TINS

PIPING NOZZLES

DRINKING STRAWS

COCKTAIL STICKS

ROLLING PIN

COOLING RACK

CAKE SMOOTHER

CUTTERS

SOFT PASTRY BRUSH

PAINTBRUSHES

BOARD

SMALL KNIFE

SCALPEL

MIXING BOWL

GREASEPROOF
PAPER

BREAD KNIFE

PALETTE KNIFE

WOODEN SPOON

Troubleshooting

1 BURNT FRUIT CAKE

This can occur if the oven is too hot or if the cake itself is cooked too near the top of the oven. Always try to bake cakes in the centre of the oven. If, despite these precautions, the cake appears to be browning too fast, or you prefer a lighter coloured appearance, place a circle of greaseproof paper with a small hole cut out of the centre over the top of the cake and continue baking.

2 SPONGE CAKES NOT RISING

Again, the usual culprit behind this is a too hot oven or the cake placed too near the top. It could also be caused by too much egg in the mixture. If you are using large eggs instead of medium, beat the eggs together first then take out a couple of spoonfuls before adding the rest to the cake mixture.

3 FRUIT CAKE NOT RISING

The reason for this happening is usually too much flour, so use slightly less in future cakes. It could also be because your ingredients were too cold. Try to use eggs and butter at room temperature.

4 SUGARPASTE/MODELLING PASTE/MARZIPAN TOO HARD

When not in use, always keep these ingredients tightly wrapped in small plastic bags to prevent them hardening. If a solid crust has formed, there is no alternative but to cut this off and discard. You can microwave any of the above for a few seconds to soften them slightly if you find them hard to knead, but be careful when doing this to sugarpaste as it can cause the icing to fracture slightly when you lay it over the cake.

5 CRACKS AND FRACTURES IN SUGARPASTE

These sometimes occur on the edges of a sugarpasted cake and seem most likely to happen if you overwork the sugarpaste with too much kneading or microwaving beforehand. Unless you find them particularly offensive, these cracks are usually best left alone or covered with a decoration, but here are two solutions you could try if you wish. On recently applied sugarpaste, take a small lump of the same colour sugarpaste and polish it on a shiny surface. Then gently rub the area using small circular motions and the tiny cracks should disappear. Alternatively, wait until the sugarpaste has dried, then spread a little royal icing in the same colour as the sugarpaste over the cracks. Carefully scrape away the excess using a knife and you should find the fractures have filled.

6 WATERMARKS

It is important to remove any accidental splashes of water you may get on your cake as soon as they happen as they will quickly start to dissolve the sugarpaste underneath, leaving an unsightly dent in your icing. If this does happen in a particularly noticeable area, dab off any remaining water then gently rub the area with the tip of your finger in a circular motion. Alternatively, use same-colour royal icing to fill the hole as described in the previous solution or place a decoration over the top of the damaged area.

7 FRAYED EDGES WHEN CUTTING SUGARPASTE

To cut sugarpaste cleanly, you need a small, sharp, non-serrated knife. A scalpel (available from stationery as well as cake decoration shops) is also useful for trimming untidy edges and making intricate cuts.

8 AIR BUBBLES

An air bubble trapped underneath a sugarpasted cake has to be removed before the icing has hardened. Hold either a clean dressmaking pin or a cocktail stick at an angle and poke it into the bubble. Then gently press out the excess air and run a cake smoother over the surface. If the area still looks unsightly, then do what I do and cover the area with a decoration. This was how I came to have a cat on the armchair cake and this in fact added extra charm to the cake as well as hiding a problem area underneath.

9 COLOURS FADING

The usual villain for this is sunlight causing the vegetable dyes to fade. Keep your finished cake in a box, tin (never a plastic container), dark cupboard or somewhere out of strong daylight until it is required.

10 FOOD COLOURS BLEEDING WHEN PAINTING

This happens when there is excess icing sugar on the sugarpaste surface you are painting on. Dust the area first with a large, dry brush (a pastry brush is ideal) before you begin.

11 BLOCKED ICING NOZZLES

To stop nozzles getting blocked with old icing, use a small paintbrush to give them a good clean when washing up. Also, try to avoid poking things such as cocktail sticks into the ends as this can force them out of shape. Make sure you sift the icing sugar before making up royal icing to get rid of lumps, and don't mix any crusty bits of dried royal icing into fresh before piping as this can cause blockages too.

Glossary of terms used

ENGLISH	AMERICAN
Baking tin	Pan
Caster sugar	Superfine sugar
Cling-film	Plastic wrap
Cocktail stick	Toothpick
Cornflour	Cornstarch
Desiccated coconut	Shredded coconut
Dried egg white	Meringue powder
Fish slice	Pancake turner
Flaked almonds	Slivered almonds
Greaseproof paper	Waxed paper
Icing sugar	Confectioner's sugar
Marzipan	Almond paste
Mixed spice	Apple pie spice
Palette knife	Metal spatula
Piping nozzle	Tip
Plain chocolate	Semi-sweet chocolate
Plain flour	All-purpose flour
Sausage	Rope
Self-raising flour	Self-rising flour
Sieve	Strainer
Sugarpaste	Rolled fondant icing
Sultanas	Golden raisins

Really Easy Novelty Cakes

From man-eating dinosaurs, to burgers, U.F.O.s, a graduation cake or a wedding present cake, there should be something amongst the designs featured in this section to appeal to most people. And if the recipient has been a bit naughty, and doesn't really deserve a cake at all, you could always make them a 'Horrible Child' cake!

Teddy cake

Not only would this make the ideal birthday cake for a first birthday but it could be used as a Christening cake too. If you are making it for a boy, simply substitute different hues of blue or yellow instead of the pink. Of course some adults are keen on teddies too – so don't restrict this cake to the children.

INGREDIENTS

15 cm (6 in) round cake
1 quantity buttercream (see page 14)
500 g (1 lb 2 oz) pale pink sugarpaste (rolled fondant icing)
375 g (13 oz) dark pink sugarpaste (rolled fondant icing)
100 g (3 oz) white sugarpaste (rolled fondant icing)
10 g (¼ oz) black sugarpaste (rolled fondant icing)
Black food colour
Water
Icing (confectioners') sugar, for rolling out

UTENSILS

20 cm (8 in) round cake board
Carving knife
Palette knife (metal spatula)
Small sharp knife
Rolling pin
Cake smoothers
Templates (see page 184)
Paintbrush

1 Slice off the top of the cake to level it if necessary and turn the cake upside down. Cut the cake in half.

2 Fill the centre with buttercream. Reassemble the cake and place it in the middle of the cake board. Spread buttercream around the sides and top using a palette knife (metal spatula).

3 Roll out the pale pink sugarpaste on a icing (confectioners') sugared surface to a thickness of about 1 cm (½ in). Lift and place over the cake. Smooth down the top and sides using your hands and a pair of cake smoothers. Trim and neaten the base.

4 Knead 75 g (3 oz) dark pink sugarpaste and roll out thinly. Using the templates, cut out a 10 cm (4 in) circle for the teddy's head, a 7.5 cm (3 in) semi-circle for the bear's body. Cut a 4 cm (1 ½ in) circle cut into two halves for the bear's ears. Re-knead the leftover icing and cut out the shape for the bear's arms. Cut this in two.

5 Stick the pieces onto the top of the cake and secure with water (*fig 1*).

6 Roll out the white sugarpaste and cut out an oval about 7 cm (2 ¾ in) wide for the muzzle. Cut out two circles for the eyes and another for the centre of the ears. Slice this last one in half and stick one half onto each ear. Cut out three small curves and stick onto the bear's forehead.

7 Roll out the black sugarpaste and cut out two circles for the eyes. Cut a slightly larger one for the nose.

8 Stick a tiny flattened ball of white onto both the eyes and the nose.

fig 2

9 Paint in the eyelashes and mouth using black food colour and a fine paintbrush.
Make a small bow out of white sugarpaste (*fig 2*) and press the back of a knife into the icing a few times to make creases. Finish off with a small flattened ball of white icing. Stick onto the bear's chin. Make a smaller bow of dark pink sugarpaste and put aside.

11 Roll 150 g (5 oz) dark pink sugarpaste into strip 60 cm x 1 cm (24 in x ½ in). Moisten the top edge of the cake with a little water. Roll the sugarpaste up like a miniature bandage. Starting from the back of the cake, feed it out around the cake twisting the icing as you go (*fig 3*). Roll the remaining dark pink sugarpaste into a strip 60 cm x 2 cm (24 in x ¾ in) and roll into a miniature bandage. Moisten the cake board with a little water and repeat the twisted effect around the base.

12 Finally hide the join at the top of the cake with the small dark pink bow you made earlier.

> *TIP: Trace and cut out the templates before you begin assembling the cake. It will make it quicker.*

fig 1

fig 3

U.F.O.

Most children (and a lot of the adults I know) have a fascination with the unexplained mysteries of the ether. So an unidentified flying cake landing on the tea table should cause a lot of interest. If it's for someone's birthday, insert birthday candles into the monster's tentacles and then turn down the lights for the full eerie effect.

INGREDIENTS

20 cm (8 in) round cake
1 quantity buttercream
(see page 14)
750 g (1 lb 10 oz) white
sugarpaste (rolled fondant
icing)
50 g (2 oz) black sugarpaste
(rolled fondant icing)
25 g (1 oz) yellow sugarpaste
(rolled fondant icing)
20 g (¾ oz) red sugarpaste
(rolled fondant icing)
40 g (1 ¾ oz) dark green
sugarpaste (rolled fondant
icing)
250 g (9 oz) dark blue
sugarpaste (rolled fondant
icing)
Small bit of liquorice (licorice)
bootlace
Water
Icing (confectioners') sugar,
for rolling out

UTENSILS

25 cm (10 in) square cake
board
Carving knife
Small sharp knife
Palette knife
Rolling pin
Cake smoothers
Small circle cutter
Paintbrush
Small plastic bags

fig 2

1 Slice about 2.5 cm (1 in) horizontally from the base of the cake. Turn this slice upside down and place it on the centre of the board. Carve and shape the remaining section of cake into a dome no bigger than 13 cm (5 in) diameter at the base. Place this in the middle of the first section of cake (*fig 1*). Secure with a layer of buttercream.

fig 1

2 Cover the outside of the cake with buttercream.

3 Knead the white sugarpaste (rolled fondant icing) until pliable. Roll the icing out and cover the cake. Carefully smooth the sides and trim and keep any excess.

4 Knead the black sugarpaste and roll out thinly and using your icing nozzle or circle cutter, cut out about 50 circles. Roll out 10 g (¼ oz) of yellow sugarpaste and cut out about 8 circles.
Stick one line of black circles, interspersed occasionally by a yellow one (to look as though there's someone home!), around the base of the craft and another around the bottom of the top section (*fig 2*).

5 Roll 10 g (½ oz) of red sugarpaste into a thin string and cut it up into about twenty-four 1 cm (½ in)

segments. Put one segment to one side (this will be used for the mouth and suckers later). Stick the rest of the segments around the middle of the cake, just below the top set of windows.

6 Make the monster's body out of 20 g (¾ oz) of green sugarpaste. Shape it into a small sausage (rope) first then slightly squeeze the icing about two thirds up to make a head. Sit the monster on the front of his craft (*fig 3*). With the remaining green sugarpaste, make six legs (each about 6 cm/2 ½ in long) and six tiny flattened balls for suckers. Stick each leg into place and finish off with a sucker.

7 Make yellow balls for eyes and stick into place. Add two tiny green eyeballs. Make a tiny ball of yellow for a nose. Add a red mouth and a small red ball to each sucker.

8 Insert two tiny strips of liquorice (licorice) into the monster's head and stick a little red ball of icing onto the

end of each one. Finish the monster off with a tiny yellow belly button.

9 Stick a small flattened 10 g (¼ oz) ball of blue sugarpaste onto the top of the spaceship. Then add a red and yellow ball. Score around the edge of the blue circle with the edge of a knife.

10 Moisten the exposed cake board with a little water.

11 Knead the dark blue sugarpaste and roll out thinly. Cover the board in sections (see page 17) and trim away the excess icing from the edges. Divide 10 g (¼ oz) of white sugarpaste into small

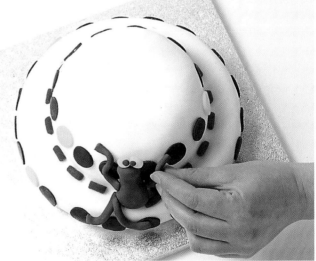
fig 3

balls. Flatten the balls slightly and stick around the board to look like planets.

> **TIP:** *If you don't possess a small circle cutter, simply use an icing nozzle (tip) or something similar instead to make the windows.*

Burger

Even the most surly teenager whose favourite meal consists of burger and French fries and who insists that they're too old for a birthday cake should find this one amusing. (Unless they become worried that it will give them even more spots than they've already got!) See the tip for an easy adaptation.

INGREDIENTS

15 cm (6 in) round cake
1 quantity buttercream (see
page 14)
800 g (12 oz) orangey-brown
coloured sugarpaste (rolled
fondant icing)
150 g (5 oz) green sugarpaste
(rolled fondant icing)
300 g (11 oz) dark brown
sugarpaste (rolled fondant
icing)
250 g (9 oz) red sugarpaste
(rolled fondant icing)
150 g (5 oz) yellow sugarpaste
(rolled fondant icing)
25 g (1 oz) orange sugarpaste
(rolled fondant icing)
Icing (confectioners') sugar,
for rolling out
Water

UTENSILS

25 cm (10 in) round cake
board
Carving knife
Small sharp knife
Palette knife
Rolling pin
Cake smoothers
Tin (aluminium) foil
Drinking straw
No 3 piping nozzle (round tip)
Fish slice (pancake turner)
Paintbrush
Small plastic bags

fig 1

1 Carefully carve the edges of the cake so that it forms a dome shape. Then cut the cake in half *(fig 1)*.

2 Cover the two parts of the cake on separate cake boards or clean work surfaces.

3 Beginning with the base section of the cake spread buttercream over the top and sides using a palette knife.

4 Roll 300 g (11 oz) of the orangey-brown sugarpaste into a flat strip about 3 mm (⅛ in) thick. Cut out a rectangle approximately 50 cm (20 in) long and just a bit wider than the depth of the cake.
Roll the strip up like a bandage and unroll around the sides of the cake *(fig 2)*.

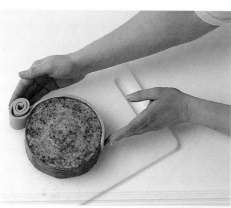

fig 2

Smooth the sides using smoothers and trim away any excess.

5 To make the lettuce, take the green sugarpaste and roll it out into a fairly thin strip. Place the strip on top of a piece of tin (aluminium) foil that has been crumpled and partially smoothed out *(fig 3)*. Run a rolling pin lightly over the sugarpaste on the tin foil and carefully peel the foil off. Cut it into strips and place around the edge of the bun allowing bits to overhang in a casual, lettucey sort of way.

6 For the burger, roll the dark brown sugarpaste into a thick circle about 15 cm (6 ¼ in) in diameter. Place this on top of the lettuce and then add texture to the burger by poking it with a drinking straw, No 3 nozzle (round tip) and the end of a paintbrush.

7 For the tomatoes, roll out the red sugarpaste and cut out six circles about 5.5 cm (2 ¼ in) in diameter. Press a line just inside each circle using either a circle cutter or the back of a knife. Then cut each circle in half *(fig 3)*. Make three lines across each segment with the back of a knife and finish off with a few pips made by pressing the tip of a No 3 piping nozzle into the tomato a few times.

8 Cover the top section of the cake with buttercream.

9 Roll out the remaining orangey-brown sugarpaste to a thickness of about 1 cm (⅜ in). Although this is a bit thicker than you would usually use to cover a cake, it makes it much easier to get a smooth rounded finish so don't over do the

rolling out. Smooth the sides with smoothers and cut away any excess. Place the top in position on the tomatoes.

fig 3

10 Make tiny oval balls out of the orange sugarpaste and stick onto the top of the burger to look like sesame seeds. Keep the rest of the orange sugarpaste to use later.

11 Roll out the yellow sugarpaste to a thickness of about 3 mm (⅛ in) and cut out a square about 25 cm (10 in) square.

12 Moisten the cake board and lay the yellow sugarpaste on it in a crumpled manner.

13 Pick up the cake using a fish slice (pancake turner) and transfer it to the board.

14 Cut 10 g (¼ oz) of orange sugarpaste up into small strips and stick onto the yellow to look like French fries.

TIP: *If you want to adapt it to a cheeseburger, simply roll out 100 g (4 oz) yellow icing and cut out a square. Place it on top of the burger so that the corners are visible just below the tomatoes.*

Horrible child

If your child has a tendency towards cheekiness and you want to get your own back, this cake could well be the answer. Personalise it with your child's hair colour, perhaps making it longer if it's to be for a girl. You could also change the blue and white sweater to the colour of their favourite garment.

INGREDIENTS

20 cm (8 in) round cake
2 quantities buttercream
(see page 14)
950 g (1 lb 15 oz) flesh-coloured sugarpaste
(rolled fondant icing)
215 g (7 ½ oz) white sugarpaste
(rolled fondant icing)
25 g (1 oz) black sugarpaste
(rolled fondant icing)
50 g (2 oz) brown sugarpaste
(rolled fondant icing)
25 g (1 oz) red sugarpaste
(rolled fondant icing)
50 g (2 oz) blue sugarpaste
(rolled fondant icing)
Icing (confectioners') sugar,
for rolling out
Water

UTENSILS

25 cm (10 in) round cake
board
Carving knife
Palette knife (metal spatula)
Small sharp knife
Rolling pin
Cake smoothers
4 cm (1 ¾ in) round cutter or
equivalent
2.5 cm (1 in) round cutter or
equivalent
Templates (see page 184)
Wooden spoon

1 Level the top of the cake if necessary and turn the cake upside down. Slice and fill the centre with buttercream. Place the cake onto the cake board. Spread buttercream around the top and sides of the cake.

2 Roll out 800 g (1 lb 2 oz) of the flesh-coloured sugarpaste (rolled fondant icing) on a surface dusted with icing (confectioners') sugar. Cover the cake and smooth over the top and sides with your hands. Repeat using a pair of cake smoothers and trim away any excess from the base of the cake.

3 Thinly roll out 10 g (¼ oz) white sugarpaste. Cut out two 4 cm (1 ½ in) circles for the eyes. Stick onto the face with a little water. Roll out 10 g (¼ oz) black sugarpaste and cut out two 2.5 cm (1 in) circles. Stick these onto the white ones. Then stick a small flattened ball of white onto each eye to make a highlight.

4 Thinly roll out the brown sugarpaste. Place the hair template on top and cut around the edges with a scalpel. Lightly moisten the forehead with a little water and place the hair into position (*fig 1*).

5 Make a nose by rolling 50 g (1 ½ oz) of flesh-coloured sugarpaste into a ball. Stick this under the eyes.

6 To make the ears, cut a 4 cm (1 ½ in) circle out of a flat piece of flesh-coloured sugarpaste. Cut the circle in half and press the end of a wooden spoon into both ears to make an oval indent. Draw a small line around the dent

using the tip of a sharp knife. Stretch both ears slightly and stick these into position with a little water.

7 Make a mouth out of a small flattened circle of black. Mould a tongue out of the red sugarpaste and stick into position (*fig 2*).

8 To make the hands, thinly roll out 100 g (4 oz) flesh-coloured sugarpaste. Position the hand template on top and cut around it. Repeat for the other hand (*see TIP*). Stick in place, lining up the edge of the wrists with the edge of the cake. Trim if necessary.

9 Roll out the remaining white sugarpaste into a thick sausage (rope) shape about 26 cm (10 in) long. Now moisten the cake board and lay the icing at the front of the cake (*fig 3*).

fig 2

10 Thinly roll out the blue sugarpaste. Cut out two stripes 25 cm x 1 cm (10 in x ½ in). Stick these onto the white using water.

fig 3

TIP: *When cutting out the hands, turn the template over before starting the second one. Otherwise you'll end up with two right (or left) hands.*

fig 1

Snake

A rare sighting of the tea time snake, Latin name 'Snakeus Cakeus'. He only ventures out once a year for birthdays and then tends to vanish quite quickly! You could substitute spots for the stripes if you prefer or even write the child's name along his back. Scatter a few sweet (candy) treats amongst the sand as well.

INGREDIENTS

Ingredients
23 cm (9 in) round sponge
2 quantities buttercream (see page 14)
1 kg (2 lb 4 oz) green sugarpaste (rolled fondant icing)
100 g (4 oz) red sugarpaste (rolled fondant icing)
100 g (4 oz) yellow sugarpaste (rolled fondant icing)
20 g (¾ oz) blue sugarpaste (rolled fondant icing)
250 g (9 oz) white sugarpaste (rolled fondant icing)
25 g (1 oz) black sugarpaste (rolled fondant icing)
175 g (6 oz/1¾ cups) soft brown sugar
Icing (confectioners') sugar, for rolling out
Water

UTENSILS

45 cm x 30 cm (18 in x 12 in) rectangular cake board
Carving knife
Small sharp knife
Palette knife (metal spatula)
Rolling pin
Cake smoothers
Paintbrush
Icing nozzle (tip) and drinking straw
About 30 jelly sweets (candies)
Small plastic bags

fig 1

1 Shape the cake by first cutting it in half. Keeping the flat edges together, slide one semi-circle just over halfway along the other (*fig 1*). Cut another semi-circle out of each half so that the remaining cake forms an 'S' shape. Keep the two cut out centres. Round the edges of the snake. Carve the tail end into a point but leave the head end flat. Put the two small semi-circles of cake together to form a head and place this into position.

2 Slice the cake in half and fill the middle with buttercream. Spread buttercream along the sides and top as well.

3 Knead and roll out green sugarpaste (rolled fondant icing) into a strip about 60 cm (24 in) long. Wind the strip around a rolling pin. Lift it and unroll over the cake (*fig 2*). Ease the icing down over the sides and smooth with the cake smoothers. Trim away excess icing.

4 Knead the red and 100 g (4 oz) yellow sugarpaste and roll out thinly. Cut about eight strips out of both. (Keep the excess red for the tongue.)

5 Moisten the snake's back with a little water and lay the

fig 2

strips over the cake, trimming them when necessary.

6 Add scales by holding an icing nozzle (tip) at a slight angle and pressing it into the still soft icing. Repeat with a drinking straw (*fig 3*).

7 Knead and roll the blue sugarpaste into a thin string and stick small sections onto the yellow stripes. Stick jelly sweets (candies) onto the snake's back. (They should stay in position with just a little water, but if your snake has a long way to slither to his party, it might be worth securing them with a little royal icing.)

8 Make two 50 g (2 oz) balls of white sugarpaste for eyes. Stick onto head.

9 Knead and roll out 10 g (¼ oz) black sugarpaste and cut out two black circles and a crescent for the eyes and mouth. Stick the circles onto the eyes and the mouth onto

the front of the face. Stick two tiny white circles onto the black eyes securing with a little water.

10 Cut a 'Y' shape out of red icing and stick onto the mouth with a little water.

fig 3

11 Partially knead the remaining black sugarpaste into the remaining white sugarpaste. Pull off small sections and mould into pebbles.

12 Moisten the cake board and spoon the soft brown sugar over the board.

13 Place the pebbles into position.

TIP: *Don't panic if the icing cracks or creases slightly around the bends when you're covering the cake. Any slight blemishes can be covered by the stripes later.*

Pony cake

Abright, bold eye-catching cake for horse-mad kids of all ages. If the young rider in question is lucky enough to own their own pony, give the icing horse similar markings. If you can get hold of any competition rosettes, these can be positioned around the cake board for an 'ambitious' finishing touch.

INGREDIENTS

15 cm (6 in) round cake
1 quantity buttercream (see page 14)
600 g (1 lb 6 oz) mid-green sugarpaste (rolled fondant icing)
65 g (2 ½ oz) light brown sugarpaste (rolled fondant icing)
25 g (1 oz) dark brown sugarpaste (rolled fondant icing)
20 g (¾ oz) white sugarpaste (rolled fondant icing)
10 g (¼ oz) black sugarpaste (rolled fondant icing)
25 g (1 oz) biscuit yellow sugarpaste (rolled fondant icing)
150 g (5 oz) orange sugarpaste (rolled fondant icing)
25 g (1 oz) dark green sugarpaste (rolled fondant icing)
Icing (confectioners') sugar, for rolling out
Water

UTENSILS

20 cm (8 in) round cake board
Carving knife
Small sharp knife
Palette knife (metal spatula)
Rolling pin
Cake smoothers
Templates (see page 185)
Scalpel
Paintbrush
Small plastic bags

1 Slice off the top of the cake to level it if necessary and turn it upside down on the cake board. Slice the cake and fill the middle with buttercream. Spread a layer of buttercream over the top and sides as well.

2 Knead and roll out 500 g (1 lb 2 oz) of the mid-green sugarpaste (rolled fondant icing) and cover the cake. Smooth the top and sides and trim away any excess icing and put this with the remainder of the mid-green icing.

3 Roll out the light brown sugarpaste to a thickness of about 3 mm (⅛ in). Place the horse's head template onto the sugarpaste and trace around it with a scalpel or the tip of a sharp knife (*fig 1*). Moisten the top of the cake and place the head in position.

fig 1

4 Roll out the dark brown icing to a thickness of 1.5 mm (¹⁄₁₆ in) and cut out three small strips for the pony's bridle. Stick them into position with a little water and trim to fit.

5 Roll out about half of the white sugarpaste until it's

fig 2

about 3mm (⅛ in) thick and cut out a 3 cm (1¼ in) circle for the horse's eye. Stick this into position and then add a thin black circle about 2 cm (¾ in) Finally add a highlight made out of a tiny flattened ball of white sugarpaste. Cut a semi-circle the same diameter as the eye out of the light brown sugarpaste and place over the eye (*fig 2*).

6 To make the horse's bit, cut out a small white circle and stick it just to the side of the horse's mouth. Stick a smaller circle of black in the centre and place another flattened ball of black just above to form the horse's nostril. Add a thin string of black sugarpaste along the base of the horse's eyelid to make an eyelash.

7 Roll out the biscuit-yellow sugarpaste and cut out the mane using the template if necessary. Stick this onto the neck with a little water.

8 Add two ears made from light brown sugarpaste.

9 To cover the cake board, roll the remaining mid-green sugarpaste into a strip about

60 cm (24 in) long. Cut away one long edge and roll the icing up like a bandage (see page 16). Moisten the exposed cake board and starting at the back, unwind the strip around the base of the cake. Trim away the excess.

10 Divide the orange sugarpaste into about fifteen pieces. Roll each one into a tapering carrot shape and press about five lines into the top of each carrot with back of a knife (*fig 3*).

fig 3

11 Using the dark green sugarpaste, make a small green flattish triangle. Make three cuts and splay the three 'fingers'.

12 Make a small dent in the end of each carrot with the tip of a paintbrush and insert a carrot top. Repeat with the rest of the carrots and position them around the top and base of the cake.

TIP: *If stored in a box with a lid to keep the dust off, the carrots can be made up to a week before.*

Computer game

The perfect cake with which to tempt junior away from his computer game for a while. If you don't feel competent about painting onto the screen, substitute a photograph or a picture cut out of a comic or magazine instead. Stick it onto a thin bit of cardboard and secure onto the cake with a little royal icing.

INGREDIENTS

18 cm (7 in) square cake
1 quantity buttercream (see page 14)
400 g (14 oz) black sugarpaste (rolled fondant icing)
800 g (1 lb 12 oz) blue sugarpaste (rolled fondant icing)
50 g (2 oz) grey sugarpaste (rolled fondant icing)
20 g (¾ oz) red sugarpaste (rolled fondant icing)
10 g (¼ oz) yellow sugarpaste (rolled fondant icing)
black food colour
Icing (confectioners') sugar, for rolling out
Water

UTENSILS

25 cm (10 in) square cake board
Carving knife
Small sharp knife
Palette knife (metal spatula)
Rolling pin
Cake smoothers
Fish slice (pancake turner)
Circle cutters or equivalent
Paintbrushes, one medium, one fine

1 Cover the cake board with 350 g (12 oz) black sugarpaste (rolled fondant icing) (see page 16). Put the board to one side.

fig 1

2 Cut about a third off one side of the cake. Place the cut off section against one of the shorter sides of the cake to increase the length of the cake *(fig 1)*. Trim to fit.

3 Cut a small semi-circle out of one of the longer sides and place this against the opposite side of the cake *(fig 2)*.

4 Run a sharp knife around the edges of the cake to make them rounded.

5 Slice the cake in half and fill the centre with buttercream. Spread buttercream over the top and sides with a palette knife (metal spatula).

6 Knead the blue sugarpaste until pliable. Roll it out and cover the cake. Smooth the sides with cake smoothers and trim away any excess.

7 Carefully lift the cake using a fish slice and place it diagonally on the black sugarpasted cake board.

8 Roll out the grey sugarpaste and cut out a rectangle for the screen 7.5 cm x 5 cm (3 in x 2 in). Stick this in the centre of the cake using a little water.

9 Using the back of a knife, indent five lines each side of the screen.

10 Thinly roll out the red sugarpaste and cut out two circles 4 cm (1 ½ in) in diameter. Stick one either side of the screen below the indented lines.

11 Paint the design onto the screen using black food colour and a fine paintbrush *(fig 3)*.

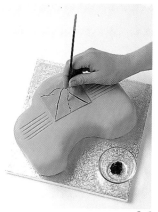

fig 3

12 Roll out the yellow sugarpaste and cut out a small cross and stick this onto one of the red circles. Stick a small yellow circle onto the other one. Cut out two yellow rectangles and one red one and stick these below the screen with a little water.

13 Roll 10 g (¼ oz) of black sugarpaste into a thin string and stick along the edge of the screen.

14 Roll the rest of the black sugarpaste into a slightly thicker string about 28 cm (11 in) long and lay this along the bottom edge of the game.

15 Roll out the rest of the blue sugarpaste and cut out about 16 circles. Use these to decorate the board.

TIP: *Add the ultimate psychedelic touch to the inside too by swirling a bit of food colour into the cake mixture before baking.*

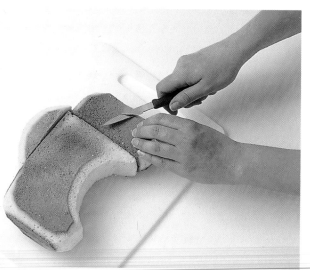

fig 2

Do-it-yourself

The ideal cake for anyone to who likes to wield a hammer or the perfect hint for someone you wish would! Give the sponge itself a 'wood' effect by partially mixing a couple of teaspoons of cocoa into the madeira mixture before it's cooked. Once baked, it should have an interesting marbled look to it.

INGREDIENTS

15 cm (6 in) square cake
1 quantity buttercream (see page 14)
60 g (2¼ oz) orange gelatin icing (see page 15)
50 g (2 oz) grey gelatin icing (see page 15)
600 g (1 lb 6 oz) white sugarpaste (rolled fondant icing)
20 g (¾ oz) grey sugarpaste (rolled fondant icing)
50 g (2 oz) red sugarpaste (rolled fondant icing)
50 g (2 oz) black sugarpaste (rolled fondant icing)
50 g (2 oz) tan sugarpaste (rolled fondant icing)
10 g (¼ oz) blue sugarpaste (rolled fondant icing)
20 g (¾ oz) orange sugarpaste (rolled fondant icing)
Royal icing, (optional, see page 15)
Cornflour (cornstarch)
Dark brown, chestnut and black food colours
Icing (confectioners') sugar, for rolling out
Water

UTENSILS

20 cm (8 in) square cake board
Templates for saw (page 185)
Scalpel
Spare cake board
Rolling pin
Carving knife
Sharp knife
Palette knife (metal spatula)
Cake smoothers
Paintbrushes, one medium, one fine

1 Roll out the grey gelatin icing to a thickness of 3 mm (⅛ in). Place the saw template onto the icing and cut out the shape using a scalpel. (Although a sharp knife will do the job adequately, it's a lot easier with a scalpel.)

2 Roll out the orange gelatin icing and, using the templates, cut out two handle shapes. Place the three gelatin icing pieces onto a spare cake board that has been lightly dusted with cornflour (cornstarch) and leave to dry overnight.

3 Slice the top off the cake to level it and turn it upside down. Cut the cake in half and fill the centre with buttercream. Spread more buttercream around the sides and over the top.

4 Place the cake slightly off centre on the cake board so that there is a wider expanse of cake board showing at the front and on the right-hand side.

5 Put 20 g (¾ oz) of the white sugarpaste (rolled fondant icing) to one side. Carefully roll the dark brown and chestnut food colours into the icing to achieve a nice wood-grain effect (see page 19). Roll out the icing and cover the cake and smooth the sides. Trim away and keep the excess. Finish neatening the sides with a pair of cake smoothers.

6 Cut a thin strip out of the cake, ready for the saw, while the icing is still soft. Make a 5 mm (¼ in) wide cut from the base of the cake to about halfway across the top of the cake. Lift this section of cake out and discard (*fig 1*).

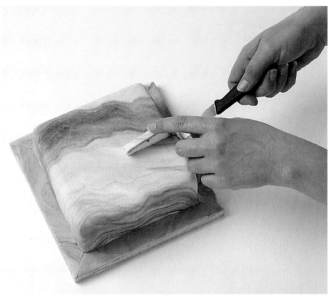

fig 1

7 Moisten the exposed cake board. Roll out the excess 'woodgrain' icing to a thickness of about 3 mm (⅛ in) and cut out four strips. Lay one strip down each edge. Trim to fit (see page 17).

8 Now make the tools (*fig 2*). To make the screwdriver, roll 10 g (¼ oz) of grey sugarpaste into a sausage (rope) approximately 10 cm (4 in) long and squash one end. Make a small flattened grey ball, and place this against the blunt end. Make a handle by rolling the red sugarpaste into

fig 2

a pear shape. Place the screwdriver into position on the cake and adhere with a little water.

9 For the ruler, roll 20 g (¾ oz) of white sugarpaste into a flat strip and cut out a rectangle 13 cm x 2.5 cm (5 in x 1 in). Carefully paint on a few lines for markings with black food colour and a fine paint brush. Stick the ruler onto the cake.

10 To make the hammer, first roll the black sugarpaste into an exaggerated pear shape. Slice a strip off the larger end and place onto the cake board. For the handle, roll the tan sugarpaste into a slightly tapering sausage approximately 18 cm (7 in) long. Place the handle into position, and stick with a little water using the side of the cake as support.

11 For the pencil, roll the blue sugarpaste into a thin sausage about 10 cm (4 in) long. Stick this onto the cake board. Finish it off with a tiny cone of flesh-coloured icing and paint in a tiny point with black food colour.

12 To put the saw together, sandwich the grey blade between the two orange handles (*fig 3*). A little water should be enough to cement the sections together but if you find they won't stick, use a few dabs of royal icing. Lightly moisten the edge of the saw handle and the inside of the

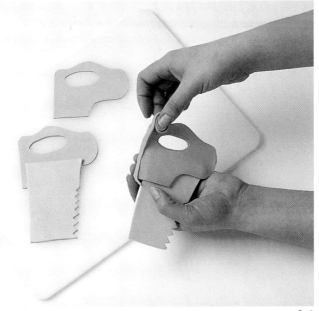

hole. Roll out the orange sugarpaste into a strip and wind this round to neaten the appearance of the handle. Trim away any excess.

13 Put the saw into the slot.

TIP: *Make the saw at least a day before the rest of the cake so you won't have to wait for it to dry when everything else is ready.*

fig 3

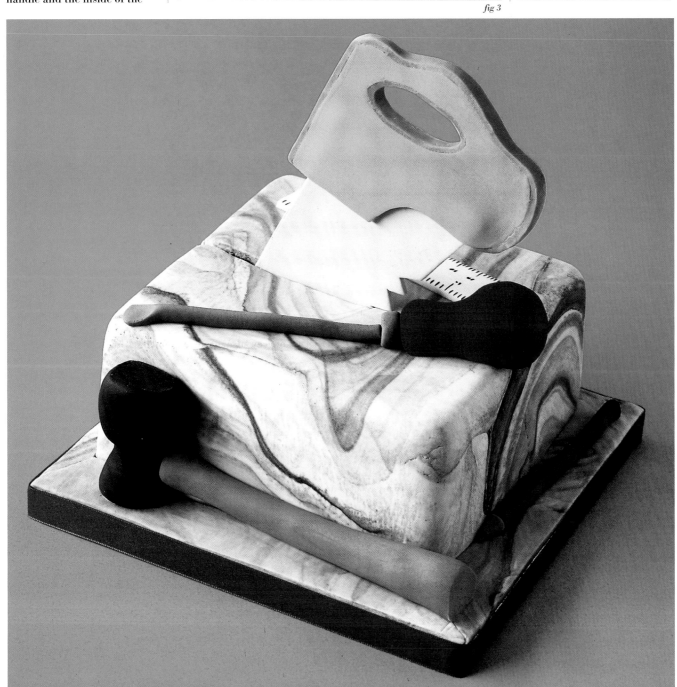

Spend, spend, spend

A dazzling cake piled up with gold coins that would suit either an accountant or someone who just likes to spend, spend, spend! This makes a nice cake for a man and let's face it, is a lot more original than a pair of socks! If you're making it for a woman, you might like to substitute small purses for the drawstring pouches.

INGREDIENTS

18 cm (7 in) square cake
1 quantity buttercream (see page 14)
500 g (1 lb 2 oz) emerald green sugarpaste (rolled fondant icing)
100 g (4 oz) dark brown sugarpaste (rolled fondant icing)
100 g (4 oz) light brown sugarpaste (rolled fondant icing)
10 g (¼ oz) red sugarpaste (rolled fondant icing)
10 g (¼ oz) blue sugarpaste (rolled fondant icing)
About 60 foil-covered chocolate coins
1 tbsp white royal icing (see page 15)
Icing sugar, for rolling out
Water

UTENSILS

25 cm (10 in) gold-coloured square cake board
Carving knife
Small sharp knife
Palette knife (metal spatula)
Rolling pin
Cake smoothers
Paintbrush
Piping bag fitted with a No 2 nozzle (round tip)

1 Slice off the top of the cake to level it and turn it upside down on the cake board so that the base now forms the top. Position the cake so that it sits off-centre on the board.

2 Slice the cake in half and fill it with buttercream. Spread buttercream over the top and down the sides with a palette knife.

3 Knead the emerald green sugarpaste (rolled fondant icing) and roll it out. Carefully cover the cake.

4 Smooth the sugarpaste over the top and sides with your hands and trim away any excess icing at the base. Then run over the surface of the icing using a pair of cake smoothers.

5 To make a purse, take the dark brown icing and mould it into a cone shape *(fig 1)*. Push your finger into the top of the thin end to make a slight hollow. This will become the opening of the purse. Pinch the edges around the top of the hollow to thin them slightly and bend them outwards. Squeeze the neck of the purse to re-shape it as necessary. Stand the purse in position on

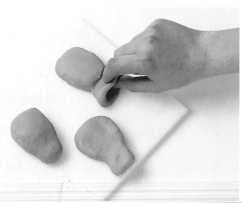

fig 1

the cake. Repeat with the lighter brown icing but this time lay it flat on the cake instead of standing up.

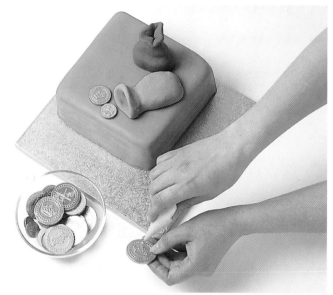

fig 2

6 Begin to position the coins around the cake, securing them into position with royal icing *(fig 2)*.

7 Finish off the purses by adding a drawstring. Poke the pointed end of a paintbrush around the neck of each purse to leave a line of small dots. (Make approximately 6-7 holes per purse about 1 cm (½ in) apart.) Using the piping bag and No 2 nozzle (round tip), pipe a line of icing between two of the holes. Leave a gap and pipe another line between the next two holes *(fig 3)*. This should give the impression of a cord being threaded through.

8 Make two tiny red balls and two tiny blue ones out of icing. Stick the two red ones on the neck of the standing up purse. Pipe two 'tails' of icing away from them. On the lying down

purse, pipe the 'tails' before adding the blue balls to look as though the purse has fallen slightly open.

9 Finish arranging the coins around the cake and board.

fig 3

TIP: *It's always worth stocking up with chocolate coins at Christmas when they are more readily available in the shops. You never know when you might need some!*

Teatime table

There are a number of ways you can cheat with this cake and yet still produce something spectacular and unique. If you don't fancy making a gelatin plate (or you haven't got the time to wait for it to dry) simply use a real one instead and pile it up with home-made (or shop-bought) goodies you know the family will love.

INGREDIENTS

20 cm (8 in) round sponge
1 quantity buttercream (see page 14)
300 g (11 oz) gelatin icing (see page 15)
550 g (1 lb 4 oz) white sugarpaste (rolled fondant icing)
750 g (1 lb 10 oz) pink sugarpaste (rolled fondant icing)
Cornflour (cornstarch)
1 tbsp white royal icing (see page 15)
Small jelly sweets (candies)
About 20 petit-four size cakes
Icing (confectioners') sugar, for rolling out on
Water

UTENSILS

30 cm (12 in) round cake board
Carving knife
Small sharp knife
Palette knife (metal spatula)
20-23 cm (8-9 in) round china plate
Rolling pin
35 cm (14 in) round cake board for use as a template
Piping (decorating) bag
Paintbrush
Clingfilm (plastic wrap)

1 Cover the china plate with clingfilm (plastic wrap) and a fine dusting of cornflour (cornstarch).

2 Roll out the gelatin icing and cover the plate. Trim the edges. Leave to dry for at least 24 hours, turning the icing plate over when it has hardened enough to support itself.

3 Level the top of the cake and turn it upside down on to the cake board. Slice it in half and fill the centre with buttercream. Reassemble the cake and spread additional buttercream around the top and sides.

4 Knead and roll out the white sugarpaste (rolled fondant icing). Place it over the cake and cover it. Smooth down the top and sides with cake smoothers and trim away any excess.

5 Knead and roll out the pink sugarpaste to a thickness of about 5mm (¼ in). Using the larger cake board or equivalent as a template, cut out a circle.

6 Lay the pink icing on top of the white and allow it to fall into folds down the sides (*fig 1*).

7 Using the end of a paint-brush, poke a pattern into the edges of the cloth (*fig 2*).

8 When the plate is dry, place it on top of the tablecloth.

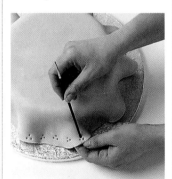

fig 2

Secure it firmly with a dab of royal icing.

9 Put the royal icing into a piping (decorating) bag and snip off the end. Decorate the edge of the plate with small jelly sweets (candies). Secure them into position with the royal icing (*fig 3*).

10 Fill the plate with small cakes, biscuits (cookies) or whatever takes your fancy.

TIP: *To ensure that the plate does not crack when you turn it over to dry the underside, place some scrunched up clingfilm (plastic wrap) under the plate to provide support.*

fig 1

fig 3

Yacht

A fun cake for anyone who fancies themselves as a bit of a sailor. Paint the recipient's name or age on the sails and if they actually own their own boat, copy those colours. Have fun with the sea as well. Add jelly (candy) or icing fish or, if your sense of humour veers towards the wicked, maybe a shark's fin or two.

INGREDIENTS

15 cm (6 in) square cake
1 quantity buttercream (see page 14)
550 g (1 lb 3 oz) red sugarpaste (rolled fondant icing)
110 g (4 ¼ oz) black sugarpaste (rolled fondant icing)
100 g (4 oz) white sugarpaste (rolled fondant icing)
50 g (2 oz) blue sugarpaste (rolled fondant icing)
25 g (1 oz) flesh-coloured sugarpaste (rolled fondant icing)
150 g (5 oz) green sugarpaste (rolled fondant icing)
Black and blue food colours
5 tbsp royal icing (see page 15)
Icing (confectioners') sugar, for rolling out
Water

UTENSILS

25 cm (10 in) round cake board
Carving knife
Small sharp knife
Palette knife (metal spatula)
Rolling pin
Cake smoothers
Paintbrushes, one medium, one fine
Wooden skewers x 2
Small bowl
Small plastic bags
Clear sticky tape
Cardboard sail (see template on page 186)

fig 1

1 Cut out the shape of the boat from the sponge (*fig 1*). Use strips cut from the discarded edges of the sponge to increase the boat's length. Carefully carve the sides of the cake so that they slope gently inwards and give the boat a nice rounded look. Slice and fill the centre with buttercream, then spread it around the top and sides.

2 Roll out 450 g (1 lb) red sugarpaste (rolled fondant icing) on a surface dusted with icing (confectioners') sugar. Cut out a strip approximately 50 cm (20 in) long and 5 cm (2 in) wide. (This last measurement depends on the depth of your cake so measure it first before cutting.) Roll the strip up like a bandage and starting from the straight edge at the back of the boat, unwind it around the base of the boat. Neaten the sides using smoothers and trim away any excess icing at the join (seam). Ensure that the top edge of the icing lies level with the top of the cake, trimming it if necessary.

3 To give the impression of boards around the boat, take a ruler and holding it horizontally, press the edge two or three times into both sides of the boat. (A photograph showing this technique appears in 'Enchanted House' page 78.)

4 Thinly roll out 100 g (4 oz) black sugarpaste and cut out a shape slightly larger than the top of the boat. Lay the sugarpaste on the top of the boat and run a knife around the edge to trim it to size. Roll out 100 g (4 oz) red sugarpaste and cut out two strips for the boat's seats approximately 2.5 cm (1 in) wide. Lightly moisten the black sugarpaste with a little water and place them into position.

5 Roll 100 g (4 oz) of red sugarpaste icing into a sausage about 60 cm (24 in) long. Moisten the top edge of the boat with water and lay the strip into position (*fig 2*).

6 Shape 90 g (3 ½ oz) white sugarpaste into an oval for the sailor's body. Thinly roll out 25 g (1 oz) of blue sugarpaste and cut out three thin strips about 15 cm (6 in) long. Moisten the body and wrap them round to make stripes. Make two arms out of 25 g (1 oz) blue sugarpaste. Bend them slightly at the elbow and stick onto the body with water (*fig 3*). Place the sailor into position and secure with a little water. For extra security, carefully push the smaller wooden skewer through the body into the cake, leaving about 2.5 cm (1 in) protruding. Roll 10 g (¼ oz) flesh-coloured sugarpaste into a ball for the head. Moisten the neck and slide the head into position over the skewer.

To make the sailor's facial hair ('de rigeuer' for any self-respecting seaman!) take the remaining black sugarpaste. Make a tiny triangle for the beard and stick on to the face.

fig 2

fig 3

hands made out of two balls of flesh-coloured sugarpaste.

7 For the octopus, make a 100 g (4 oz) ball of green sugarpaste for the head and five 50 g (2 oz) green sausages (ropes) for the legs (*fig 3*).

8 Place 5 tbsp of royal icing in a bowl and partially mix in a small amount of blue food colour. Using a palette knife, swirl the icing around the cake board. Position the octopus' head and legs, making sure that the 'sea' covers the tops of the legs.

9 Stick two white circles of icing onto the octopus' face.

Add two smaller black ones. finish off with two tiny white flattened dots of white to make the highlights. Paint in a mouth and two eyebrows with black food colour.

10 Attach the sails to the second wooden skewer with sticky tape. Finally insert them into the boat.

> **TIP:** *If you go too far mixing the blue food colour into the 'sea' and it all turns blue, don't panic! Simply add more white royal icing to reverse the process.*

Add two tiny black ovals for the moustache. Stick a small flattened circle of white sugarpaste onto the top of his head to make his cap and finish it off with a tiny white oval of icing stuck to the front

to make a peak. Add three tiny balls of flesh-coloured icing for the ears and nose and paint in the eyes, hair and a dot for the mouth with black food colour and a fine paint-brush. Finish the arms with

Passing exams

A cake that shows how proud you are of someone's academic achievements. You could also write their name or the subject they passed on the certificate. If you can't get hold of ready-coloured black sugarpaste and have to colour your own, invest in some disposable polythene gloves to save discolouring your hands.

1 Knead paprika and dark brown food colour into 250 g (9 oz) white sugarpaste (rolled fondant icing) to achieve the wood grain effect as shown on page 19.

2 Moisten the 30 cm (12 in) cake board and cover it with the 'wood' icing (see page 16). Put the board to one side.

3 Turn the cake upside down on a spare cake board or clean work surface (countertop) and round the edges with a carving knife. Place the thinner cake board on top just to check that it sits nice and flat.

4 Slice the cake in half and fill the centre with buttercream. Cover the top and sides with buttercream.

5 Knead and roll out 500 g (1 lb 2 oz) of black sugarpaste and cover the cake with it. Smooth and trim away any excess.

6 Moisten the thin cake board with a little water. Roll out the remaining black sugarpaste and use this to cover the board.

7 Lift the round base cake using a fish slice or equivalent and place in the centre of the covered cake board.

fig 1

8 Lightly moisten the top of the cake and place the thin black cake board into position on the top (*fig 1*).

9 Make a scroll out of 150 g (5 oz) white sugarpaste. Knead and roll it out and cut out a rectangle about 18 cm x 13 cm (7 in x 5 in) long. Roll it up and stick it onto the board with a little water.

fig 2

10 Cut out two thin red strips of sugarpaste and stick onto the scroll. Add a bow made out of another two red strips folded into two loops, two 'tails' and a small strip to cover the centre (*fig 2*).

11 Take the green sugarpaste. Pull off a small ball and put it to one side. Roll the rest into a tapering sausage (rope) shape approximately 23 cm (9 in) long. Flatten the sausage slightly and score lines down its length using the back of a knife (*fig 3*). Moisten the top of the mortar board and lay the tassel upon it, allowing the icing to rest on the board at the base. Add a few thin

strings of green sugarpaste to look like 'stragglers'.

12 Put the leftover ball of green sugarpaste on top and again score lines in it with the back of a knife.

13 For the pencils, simply roll the yellow sugarpaste and blue sugarpaste into 12 cm (5 in) lengths. Add a tiny

brown cone to one end and a tiny flattened ball of white to the other. Paint in the leads with black food colour.

TIP: *Clean away dusty icing (confectioners') sugar fingerprints with clean water and a damp paintbrush.*

fig 3

Hallowe'en spider

A couple of local children gave me some hints about how to make this cake more ghoulish. Although I ignored their suggestions as they were too gory, this cake does harbour one horrible surprise. Before it was cooked, the cake was coloured an awful mouldy colour with food colours. It looked bad enough to eat!

INGREDIENTS

18 cm (7 in) round cake
1 quantity buttercream (see page 14)
450 g (1 lb) green sugarpaste (rolled fondant icing)
750 g (1 lb 10 oz) black sugarpaste (rolled fondant icing)
110 g (4 ¼ oz) white sugarpaste (rolled fondant icing)
25 g (1 oz) red sugarpaste (rolled fondant icing)
10 g (¼ oz) grey sugarpaste (rolled fondant icing)
2 liquorice (licorice) bootlaces (about 1 m/39 in long)
Red food colour
Icing (confectioners') sugar, for rolling out
Water

UTENSILS

35 cm (12 in) round cake board
Spare cake board
Carving knife
Small sharp knife
Palette knife (metal spatula)
Rolling pin
Cake smoothers
Pastry brush
Fish slice (pancake turner)
Paintbrushes, one medium, one fine
Two cocktail sticks (toothpicks), optional

1 Cover the cake board with the green sugarpaste (rolled fondant icing) (see page 16). Put to one side.

2 Place the cake onto the spare cake board and carefully carve it into a rounded dome shape.

3 Slice the cake in half and fill the centre with buttercream. Spread additional buttercream around the outside.

4 Knead and roll out the black sugarpaste to a thickness of about 5 mm (¼ in). Lift and cover the cake. Pat down and smooth the sides

fig 2

with your hands, then run a pair of cake smoothers over the surface to make the spider become nice and rounded. Trim and keep the excess.

5 Lift the cake using a fish slice (pancake turner) or

fig 1

equivalent utensil and place it into the centre of the covered cake board (*fig 1*).

6 Roll and divide 100 g (4 oz) of white sugarpaste into two balls. Then slightly flatten each one to a width of about

5 cm (2 in). Stick these on with a little water to make his eyes.

7 Roll out 10 g (¼ oz) of black sugarpaste to a thickness of about 3 mm (⅛ in). Cut out two circles 3 cm (1 ¼ in) diameter. Stick these onto the whites of the eyes with a little water. Flatten two tiny white balls and stick one onto each black circle to make the highlights.

8 Roll 10 g (¼ oz) of dark grey sugarpaste into a sausage (rope) 5 cm (2 in) long. Cut in two and mould each half into an 'S' shape to make the eyebrows. Stick these into place with water (*fig 2*).

9 Thinly roll out the red sugarpaste and cut out a crescent shape for the mouth. Stick it onto the spider's face.

10 Flatten 10 g (¼ oz) of white sugarpaste and cut out two triangles for the spider's teeth. Line up the top of each tooth with the top of the mouth and allow them to fall into a curved shape.

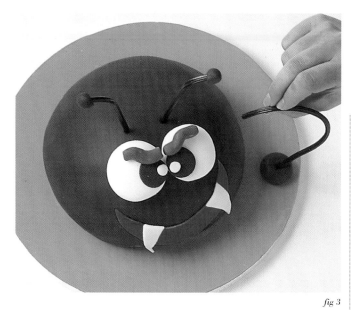

fig 3

11 Now divide the liquorice (licorice) bootlaces into eight even 20 cm (8 in) lengths for the legs and two 7.5 cm (3 in) lengths to make the spider's antennae.

12 Take 100 g (4 oz) of the leftover black sugarpaste and divide this into eight balls.

13 Moisten the base of one of the balls and position on the board. Poke one of the liquorice legs into the ball then bend it back and insert it into the spider's body. Repeat with the other seven legs *(fig 3)*.

14 Stick a little ball of black sugarpaste onto one end of both liquorice antennae. Make two small holes in the top of the spider's head and insert the liquorice.

15 Paint tiny blood vessels onto the eyes with red food colour and a fine paintbrush.

16 Finally tidy up any icing (confectioners') sugar smudges with a damp paintbrush.

TIP: *If you find the antennae won't stand up, insert a cocktail stick (toothpick) up the middle of each bit of bootlace to add support. Ensure that they are removed when the cake is cut.*

Valentine lips

If, as they say, the way to a man's (or woman's) heart is through their stomach, what better way to get there than by presenting them with this stylish, eye-catching cake. Gold cake boards are easily available from cake decorating equipment shops, and really set off the black and red icing.

INGREDIENTS

25 cm (10 in) square cake
2 quantities of buttercream
(see page 14)
1.25 kg (2 lb 12 oz) red
sugarpaste (rolled fondant
icing)
50 g (2 oz) black sugarpaste
(rolled fondant icing)
1 tbsp black royal icing (see
page 15)
Icing (confectioners') sugar,
for rolling out
Water

UTENSILS

30 cm (12 in) square gold cake
board
Cake template (see page 186)
Carving knife
Small sharp knife
Palette knife (metal spatula)
Rolling pin
Cake smoothers
Small heart-shaped cutter
Piping (decorating) bag and
No 3 piping nozzle (round tip)
Paintbrush

fig 1

1 Cut out the cake using the template as a guide *(fig 1)*.

2 Round the sides and make sure that the outside edges of the lips slope downwards towards the board. Cut a groove along the middle *(fig 2)*. Position the cake on the board.

3 Slice and fill the centre with buttercream. Reassemble and cover the outside of the cake with buttercream.

fig 2

4 Knead and roll out all the red sugarpaste (rolled fondant icing) to a thickness of 1 cm (½ in). (If it's nice and thick, it's easier to achieve a nice smooth luxurious finish.)

5 Lift and place the icing over the cake. Carefully press the icing into the groove. Then smooth and trim the sides,

keeping the excess icing. Finish off by running over the cake with a pair of smoothers.

6 Cut out two red heart shapes and make three sets of lips out of the leftover icing *(fig 3)*. For each pair of lips make two small red sausage (rope) shapes the same size. Make a small dent in the middle of the top lid and press the two sections together. Tweak the ends into points.

7 Thinly roll out the black sugarpaste and cut out eleven heart shapes using the cutter.

8 Arrange the hearts and lips around the cakes with squiggles of black royal icing.

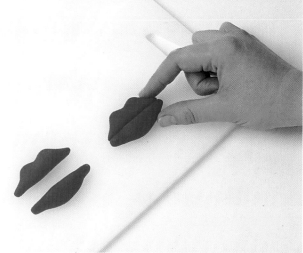

fig 3

TIP: *To save you time and effort on baking day, the small decorative lips and the hearts can easily be made a few days in advance. Store them carefully in an airtight tin until required.*

Knapsack

Not only would this be an extremely apt cake for someone about to embark on a long voyage but it would also make a good cake for someone about to leave home for the first time. Alternatively, if they show no inclinations to fly the nest, you could make it as a cheeky hint that perhaps it was about time they did!

INGREDIENTS

15 cm (6 in) round cake
1 quantity buttercream (see page 14)
600 g (1 lb 6 oz) white sugarpaste (rolled fondant icing)
600 g (1 lb 6 oz) red sugarpaste (rolled fondant icing)
10 g (¼ oz) black sugarpaste (rolled fondant icing)
100 g (4 oz) green coloured sugar (see page 14)
2 breadsticks
Icing (confectioners') sugar, for rolling out on
Water

UTENSILS

25 cm (10 in) round cake board
Small sharp knife
Carving knife
Palette knife (metal spatula)
Rolling pin
Cake smoothers
Paintbrush

fig 1

1 Shape the cake. If it rose well in the oven, trim off the outside crust but keep most of the dome shape. Turn the cake upside down on the cake board. Round the sides and build up the height with approximately 250 g (9 oz) white sugarpaste (rolled fondant icing) *(fig 1)*.

2 Split the cake and fill the centre with buttercream. Place onto the cake board and spread additional buttercream around the sides and top.

3 Knead and roll out the red sugarpaste and cover the cake with it. Smooth the sides with cake smoothers. Trim and keep the excess icing for making the tie later. Make a few crease marks with the back of a knife *(fig 2)*.

4 Measure the breadsticks and cut to size. (It'll probably take about one and a half depending on the length of the sticks you use.)

5 For the tie, roll 50 g (2 oz) of red sugarpaste into a pointed oval shape about 10 cm (4 in) long. Pinch the centre together and flatten the whole shape slightly. Place on the top of the cake.

6 Place the breadsticks on top and twist the two sugarpaste ends over, making sure that the join in the breadsticks is hidden from view by the sugarpaste *(fig 3)*.

7 Clean any dusty icing (confectioners') sugar marks off the cake with a damp paintbrush and a little water.

8 Divide 100 g (4 oz) of white sugarpaste into small flattened balls and stick onto the sides of the knapsack.

9 Make the rocks by partially kneading together the remaining white sugarpaste and the remaining black sugarpaste. Divide into misshapen balls and arrange on the board.

10 Finally moisten the cake board and carefully spoon the coloured sugar around the base of the cake.

fig 3

TIP: *Don't make the red icing too moist when cleaning it with water or it will bleed!*

fig 2

Wedding present

A bold way to decorate a single-tier cake. Tie the colours of the ribbons and mice in with the wedding colours and if you really fancy a challenge, find out what the bride and groom will be wearing and dress the mice in miniature replica outfits. Cake smoothers are essential for achieving the straight edges and neat corners required on this cake.

INGREDIENTS

30 cm (12 in) square fruit cake
2.5 kg (5 lb) marzipan
(almond paste)
3.25 kg (7 lb 4 oz) white
sugarpaste (rolled fondant
icing)
65 g (2 ½ oz) pink sugarpaste
(rolled fondant icing)
25 g (1 oz) black sugarpaste
(rolled fondant icing)
4 tbsp brandy
4 tbsp warmed apricot jam
White royal icing (see page 15)
Icing (confectioners') sugar
for rolling out
Black food colour
Water

UTENSILS

40 cm (16 in) square cake
board
Small sharp knife
Carving knife
Cocktail stick (toothpick)
Pastry brush
Rolling pin
Cake smoothers
Ruler
Heart-shaped cutters
Scissors
3 m (40 in) x 45 mm (1 ¾ in)
wide white ribbon
3 m (40 in) x 35 mm (1 ¼ in)
wide pink ribbon
3 m (40 in) x 25 mm (1 in) wide
white ribbon
3 m (40 in) x 15 mm (½ in) wide
pink ribbon
Piping bag
Paintbrushes, one medium,
one fine
Templates for mice clothes
(see page 186)

1 Level the top of the cake and place it upside down on the cake board. If there is a gap between what is now the base of the cake and the board, fill this with a sausage (rope) of marzipan. Pierce the cake a number of times with the cocktail stick (toothpick) and drizzle the brandy over the cake. Brush the warmed apricot jam over the top and sides using a pastry brush.

2 Place the marzipan onto a surface dusted with icing (confectioners') sugar. Knead it until it becomes nice and pliable then roll it out and cover the cake. Stroke the marzipan into place with your hands and trim away any excess from the base. Then run a pair of cake smoothers over the top and sides trying to get the corners as neat and squared as possible.

3 Moisten the marzipan with a little water to prepare for the next step.

4 Roll out 2.5 kg (5 lb) white sugarpaste. Lift the icing and carefully place it onto the cake. Smooth and trim the sides as necessary.

5 To make the folds in the paper, carefully press a long 'V' shape into two opposite sides of the cake using the edge of a clean ruler.

6 Press a heart-shaped cutter into the icing while it's still soft. This will make the pattern on the 'paper'. Take care not to press right into the fruit cake below as moisture from the fruit could leak through and discolour the cake *(fig 1)*.

fig 1

7 Measure the height and width of the cake and cut two strips of the widest ribbon to that length (counting the height measurement twice). Arrange the two ribbons in a criss-cross fashion across the cake and secure the centre and the ends with dabs of royal icing. Don't worry if moisture from the icing leaks through the ribbon as this will be hidden by the bow and the icing round the board later. Repeat this procedure with the other three ribbon widths *(fig 2)*.

8 To cover the board, thinly roll out 850 g (1 lb 14 oz) of white sugarpaste (see page 16). Cut this into strips wider than the width of the board. Moisten the exposed cake board with a little water. Take one of the strips and lay it onto the board, deliberately allowing it to fall into folds and creases as you do so. Continue to do this all around the cake, remembering to hide the ends of the ribbon. Trim away the excess from the edges and press down any gaping holes with your thumb.

fig 2

9 To make the groom, knead and roll 25 g (1 oz) pink sugarpaste into a cone shape (*fig 3*). Bend the pointed end over to make a nose and flatten the base. Knead and roll out 10 g (¼ oz) black sugarpaste and cut out a jacket shape using the template if necessary. Wrap it around the groom's back and stick with a little water. Make a tiny black sausage for the arm and cut a tiny pea-sized ball of black sugarpaste in half for his feet. Give the groom a hat made out of a small black circle topped with a small black circle of icing.

10 For the bride, mould 20 g (¾ oz) of white sugarpaste into a small cone. Take another 10 g (¼ oz) oval of white sugarpaste and place this on top. Place a small pink pointed cone shape on top of this for her head. Make a small pink sausage of icing for the bride's arms and stick this onto the front of her body in a 'U' shape. Stick three tiny white balls onto her 'hands' and indent each ball with the tip of a paintbrush.

11 Give the bride a veil (see template, page 186) cut out of a rolled out bit of white icing. Stick this to the back of her head and finish off with three tiny white balls of icing on top.

Give each mouse two tiny balls for ears and indent each one with the tip of a paintbrush. On the faces, give each mouse two small flattened white circles for eyes and an even tinier one for the nose. Paint in the mouth, eyeballs and eyelashes with black food colour and a fine paintbrush.

12 Place the two mice into position and make two tails out of 20 g (¾ oz) of pink icing. Stick these into position.

13 Arrange the rest of the ribbon into an attractive bow and stick in place with a little royal icing.

TIP: *Wipe your hands after using the black sugarpaste so you don't get dirty fingerprints everywhere.*

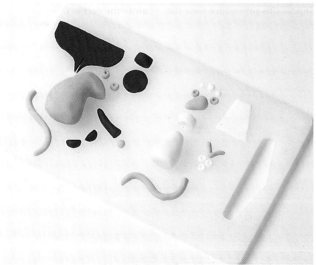

fig 3

5 9

Valentine teddies

Teddies are extremely useful because they can be used on so many cakes. For example, a couple of brightly coloured ones would be ideal for a child whilst a big surly blue one bedecked with a tie might make a good gift for Father's Day. Although the ones featured here are fairly basic, you could always add some extra features.

INGREDIENTS

18 cm (7 in) square cake
1 quantity buttercream (see page 14)
750 g (1 lb 10 oz) red sugarpaste (rolled fondant icing)
150 g (5 oz) pink sugarpaste (rolled fondant icing)
350 g (12 oz) white sugarpaste (rolled fondant icing)
2 small heart-shaped chocolates
Black food colour
Icing (confectioners') sugar, for rolling out
Water

UTENSILS

25 cm (10 in) round cake board
Template (see page 186)
Carving knife
Small sharp knife
Palette knife (metal spatula)
Rolling pin
Cake smoothers
Paintbrushes, one medium, one fine
Small heart-shaped cutter

fig 1

1 Cut the cake to shape using the template *(fig 1)*. Level the top and place the cake upside down in the middle of the cake board.

2 Slice the cake and fill the centre with buttercream. Reassemble the cake and spread additional buttercream around the top and sides.

3 Knead and roll out the red sugarpaste (rolled fondant icing) fairly thickly. (Don't roll it any thinner than 1 cm (½ in).) Lift and place the icing over the cake and smooth the sides and trim away the excess. Run over the top and sides with cake smoothers.

4 To make the teddies, knead 75 g (3 oz) pink sugarpaste until pliable. Pull off a small ball (just enough to make four tiny ears later) and put this to one side. Divide the rest into two cone shapes. Bend them slightly so that they lean together. Add two 10 g (¼ oz) balls for heads.

For the legs, roll a 20 g (¾ oz) lump of sugarpaste into a sausage (rope) about 13 cm (5 in) long. Divide this into four. Flatten one end of each leg to make a foot and bend the foot up slightly to form a sort of 'L' shape. Lightly squeeze the thigh and place the legs into position. Poke the pointed end of a paintbrush, into the base of each paw four times to make the pads of the feet *(fig 2)*.

fig 2

5 Moisten the bears' stomachs with a little water and gently press the chocolates into position. Roll 10 g (¼ oz) pink icing into a sausage about 13 cm (5 in) long. Divide into four arms. Squeeze both ends

of each arm and stick onto the bodies with the hands clasping the chocolates *(fig 3)*. Give both teddies two small balls of pink for ears and poke a small hole in each one with the end of a paintbrush. Paint two small circles for eyes using black food colour and a fine paintbrush. Add pupils and also eyelashes on the lady. Stick two small flattened balls of white below the eyes for the muzzle. Paint a nose and mouth on each one.

fig 3

6 Roll a 50 g (2 oz) lump of white sugarpaste into small balls. Use these to decorate the edge of the cake. Stick them in place with water. Position the teddies. Roll out 100 g (4 oz) white sugarpaste and cut out 6 hearts with the cutter. Use these to decorate the cake.

7 Moisten the exposed cake board with water. Thinly roll out 200 g (7 oz) white sugarpaste. Cut this into strips and drape onto the board, coaxing the icing into irregular folds like material. Trim away the excess and press down any unsightly bits (see page 17).

TIP: *Assemble the teddies away from the cake so you don't lean on, and damage, the surface.*

Get well soon

There's no prize for guessing the most apt situation this cake is aimed at. But at least bearing down on an ailing friend or relative with this humorous cake would be a bit more original than grapes! Alternatively, stick a few candles around the board and you have the perfect birthday cake for the favourite hypochondriac in your life.

INGREDIENTS

15 cm (6 in) round sponge
1 quantity buttercream (see page 14)
500 g (1 lb 2 oz) flesh-coloured sugarpaste (rolled fondant icing)
50 g (2 oz) black sugarpaste (rolled fondant icing)
20 g (¾ oz) white sugarpaste (rolled fondant icing)
75 g (3 oz) red sugarpaste (rolled fondant icing)
500 g (1 lb 2 oz) green sugarpaste (rolled fondant icing)
10 g (¼ oz) yellow sugarpaste (rolled fondant icing)
20 g (¾ oz) blue sugarpaste (rolled fondant icing)
1 candy stick
Red and black food colours
Icing (confectioners') sugar, for rolling out
Water

UTENSILS

23 cm (9 in) round cake board
Carving knife
Palette knife (metal spatula)
Small sharp knife
Rolling pin
Template for hair (see page 186)
Paintbrushes, one medium, one fine

1 Level the sponge and position it on the cake board. Split it in half and fill the middle with buttercream. Reassemble and spread buttercream around the sides and top.

2 Roll out and cover the cake with 450 g (1 lb) of flesh-coloured sugarpaste (rolled fondant icing). Trim and keep any excess.

3 Knead and roll the black sugarpaste. Cut out a fringe and keep the trimmings, using the template if necessary. Stick this into place with water.

4 Knead and roll out the white sugarpaste. Cut out two circles about 2.5 cm (1 in) in diameter for the eyes.

fig 1

5 Cut out a slightly larger circle out of 10 g (¼ oz) flesh-coloured sugarpaste. Cut this in half and stick one half over each eye (*fig 1*). Add a thin string of black along the base of both eyelids and stick a small flattened circle of black in each eye. Finish off the eyes with two tiny balls of white for the highlights.

6 Make a round nose out of 40 g (2 ½ oz) of flesh-coloured sugarpaste and stick in place.

7 Roll about 5 g (⅛ oz) of black icing into a thin string for a mouth and position this to look miserable.

fig 2

8 Make a thermometer out of a candy stick. Paint a few black marks up the stick and add a thin red line. Finish with a ball of white on the top. Paint a small curved line at the corners of the mouth and insert the thermometer (*fig 2*).

9 Stick a few red sugarpaste spots onto the face.

10 Knead and roll out the green sugarpaste into a strip about 60 cm x 7.5 cm (23 in x 3 in) long. Roll the sugarpaste into a bandage.

11 Moisten side of head and wrap the green sugarpaste round (*fig 3*).

12 Roll out and cut 50 g (2 oz) of red sugarpaste into a rectangle 7.5 cm x 5 cm (3 in x 2 in). Cut the rectangle into a fringe and stick into position on scarf.

13 Finally, add two small stripes. Make one out of blue sugarpaste and the other out of yellow.

TIP: *Rather than using red sugarpaste to make the patient's spots you could use red coloured sweets (candies).*

fig 3

Frog pond

In this cake, the pond is 'flooded' with royal icing. If you don't feel competent about trying this, simply cover the board with blue sugarpaste instead. The second new technique is modelling the waves out of piped royal icing. Don't worry if you're a bit unsure about handling a piping bag because the more wobbly the line the better.

1 Slice the cake in half and fill the centre with buttercream. Place the cake on the board and cover the top and sides with buttercream as well.

2 Knead and roll out the mid-green sugarpaste (rolled fondant icing). Lift and place over the cake. Smooth the sides using your hands and a pair of cake smoothers and trim and keep any excess from the base.

3 Using the back of a knife, score a central vein down the centre of the leaf and add a couple leading away from it. Use about 10 g (¼ oz) of the leftover icing to make a sausage about 10 cm (4 in) long for the stem. Drape this from the back of the leaf onto the cake board.

4 Now make the frogs *(fig 1)*. Make a 50 g (2 oz) ball of dark green sugarpaste for the male frog's body. Stick this onto the edge of the leaf and insert a cocktail (toothpick) stick or couple of strands of uncooked spaghetti.

fig 1

5 Moisten the neck and stick on a 25 g (1 oz) ball of dark green sugarpaste for the head.

6 To make the mouth, roll 10 g (¼ oz) of dark green sugarpaste into a longish oval

and press a line down the centre using the back of a knife. Tweak the ends and stick onto the head.

7 Make each leg out of 10 g (¼ oz) of green sugarpaste. Roll each one into a slightly tapered 10 cm (4 in) sausage (rope). Press and flatten about 2.5 cm (1 in) of the thicker end. The leg should now look like a small paddle. Cut 2 small triangles out of the foot to give the impression of webbed feet. Bend the leg into an 'S' shape and press against the frog's body, allowing the

end of the foot to just dangle over the side of the lily leaf. Repeat with the other foot.

8 For the lady frog, again make another 25 g (1 oz) ball of dark green sugarpaste for the head. Add a 10 g (¼ oz) strip for the mouth and score a line across the middle.

9 Make four small white sugarpaste balls and stick two

onto each frog for eyes. Add a small flattened circle of black to each eye and finish with a small ball of white for a highlight.

10 Add a little strip of yellow sugarpaste for Mrs Frog's hair. Cut out a pink bow and secure this to her head with a little water.

11 Divide 15 g (½ oz) dark green sugarpaste into four and make four small sausage-shaped arms, two for each frog. Secure these in position with a little water.

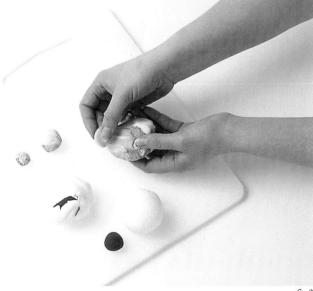

fig 2

12 Make the rocks by partially kneading 25 g (1 oz) black sugarpaste into 50 g (2 oz) white. Pull bits off and roll into small misshapen ball shapes *(fig 2)*. Moisten the cake board and stick the rocks, close together, around the edge.

13 Put 5 tbsp royal icing into a small bowl. Stir in enough blue food colour to make it a

rich blue. Add just enough water so that when the knife is lifted out, the icing begins to fall back on itself and loses its shape. Spoon it into an empty piping (decorating) bag. Snip the end off the bag and starting from the pointed end of the lily, begin to fill pool with 'water'. Move the piping bag from side to side across the exposed cake board in a wiggly motion. Push the icing into any reluctant corners with the tip of a damp paint brush. Leave to dry for at least a few hours, or over night.

14 Make the lily flowers by cutting out 5 white petals per flower using a small circle cutter or piping nozzle (tip). Stick the petals around the lily pad. Now make yellow sugarpaste circles and stick these securely in the centre of each flower.

15 Put 1 tbsp white royal icing into a bag with No 4

nozzle (tip). Pipe a line around base of the lily leaf. Using a damp paintbrush, stroke the icing back away from the leaf to achieve the wave effect (fig 3).

TIP: *Don't worry if you get a few trapped air bubbles in your 'flooded' water. They will enhance the pond by making it look authentic.*

fig 3

Shopping bag

The ideal cake for anyone who shops 'til they drop. If the recipient favours a certain shop, have their bags poking out amongst the shopping. You could also paint small rectangles of icing with food colour to look like credit cards. If you really want to cheat, simply stuff the top of the bag with a couple of real (and clean!) scarves.

INGREDIENTS

18 cm (7 in) square cake
1 quantity buttercream (see page 14)
750 g (1 lb 10 oz) mid-blue sugarpaste (rolled fondant icing)
100 g (4 oz) green sugarpaste (rolled fondant icing)
150 g (5 oz) pink sugarpaste (rolled fondant icing)
100 g (4 oz) white sugarpaste (rolled fondant icing)
90 g (3 ½ oz) dark blue sugarpaste (rolled fondant icing)
90 g (3 ½ oz) yellow sugarpaste (rolled fondant icing)
90 g (3 ½ oz) red sugarpaste (rolled fondant icing)
200 g (7 oz) black sugarpaste (rolled fondant icing)
30 g (1 ¼ oz) light orange sugarpaste (rolled fondant icing)
Black food colour
Icing (confectioners') sugar, for rolling out
Water

UTENSILS

20 cm (8 in) square cake board
Carving knife
Palette knife (metal spatula)
Small sharp knife
Rolling pin
Cake smoothers
Template (see page 185)
Drinking straw
Paintbrush

fig 1

1 Lay the cake flat and cut a long tapering triangle off two opposite sides (*fig 1*). Stand the cake upright so that the shortest edge is at the top of the cake and check that it balances. If it doesn't, shave bits of cake off the bottom. Place bits of the off-cuts against the wider sides of the cake. These will look like exciting bulges when the cake is covered.

2 Place the cake diagonally on the cake board. Slice and fill the centre with buttercream. Use the buttercream to 'glue' the off-cuts to the side of the cake. Then spread the buttercream over the top and sides.

3 Knead and roll out the mid-blue sugarpaste (rolled fondant icing). Cut out a thick strip approximately 55 cm (22 in) long and 2.5 cm (1 in) deeper than the height of the cake. Keep the excess. Starting from the back, carefully wrap the sugarpaste around the cake, making sure that the top edge of the icing is higher than the top edge of the cake. Trim and keep any excess icing from the base and neaten the top edge.

4 Begin to fill the top of the bag (*fig 2*). Make two 50 g (2 oz) green sugarpaste squares. Make a bottle out of 50 g (2 oz) pink topped with a small, slightly flattened 20 g (¾ oz) ball of white. Place these into the top of the bag and fill the empty spaces with flat squares of dark blue, yellow, red and pink sugarpaste slightly scrunched up and allowed to fall over the sides of the bag. Roll out 50 g (2 oz) white and cut out a glove

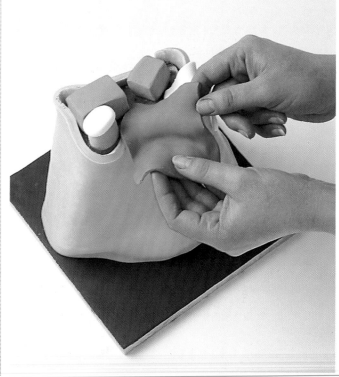

fig 2

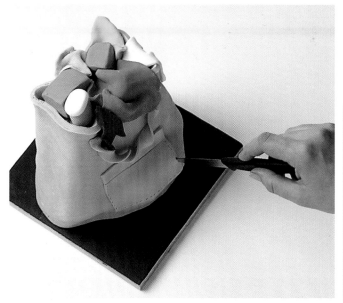

9 Cut a second glove shape out of 20 g (¾ oz) white sugarpaste. Cut out a pink and an orange square. Arrange and stick onto the board with water.

10 Make a necklace by partially mixing a tiny ball of blue and pink sugarpaste into 25 g (1 oz) of white. Roll the icing into tiny balls. Arrange in a wavy line around the board and secure. Add a small yellow oval for a clasp.

fig 3

11 Using black food colour, carefully paint small irregular oval shapes onto the orange scarf to achieve a leopard skin effect.

TIP: *When butter-creaming the cake, cover the sides of the cake first. This allows you to hold the cake steady by the top and stops you getting sticky.*

shape using the template. Insert this into the top of the bag and allow the fingers to fall over the side. Secure everything with a little water.

5 Roll the remaining mid-blue sugarpaste out flat and cut out two strips about 23 cm x 2 cm (9 in x ¾ in). Twist the sugarpaste to form a handle and stick to the side of the cake with water. Repeat on the other side. Cut out a pocket and stick it to the front of the cake. Score a line using the back of a knife about 2 cm (¾ in) from the top of the pocket. Using just the tip of a sharp, pointed knife, make a line of tiny incisions around the edge of the pocket and the tops of the handles to look like stitching *(fig 3)*.

6 Decorate the pocket with a button made out of a small flattened ball of yellow. Press a drinking straw and the end of a paintbrush into the centre of the button.

7 Moisten the cake board with a little water. Roll out the black sugarpaste and cover the board in sections (see page 17). Trim the edges.

8 Make the purse out of the red sugarpaste rolled into a slightly misshapen oval. Score a few creases into the sugar-paste using the back of a knife. Stick a thin strip of yellow onto the top and two small yellow pearls for the clasp. Place against the bag.

Stuffed elephant

Now here's a real party animal! Although I originally designed this cake for children, I rather suspect he will appeal to many adults as well as we have all felt how he looks at some time or another. If you wanted to dress him up a bit, you could attach a bow around his neck or place a few party streamers around the board.

INGREDIENTS

15 cm (6 in) round cake
1 quantity buttercream (see page 14)
350 (12 oz) pale blue sugarpaste (rolled fondant icing)
1.15 kg (2 lb 5 oz) pale pink sugarpaste (rolled fondant icing)
50 g (2 oz) white sugarpaste (rolled fondant icing)
20 g (¾ oz) black sugarpaste (rolled fondant icing)
10 g (¼ oz) dark pink sugarpaste (rolled fondant icing)
1 tbsp dark pink royal icing (see page 15)
Icing (confectioners') sugar, for rolling out
Water

UTENSILS

30 cm (12 in) round cake board
Carving knife
Small sharp knife
Palette knife (metal spatula)
Rolling pin
Cake smoothers
Wooden spoon
Fish slice (pancake turner)
Piping bag fitted with No 2 (round tip) nozzle
Paintbrush
Clingfilm (plastic wrap)

1 Lightly moisten the cake board with a little water. Roll out the pale blue sugarpaste (rolled fondant icing) and use this to cover the board (see page 16). Trim and neaten the edges and place the board to one side.

fig 1

2 Carve the cake into a rounded shape on a spare cake board or clean work surface (countertop). Slice it in half and fill the centre with buttercream. Spread buttercream around the sides and top as well and cover the cake using 500 g (1 lb 2 oz) of pale pink sugarpaste. Smooth and trim away any excess and lift the cake and place it towards the rear of the covered cake board using a fish slice (pancake turner). Be careful not to get any indents or fingerprints on the sugarpaste *(fig 1)*.

3 Make a head using 300 g (11 oz) of pale pink icing. Mould it into a chunky tennis racquet sort of shape. Flatten the head slightly and pinch around the edge of the trunk to make a slight rim. Moisten the body and cake board and place the head into position. Press the end of a wooden spoon into the end of the trunk to make the nostrils and

use the back of a knife to make a few creases across the top of the trunk.

4 Make four pink 50 g (2 oz) chunky carrot shapes for the legs and stick into position. Cut out four 2.5 cm (1 in) white circles and stick one to the pad of each foot.

5 Make two 50 g (2 oz) pale pink ovals for the ears and stick one either side of the head using a couple of scrunched up balls of clingfilm (plastic wrap) to support the backs of the ears whilst they are drying *(fig 2)*. Cut out two smaller white ovals and stick these inside the ears.

6 Make a thin, tapering sausage (rope) shape for the tail out of 20 g (¾ oz) of pale pink sugarpaste.

7 For the eyes, cut out two 2.5 cm (1 in) round circles of white sugarpaste and stick these in place. Add two 2 cm (¾ in) black circles and finish with two tiny flattened balls of white as highlights.

8 Add two thin black sausage shapes as eyebrows and a fringe (bangs) cut out of the dark pink sugarpaste.

9 Put the pink royal icing into a piping (decorating) bag fitted with a No 2 piping nozzle (round tip) and and pipe dots onto the board *(fig 3)*.

fig 3

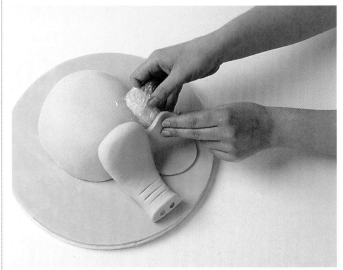

fig 2

TIP: *If you feel that piping all those spots would make you go 'dotty', substitute sweets (candies) instead.*

Dopey dog

The way to give someone who wants a puppy for their birthday a dog – without all the chewed slippers and 'little presents' that usually accompany the real thing. This is the ideal cake and for both dog and cake lovers alike. If you're feeling adventurous, try and base the markings of the dog on the family pet or a favourite breed.

INGREDIENTS

18 cm (7 in) round cake
1 quantity buttercream (see page 14)
600 g (1 lb 6 oz) brown sugarpaste (rolled fondant icing)
50 g (2 oz) flesh-coloured sugarpaste (rolled fondant icing)
165 g (5½ oz) black sugarpaste (rolled fondant icing)
25 g (1 oz) white sugarpaste (rolled fondant icing)
150 g (5 oz) red sugarpaste (rolled fondant icing)
About 12 edible silver coloured balls
Icing (confectioners') sugar, for rolling out
Water

UTENSILS

23 cm (9 in) round cake board
Small sharp knife
Carving knife
Palette knife (metal spatula)
Rolling pin
Template (see page 185)
Cake smoothers
Paintbrush
Small plastic bags

fig 1

1 Level the top of the cake if necessary and turn the cake upside down. Cut the shape of the dog's head out of the cake using the template (*fig 1*).

2 Slice the cake in half and fill the centre with buttercream. Spread buttercream over the top and sides and place the cake onto the board.

3 Roll out the brown sugarpaste (rolled fondant icing) and cover the cake with it. Neaten and flatten the sides using smoothers. Trim away and keep the excess.

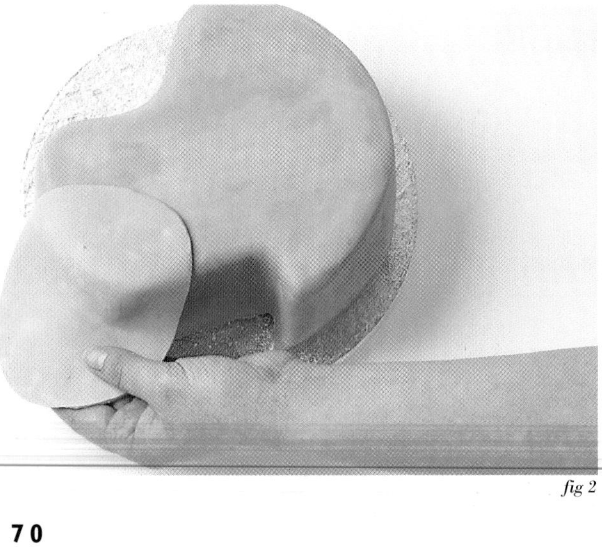

4 Knead and roll out the flesh-coloured sugarpaste and cut out a large oval shape. Stick this onto the muzzle area with water and trim away any excess from the bottom (*fig 2*).

5 Make a 20 g (¾ oz) ball of black sugarpaste for the nose and stick into position with a little water.

6 Use 10 g (¼ oz) of black sugarpaste for the mouth. Roll the icing into a thin string approximately 10 cm (4 in) – the length will depend on the depth of your cake – and stick it onto the muzzle and down the side of the cake.

7 Mould 75 g (3 oz) of red sugarpaste into a tongue and stick this onto the mouth, with the thickest part resting on the brown sugarpaste beneath the eye.

8 Make three small flattened balls out of black sugarpaste and stick above the tongue.

9 Roll out 10 g (¼ oz) white sugarpaste and cut out an oval shape for the eye. Slice the base off the oval and stick this into position on the dog's head, securing with water.

10 Roll 10 g (¼ oz) black sugarpaste into a thin string and cut off a section about 13 cm (5 in) long. Now place this round the eye, trimming the ends if necessary so that they line up with the base of the eye.

11 Place another black sugarpaste 'string' about 6 cm (2 ½ in) long under the eye.

12 Add a black eyeball and finish with a flattened white ball of icing as a highlight.

fig 2

13 Make an ear by cutting a leaf shape out of 40 g (1 ½ oz) black sugarpaste. Moisten the cake board above the dog's nose and ease the ear into position. Make another ear out of 65 g (2 ½ oz) black sugarpaste and stick this onto the top of the cake, bending the top of the ear slightly back on itself as you lay it down (*fig 3*).

Knead the remaining red sugarpaste until pliable and roll out. Cut a strip approximately 23 cm x 2.5 cm (9 in x 1 in) and place around the dog's neck. Press the silver balls into the collar and secure with a little water.

Make a couple of dog biscuits by kneading a little brown icing into 20 g (¾ oz) white sugarpaste. Divide into two slightly flattened balls and poke six holes into the top of each biscuit with the end of a paintbrush. Stick onto the board with water (*fig 3*).

fig 3

TIP: *If the silver balls refuse to stay put, stick them with a little red-coloured royal icing.*

Cat and mouse

Who says that mice are always scared of cats? This one certainly isn't! Make the markings on the cat similar to those of your own pet, or the intended recipient's, and save time on 'cake decorating day' by making the mouse a few days in advance or even substituting a shop-bought sugar one instead.

INGREDIENTS

18 cm (7 in) round cake
1½ quantities of buttercream (see page 14)
350 g (12 oz) red sugarpaste (rolled fondant icing)
1 kg (2 lb 4 oz) orangey-brown sugarpaste (rolled fondant icing)
10 g (¼ oz) green sugarpaste (rolled fondant icing)
20 g (¾ oz) pink sugarpaste (rolled fondant icing)
20 g (¾ oz) black sugarpaste (rolled fondant icing)
100 g (4 oz) dark brown sugarpaste (rolled fondant icing)
25 g (1 oz) grey sugarpaste (rolled fondant icing)
Liquorice (licorice) bootlace
Icing (confectioners') sugar, for rolling out
Water

UTENSILS

30 cm (12 in) round cake board
Carving knife
Small sharp knife
Palette knife (metal spatula)
Fish slice (pancake turner)
Rolling pin
Cake smoothers
Paintbrush
Cocktail stick (toothpick)

1 Cover the 30 cm (12 in) round cake board with the red sugarpaste (rolled fondant icing) (see page 16). Place this board to one side.

fig 1

2 On either a spare cake board or a clean work surface (counter top), cut the cake into an oval shape that tapers and slopes towards the front *(fig 1)*. Slice and fill the centre with buttercream and continue to spread the buttercream carefully over the top and sides.

3 Roll out 500 g (1 lb 2 oz) of the orangey-brown sugarpaste to a 5 mm (¼ in) thickness. Lift and place over the cake. Smooth down the icing first with your hands, then with a pair of cake smoothers and trim away any excess.

4 Lift the cake using a fish slice (pancake turner). Slide

the fish slice under the back and place the cake towards the rear of the sugarpasted board. Be careful not to damage the sugarpaste.

5 To make the head *(fig 2)*, roll 300 g (11 oz) of the orangey-brown sugarpaste into a large flattish oval shape. Place into position and stick with a little water.

6 Cut two flat almond shapes out of the green sugarpaste and stick onto the face.

7 To make the ears, cut two small orangey-brown triangles and stick these onto the top of the head.

Thinly roll out 10 g (¼ oz) pink sugarpaste and cut out two smaller triangles and stick these inside the ears. Bend the tips of the ears forward slightly.

8 Make the eyebrows by rolling 10 g (¼ oz) of black sugarpaste into a thin sausage (rope). Cut this in half and bend each half into an 'S' shape. Stick one above each eye.

9 Stick a small flattened black circle onto each eye and finish off with a tiny ball of white for a highlight.

10 Make a nose out of a small rounded pink triangle. Then make a flattened black circle for a mouth.

11 For the whiskers, cut a liquorice (licorice) bootlace into short lengths about 9 cm (3 ½ in) long. Insert these into the cat's face while the icing is still soft. (See TIP.)

fig 2

12 To make the cat's tail, roll 100 g (4 oz) of the orangey-brown sugarpaste into a thick sausage and stick this into position.

13 To make the stripes, thinly roll out the brown sugarpaste. Cut out four strips for the cat's back and about 10 small strips for the tail. Also cut out a triangle for the cat's head and stick this between the cat's ears.

14 To make the mouse, roll 20 g (¾ oz) of grey sugarpaste into a cone shape. Bend the top forward slightly to make a

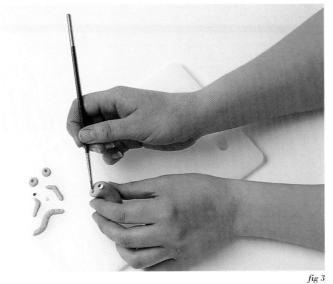

fig 3

head. Stick two tiny grey balls to the top of the head for ears and indent each ear with the end of a paintbrush. For the arms, make two small grey

strands. Flatten and bend the ends to form hands and stick one either side of the head. Secure with a little water if necessary.

15 Make two eyes out of two tiny white and two even tinier balls of black. Add a pink nose and a pink triangle for his sticking out tongue *(fig 3)*.

Make a small tail out of a thin pink sausage and stick behind the mouse's body. Indent the tail using the back of a knife.

TIP: *To prevent the icing from cracking when inserting the liquorice, first make a small hole using a cocktail stick (toothpick).*

Soccer

Colour the scarf in the recipient's favourite team's sporting colours and use it to hide any mistakes you might make when carving and covering the cake. If you really don't fancy the idea of shaping a rounded cake, it is possible to buy circular baking tins (pans) that do all the hard work for you.

INGREDIENTS

15 cm (6 in) round cake
1 quantity of buttercream (see page 14)
1 kg (2 lb 4 oz) white sugarpaste (rolled fondant icing)
50 g (2 oz) black sugarpaste (rolled fondant icing)
200 g (7 oz) blue (or the favoured team's colours) sugarpaste (rolled fondant icing)
50 g (2 oz) green coloured sugar (see page 14)
Icing (confectioners') sugar, for rolling out
Water

UTENSILS

23 cm (9 in) round cake board
Carving knife
Small sharp knife
Palette knife (metal spatula)
Rolling pin
Cake smoothers
Template for hexagon (see page 185)
Scalpel
Paintbrush
Teaspoons
Small plastic bags

fig 1

fig 3

1 Carve the cake into a rounded dome shape (*fig 1*).

2 Slice the cake in half and fill the centre with buttercream. Continue to spread the buttercream around the top and sides. Place the cake in the centre of the board.

3 Knead and roll out half of the white sugarpaste (rolled fondant icing) and cover the cake. Trim away and keep any excess from the base. Run over the surface with a cake smoother.

4 Roll out the black sugarpaste and 200 g (7 oz) of white. Using the template and a scalpel or sharp knife, cut out 20 white hexagons and seven black hexagons.

5 Starting with a black hexagon in the centre of the cake, surround it with a circle of white ones. Build up the pattern, securing the hexagons with water (*fig 2*). When all the hexagons are in place, run over the surface with a cake

smoother again to make them lie neat and flat.

6 Knead the remainder of the white sugarpaste until pliable. Roll it out and cut a strip about 50 cm x 7.5 cm (20 in x 3 in) to form the scarf.

7 Moisten the sides of the cake and wrap the scarf around (*fig 3*).

8 Roll out the blue sugarpaste and cut into stripes. Stick these onto the scarf securing them with water. Roll out and cut a white rectangle into a fringe. Stick onto the end of the scarf.

9 Moisten the exposed cake board and spoon the coloured sugar around the scarf.

TIP: *When you have cut out the hexagons, place a sheet of clingfilm (plastic wrap) over the top of them to stop them drying out and cracking before you stick them on.*

fig 2

Rag doll

Asmiling, edible doll that should please any little girl. Dress the doll in the child's favourite colours – or you could even copy her favourite dress if you're feeling particularly enterprising. If you find the sugar flowers a bit fiddly, arrange sweets (candies) or small biscuits (cookies) around the board instead.

INGREDIENTS

15 cm (6 in) round cake
15 cm (6 in) square cake
2 quantities of buttercream
(see page 14)
500 g (1 lb 2 oz) pale pink
sugarpaste (rolled fondant
icing)
450 g (1 lb) flesh-coloured
sugarpaste (rolled fondant
icing)
250 g (9 oz) white sugarpaste
(rolled fondant icing)
500 g (1 lb 2 oz) yellow
sugarpaste (rolled fondant
icing)
350 g (12 oz) brown sugarpaste
(rolled fondant icing)
20 g (¾ oz) dark pink
sugarpaste (rolled fondant
icing)
50 g (2 oz) black sugarpaste
(rolled fondant icing)
Black and blue food colours
Icing (confectioners') sugar,
for rolling out
Water

UTENSILS

30 cm x 40 cm (12 in x 16 in)
rectangular cake board
Carving knife
Small sharp knife
Palette knife (metal spatula)
Rolling pin
Cake smoothers
Fish slice (pancake turner)
No 3 piping nozzle (round tip)
Paintbrushes, one medium,
one fine
Small plastic bags

1 Moisten the entire cake board with a little water and cover with the pale pink sugarpaste (see page 16). Trim away the excess and put the board to one side.

2 Cut the round cake into a rounded dome shape for the head. The diameter at the base should measure about 12.5 cm (5 in).

3 To make the doll's body, cut two triangles off the sides of the square cake to leave a shape that resembles a roof. Then cut a slope into the neck end (fig 1).

fig 1

4 Slice and fill the centres of both cakes with buttercream. Then cover the tops and sides of the cakes with buttercream.

5 Cover the head with 250 g (9 oz) flesh-coloured icing. Trim off any excess and smooth it. Lift it with a fish slice (pancake turner) into position on the board. Place the buttercreamed body into position beneath the head.

6 Add two legs, each made from a 100 g (4 oz) sausage (rope) of white sugarpaste. Stick to the board with a little water.

7 Knead and roll out the yellow sugarpaste. Cut out a sort of roof shape for the dress, 15 cm (6 in) wide at the top, 30 cm (12 in) wide at the bottom and 23 cm (9 in) long. Drape it over the doll's body allowing it to fall onto the legs. Neaten the sides if necessary

8 Press the tip of a No 3 nozzle (round tip) along the base of the hem to produce a pattern (fig 2). Keep the excess yellow icing to one side.

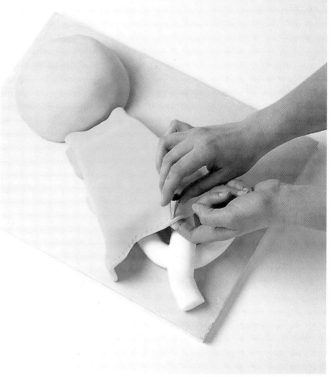
fig 2

9 Make two arms, each one made out of 100 g (4 oz) flesh-coloured icing. Flatten the hands slightly and make two partial cuts for fingers. Make another cut right through the icing for the thumb. Splay the thumb slightly. Place the arms into position using water.

10 To make the collar, roll out 50 g (2 oz) yellow icing and cut a strip 18 cm x 2.5 cm (7 in x 1 in) long. Stick along the top of the dress. Press the tip of a No 3 nozzle along the base of the collar.

11 Roll out 200 g (7 oz) of brown icing and cut out two large almond shapes and stick one to each side of the head. Score four lines down each side of the hair with the back of a knife. Cut a triangle out of the excess and cut it to make a fringe (bangs).

12 Make a plait (braid) out of 50 g (2 oz) brown sugarpaste. Roll it into a sausage (rope) about 33 cm (13 in) long. Fold the sausage in half and twist the icing together (fig 3). Moisten the side of the head and board with water and stick into

fig 3

position. Repeat on the other side. Add a small fringe to the end of each plait using about 10 g (¼ oz).

13 Make two small bows out of four small triangles and two flattened balls of dark pink icing. Position them on the the end of the plaits.

14 Cut out two flat circles about 2.5 cm (1 in) diameter of white sugarpaste for the eyes. Stick them into position. Add two smaller black circles and a flattened ball of white. Position a small ball of flesh-coloured icing for a nose. Paint the mouth and eyelashes with a fine paintbrush and black food colour.

15 Paint the stripes onto the legs with blue food colour.

16 Make flowers out of the remaining white and yellow sugarpaste. Using the No 3 piping nozzle as a cutter, cut out five white circles and one yellow per flower. Stick the five white circles in a ring and top with a yellow centre.

TIP: *Use the flowers to cover up any marks or blemishes on the board.*

Enchanted house

You can make this cake as colourful as you like. Use whatever sweets (candies) take your fancy and if, after constructing the house, you find blemishes on the brickwork, use the sweets to hide them. If you can't get hold of 'hundreds and thousands' (rainbow nonpareils) for the path, use coloured sugar instead.

INGREDIENTS

2 x 15 cm (6 in) square sponges
2 quantities of buttercream (see page 14)
800 g (1 lb 12 oz) pink sugarpaste (rolled fondant icing)
50 g (2 oz) black sugarpaste (rolled fondant icing)
200 g (7 oz) white sugarpaste (rolled fondant icing)
50 g (2 oz) brown sugarpaste (rolled fondant icing)
10 g (¼ oz) grey sugarpaste (rolled fondant icing)
500 g (1 lb 2 oz) green sugarpaste (rolled fondant icing)
31 plain finger biscuits (cookies) (but have spares in case of breakages)
3 chocolate cream biscuits (cookies)
2 tbsp white royal icing (see page 15)
Edible gold balls
Assorted sweets, lollipops, candy canes
3 tsp 'hundreds and thousands' (rainbow nonpareils)
Water
Icing (confectioners') sugar, for rolling out on

UTENSILS

Utensils
30 cm (12 in) round cake board
Carving knife
Palette knife (metal spatula)
Rolling pin
Cake smoothers
Small sharp knife
Ruler
Piping (decorating) bag fitted with a No 3 nozzle (round tip)
Paintbrush

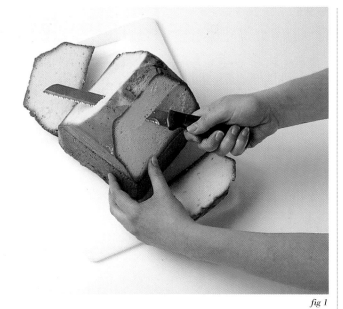

fig 1

1 Stack the two sponges on top of each other and cut the top one into a roof shape *(fig 1)*. Slice the cakes and fill the layers with buttercream. Spread buttercream around the top and sides.

2 Knead the pink sugarpaste (rolled fondant icing) on a surface dusted with icing sugar until it's pliable. Roll it out and place it over the cake. Smooth the sides, first with your hands and then with a pair of cake smoothers. Trim away any excess.

3 Make the brickwork by holding a ruler horizontally and pressing it into the icing while it's still soft *(fig 2)*. Press three lines into the sides of the house and six into the front and back. Press the back of a small knife vertically into the icing to pick out the individual bricks.

4 Split the chocolate cream biscuits in half to make the shutters. Roll the black icing out to a 3 mm (⅛ in) thickness. Measure the height of the biscuits (cookies) and make the height of the windows slightly shorter. Cut out three windows with a width of 2.5 cm (1 in) Stick the black icing windows into position with a little water. Roll out 10 g (¼ oz) white sugarpaste and cut out six strips. Place two on each window in the shape of a cross. Trim to fit and secure into position with a little

water. Using a little royal icing stick half a chocolate cream biscuit each side of each window to make the shutters.

5 Roll out the brown sugarpaste and cut out a rectangle 5 cm x 2.5 cm (2 in x 1 in). Stick this to the front of the house to make a door and holding a knife vertically, press the back of it into the icing to make the wooden slats of the door.

6 Divide the grey sugarpaste into two slightly misshapen rectangles and stick these against the door, one on top of the other to make the steps.

7 For the roof, break 25 finger biscuits in half. Starting at the bottom of one slope, make a line of five half biscuits, securing them with dabs of royal icing. Now add another line of biscuits above these and repeat a further three times. Do this again on the other side *(fig 3)*. Lay five whole biscuits across the top of the roof.

8 Make a small chimney out of either a sweet (candy) or a small white and pink icing

fig 2

fig 3

'sandwich' and position with royal icing. Stick a line of pink sweets along the top of the roof to decorate.

9 Decorate the shutters with sweets securing them with a little royal icing.

10 Pipe a line of royal icing above the door and press a finger biscuit into this to make the porch. Stick an edible gold ball in place for a door handle.

11 Pipe dots along the top and bottom of the windows.

12 Stick two 65 g (2 ½ oz) and one 50 g (2 oz) lumps of white sugarpaste onto the cake board with a little water.

13 Knead and roll out the green sugarpaste. Moisten the white 'lumps' and the exposed cake board.

Lay the green around the house in sections (see page 17). Trim the edges of the board and cut and lift away a section at the front of the house to make a path.

14 Moisten the path with a little water and sprinkle with 'hundreds and thousands' (rainbow nonpareils). Edge the sides of the path with small sweets inserted into the icing. Stick a few sweets to the side of the house and around the garden and secure with royal icing if necessary. Insert a couple of candy canes and lollipops into the green lumps.

TIP: *Score a thin line across the middle of each finger biscuit with a sharp knife before breaking them in half.*

Fisherman

Fishing is apparently one of the most popular hobbies so there must be hundreds of wet and bedraggled fishermen sitting out there in the wind and the rain who would appreciate a cake like this when they get home. If it's the fisherman's birthday, the rocks double up as ideal candle holders.

INGREDIENTS

15 cm (6 in) round cake
1 quantity buttercream (see page 14)
550 g (1 lb 4 oz) brown sugarpaste (rolled fondant icing)
50 g (2 oz) black sugarpaste (rolled fondant icing)
40 g (1½ oz) flesh-coloured sugarpaste (rolled fondant icing)
185 g (6 oz) dark green sugarpaste (rolled fondant icing)
100 g (4 oz) white sugarpaste (rolled fondant icing)
50 g (2 oz) green sugarpaste (rolled fondant icing)
3 tbsp royal icing, (see page 15)
Green and blue food colours
Water
Icing (confectioners') sugar, for rolling out

UTENSILS

25 cm (10 in) round cake board
Carving knife
Small sharp knife
Palette knife (metal spatula)
Rolling pin
Cake smoothers
Cocktail stick (toothpick)
No 3 piping nozzle (round tip)
Sieve (strainer)
Small bowl
8 jelly (candy) fish
Needle and thread
Black boot cut out of a small piece of thin cardboard
Wooden skewer, trimmed to about 20 cm (8 in)

1 Carve the cake into shape (*fig 1*). Cut slopes into the sides and then cut a small semi-circle out of the side of the cake to make a bit of an inlet. Place the cut-out bits on top of the cake to make a hill.

fig 1

2 Place the cake onto the board. Slice it in half, fill and cover with buttercream.

3 Roll out 500 g (1 lb 2 oz) of brown sugarpaste (rolled fondant icing) to a thickness of about 1 cm (½ in). Lift and cover the cake. Smooth the sides. Trim and keep the excess.

4 To make the fisherman's body, knead the remaining brown sugarpaste into a ball. Place it in position on the cake and secure with a little water.

5 To make the legs, take two 20 g (¾ oz) lumps of black sugarpaste and roll each one into a sausage (rope) about 7.5 cm (3 in) long. Bend the end of each leg into an 'L' shape to make the feet. Stick the legs into position. Insert a cocktail stick into the top of the body, leaving about 1 cm (½ in) protruding.

6 Roll 25 g (1 oz) flesh-coloured sugarpaste into a ball for the head. Moisten the neck and thread onto the stick.

7 Roll out 150 g (5 oz) dark green sugarpaste to a thick-

fig 2

ness of about 3 mm (⅛ in). Cut out a strip approximately 23 cm x 7.5 cm (9 in x 3 in). Moisten the body and wrap it round (*fig 2*). Press the tip of a No 3 piping nozzle (round tip) into the sugarpaste to make a line of buttons up the front of the coat. Make two sausages out of 10 g (¼ oz) of green sugarpaste for the arms. Stick into place. Add two small ovals of flesh-coloured sugarpaste for hands and

another ball for a nose and a strip of brown sugarpaste for the hair. Moisten the top of the head and stick a small flat 5 cm (2 in) circle onto it for a hat. Bend the front up slightly to make a peak.

8 Partially knead the remaining black sugarpaste into 50 g (2 oz) white. Mould the marbled sugarpaste into odd-sized balls for rocks.

9 Moisten the area of land behind the fisherman. Knead the green sugarpaste until pliable then push bits through a sieve (strainer). Cut off the strands and place into position.

10 Put 3 tbsp royal icing into a bowl and partially mix in a little green and blue food colours. Swirl the coloured icing around the cake board using a small palette knife (metal spatula) and place the rocks and jelly (candy) fish into position (*fig 3*). Wipe round the edge of the board with a damp cloth.

11 Using a needle, thread the cotton through the top of the cardboard wellington boot and tie a knot. Tie the other end to the wooden skewer.

fig 3

12 Carefully insert the wooden skewer through the fisherman's lap and make sure that the wellington boot is positioned properly.

TIP: *A few strands of spaghetti can be used instead of a cocktail stick, inside the fisherman's body if preferred.*

Bouquet

The wonderful thing about this cake is its versatility. Not only would it make a lovely birthday cake but it could also be used for Mother's Day, Easter, Anniversaries or Valentine's Day. These roses are the fastest and easiest you'll ever see in icing. Colour them the recipient's favourite colour or, if rushed, use silk blooms instead.

INGREDIENTS

15 cm x 20 cm (6 in x 8 in) cake (Don't rush out to buy a special tin, simply trim a 20 cm (8 in) square cake instead.)
1 quantity buttercream (see page 14)
1 kg (2 lb 4 oz) white sugarpaste (rolled fondant icing)
50 g (2 oz) pale green sugarpaste (rolled fondant icing)
50 g (2 oz) mid-green sugarpaste (rolled fondant icing)
50 g (2 oz) dark green sugarpaste (rolled fondant icing)
100 g (4 oz) yellow sugarpaste (rolled fondant icing)
25 g (1 oz) violet sugarpaste (rolled fondant icing)
2 tbsp green royal icing (see page 15)
Icing (confectioners') sugar, for rolling out
Water

UTENSILS

35 cm (12 in) square cake board
Carving knife
Small sharp knife
Palette knife (metal spatula)
Rolling pin
Wooden spoon
Clingfilm (plastic wrap)
Paintbrush
Piping (decorating) bag with No 3 nozzle (round tip)
Tin foil
Cellophane (approximately 38 cm x 43 cm/15 in x 17 in)
If you can't find cellophane in your local craft shop, buy some of the real thing from a florist instead.
Clear sticky tape
1 metre (39 in) yellow ribbon

fig 1

1 Shape the cake by slicing two long triangles off the sides and a slope into the front *(fig 1)*. Place the cake diagonally onto the cake board.

2 Slice the cake in half and fill the centre with buttercream and then cover the top and sides with buttercream as well.

3 Knead and roll the white sugarpaste (rolled fondant icing) until it's about 3 mm (⅛ in) thick. Now carefully lift the icing and place over the cake, making sure that enough icing falls onto the board at the front of the cake for you to be able to make the folds later on.

4 Gather the icing up at the front and using a wooden spoon, coax the icing into folds *(fig 2)*.

5 Wriggle your finger under the point at which the gathers meet the cake to make a tunnel through which you will thread

the ribbon later. Support the tunnel while it's drying by placing a bit of scrunched up clingfilm (plastic wrap) under the arch.

6 Trim and neaten the rest of the icing around the edges of the cake and secure the bits that rest on the board with a little water.

7 Make the leaves by rolling out about half of one of the green sugarpastes. Using a the tip of a sharp knife, cut out a simple leaf shape. Turn the knife over and press the back of it into the leaf to make a couple of simple veins. Place the leaf on a bit of partially crumpled tin (aluminium) foil so that it dries in a slightly irregular shape. Repeat with the other green sugarpastes, making a total of about fifty leaves in all.

8 To make the roses, take a 10 g (¼ oz) ball of yellow sugarpaste and roll it into a

fig 2

strip about 15 cm (6 in) long. Paint a line of water down the centre of the strip and roll it up (not too tightly) like a miniature Swiss roll. Tweak the rose into a point at the base and carefully bend back

fig 3

the top of the rose petals *(fig 3)*. Put a tiny ball of yellow sugarpaste to one side to make the iris centres later and use the rest to make a further eleven roses. Leave them to dry on their sides.

9 For the irises, take a pea-sized ball of violet sugarpaste and press it into a flat oval shape. Dab a little water in the centre and fold the icing almost in half. Bend the two ends back slightly and tweak the base into a point. Stick a tiny ball of yellow into the centre and place to dry on its side. Make another nine irises.

10 Place two tablespoons of green royal icing into a piping

bag fitted with a No 3 nozzle (round tip). Starting from just inside the folds at the front of the cake, pipe about eight flower stems.

11 Beginning from the top of the cake and working down, stick the roses and leaves into position with the royal icing.

12 Insert the irises into any gaps.

13 Tidy up any dusty icing (confectioners') sugar smudges with a damp paintbrush.

14 Place the cellophane over the cake. Secure the far end of the cellophane to the cake board with a couple of small

pieces of clear sticky tape. Gather the rest up at the front.

15 Thread the ribbon through the hole and tie a neat bow over the top of the cellophane.

16 Tweak the cellophane into place and secure at the sides with sticky tape.

TIP: *To give your bouquet that final touch, buy a card from a real florist complete with its own miniature envelope. Write your message and tuck it into the bow.*

Racetrack

A fun race track suitable for boys (or girls!) from eight to eighty. To make it a little more personal, paint 'Birthday Boy's' age on the winning car (or perhaps the losing one if he's really depressed about the relentless passing of the years!) and model it in his favourite colour or those of his favoured racing team.

INGREDIENTS

20 cm x 18 cm (8 in x 7 in) cake (trim down an 20 cm (8 in) square cake)
1 quantity buttercream (see page 14)
1.15 kg (2 lb 6 oz) mid-green sugarpaste (rolled fondant icing)
10 g (¼ oz) red sugarpaste (rolled fondant icing)
10 g (¼ oz) blue sugarpaste (rolled fondant icing)
10 g (¼ oz) yellow sugarpaste (rolled fondant icing)
25 g (1 oz) black sugarpaste (rolled fondant icing)
25 g (1 oz) white sugarpaste (rolled fondant icing)
100 g (4 oz) grey sugarpaste (rolled fondant icing)
100 g (4 oz) dark green sugarpaste (rolled fondant icing)
Black food colour
Icing (confectioners') sugar, for rolling out
Water

UTENSILS

25 cm (10 in) square cake board
Carving knife
Small sharp knife
Palette knife (metal spatula)
Rolling pin
Cake smoothers
Drinking straw
Paintbrushes, one medium, one fine
Wooden skewer trimmed to a length of about 13 cm (5 in)
Sieve (strainer)
Small plastic bags

1 Slice off the top of the cake to level it if necessary and place the cake upside down on the board. Cut the cake in half and fill the middle with buttercream. Coat the top and sides of the cake with buttercream as well.

2 Dust your work surface with icing (confectioners') sugar and roll out 1 kg (2 lb 4 oz) of the mid-green sugarpaste (rolled fondant icing) into a thick rectangle approximately 33 cm x 28 cm (13 in x 11 in) and about 8 mm (¼ in) thick.

3 Lift the icing and cover the cake. Smooth down the sides using your hands first and then the smoothers. Trim away and keep the excess to make bushes later.

fig 1

4 Cover the exposed cake board using the remaining mid-green icing cut into four strips (see page 17 for details how to do this).

5 For the cars, roll the red, blue and yellow sugarpaste into three tapered carrot shapes, each about 5 cm (2 in) long. Cut a small slice off the back of each car and re-shape these cut off bits into three small rectangles and put them to one side.

Take 10 g (¼ oz) black sugarpaste and roll it into a sausage (rope) about 7.5 cm (3 in) long. Divide this into 12 equal slices and model each slice into a small flattish round shape to make the wheels. Stick four wheels onto each car with water. Add details to the wheels by pressing the tip of a drinking straw into the centre of each wheel to leave a ring. Then make a small dot with the wooden end of a paintbrush in the middle of the ring (fig 1).

Stick a pea-sized ball of white sugarpaste onto the top of each racing car, about 1 cm (½ in) from the back end. Stick three tiny flattened black sugarpaste ovals onto the front of the helmets to make visors. Stick the three coloured rectangles onto the car behind the helmets.

fig 2

6 For the racetrack, roll out 100 g (4 oz) grey sugarpaste and cut out a rectangle about 30 cm x 7.5 cm (12 in x 3 in). Lay this diagonally across the cake and fix into position with water. Trim away any excess icing from the corners.

Knead and roll out the remaining white sugarpaste and cut out a rectangle 10 cm x 5 cm (4 in x 2 in). Place the wooden skewer into position at a slight angle. Moisten the edge of the cake and the top half of the skewer slightly with a little water. Carefully wrap one edge of the flag round the skewer and allow the rest of the icing to drape elegantly over the side of the cake, hiding the edge of the road (fig 2). Paint a chequered design onto the flag using black food colour and a fine paintbrush.

7 Now make the bushes. Put the dark green sugarpaste and any remaining mid-green sugarpaste together but don't knead them together. Pull off a lump of the icing and push it through a sieve (strainer) (fig 3). Slice off the strands with a knife and position the 'bush' on the base of the cake, sticking them down with a little water. Continue to do this all round the base of the cake and onto the top too. (This is an extremely effective way to disguise any cracks or blemishes in the icing!)

Make another six small wheels out of the remaining black sugarpaste. Press a tiny ball of grey into the centre of each one and stack them into two piles. Position one pile each side of the track. Using black food colour, paint a

fig 3

number onto each car and lines down the centre of the track. Fix the cars into position with water and paint two skid marks behind the car veering off the track using the medium paintbrush and slightly watered down food colour.

TIP: *If you want to make things easier for yourself, either substitute toy cars for the icing ones or buy some car-shaped sweets.*

Golf course

Poor old Mister Mole. He'd just found a nice ready-made hole and had settled down for a sleep in when a nasty white thing landed on his head! This cake is easier to put together than it looks. The cake can be as irregular as you like and the shrubbery can be used to hide any imperfections in the icing.

INGREDIENTS

23 cm (9 in) round cake
1 ½ quantities buttercream
(see page 14)
1 kg (2 lb 4 oz) green
sugarpaste (rolled fondant
icing)
70 g (2 ¾ oz) black sugarpaste
(rolled fondant icing)
25 g (1 oz) dark grey
sugarpaste (rolled fondant
icing)
100 g (4 oz) white sugarpaste
(rolled fondant icing)
100 g (4 oz) darker green
sugarpaste (rolled fondant
icing)
Silver and black food colours
2 tsp light golden sugar
Icing (confectioners') sugar,
for rolling out
Water

UTENSILS

25 cm (10 in) square cake
board
Carving knife
Small sharp knife
Palette knife (metal spatula)
Rolling pin
Cake smoothers
Paintbrushes, one medium,
one fine
Ball tool or wooden spoon
Two cocktail sticks
(toothpicks), optional
Sieve (strainer)
Small plastic bags

fig 1

1 Slice the top off the cake to level it if necessary and place it upside down on the cake board. Carve away part of the sides of the cake so that it now forms a slightly irregular shape. Cut out a hole slightly towards the rear of the cake approximately 5 cm (2 in) wide and 2.5 cm (1 in) deep *(fig 1)*. Slice and fill the centre of the cake with buttercream. Reassemble the cake and spread a thin layer of buttercream around the sides and top.

2 Knead and roll out the of green sugarpaste (rolled fondant icing) to a thickness of about 1 cm (½ in). Carefully lift it and place over the cake. Smooth over the top and sides, first with your hands, then with a pair of smoothers. Don't worry if the icing tears when you're pushing it into the hole as this will be hidden by the mole's body later. Trim away the excess icing (there should be about 300 g/11 oz). Store it in a plastic bag for making bushes later.

3 Now make the mole by rolling 50 g (2 oz) black sugarpaste into a ball and place this into the hole. Make a head by moulding the dark grey sugarpaste into a cone shape. Stick this onto the mole's body with a little water, making sure that the thinnest part of the cone is facing forwards.

Roll 10 g (¼ oz) white sugarpaste into a thin sausage (rope) approximately 15 cm (6 in) long. Lightly moisten the edge of the hole with a little water and lay the strip around the top edge and mole's body *(fig 2)*. Paint a disgruntled expression onto the mole's face using black food colour and a fine paintbrush.

Add two small tapering sausages of black sugarpaste for arms. Position one as though he is rubbing his eye and the other resting on the ground.

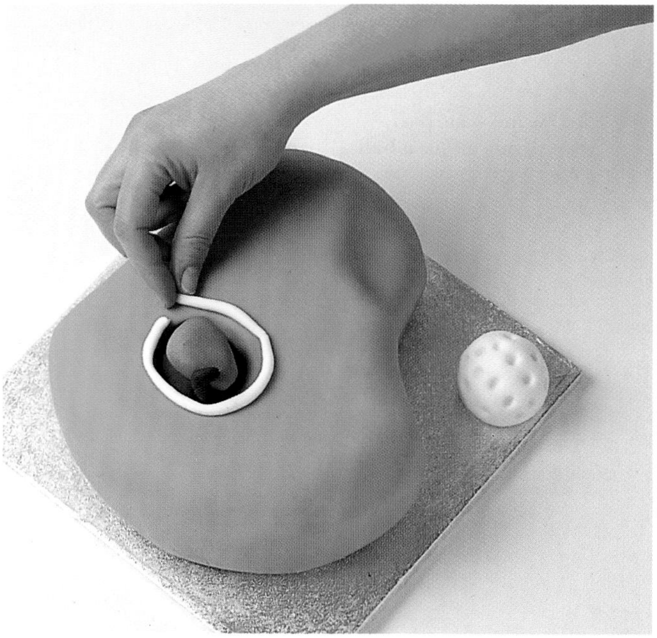

fig 2

4 To make the golf ball, roll 50 g (2 oz) white sugarpaste into a ball. Using either a ball tool or the end of a wooden spoon handle, poke small dents around the outside of the ball. Stick the ball into position.

5 For the golf club, make the metal part of the golf club out of 40 g (1 ½ oz) white sugarpaste shaped into a sort of 'L' shape. Flatten and round the edges of the base part and press a few horizontal lines into the still soft sugarpaste using the back of a knife. Make a handle out of 10 g (¼ oz) black sugarpaste rolled into a sausage. Make a few diagonal indented lines across the handle and finish with a few small holes made with the end of a paintbrush (*fig 3*). Place the golf club into

fig 3

position on the cake and paint the white metal section with silver food colour.

6 Lightly moisten the exposed cake board with a little water. Press about 200 g (7 oz) of the remaining green sugarpaste

around the board, forming small undulating slopes. Trim the edges.

7 Partially mix together the remaining mid-green sugarpaste and the dark green sugarpaste. Pull off a small ball and push it through a sieve (strainer). Cut and lift the strands of sugarpaste away from the sieve with a sharp knife and place onto the cake, sticking into place with a little water. Continue around the sides of the cake hiding the joins and any blemishes in the icing as you go.

8 Moisten the bunker area with a little water. Carefully spoon about two teaspoons of light golden (brown) sugar onto the board. Brush away any stray bits of sugar with a dry paintbrush.

TIP: *If the golf ball won't stay in position on the mole's head, remove the ball and insert two cocktail sticks (toothpicks) into the mole's head, leaving about 2.5 cm (1 in) protruding. Then place the ball back in position. The cocktail sticks will provide additional support, but please ensure that nobody tries to eat the mole without removing them first.*

N.B. *Please note that the silver food colour is inedible and therefore the golf club should be discarded when cutting the cake.*

Dinosaur

Dinosaurs can sometimes be a problem because their legs are often fairly spindly in relation to their bodies. This cake gets round that by using the rock as a support. Although technically thousands of years separated the first man from the last dinosaur, I don't think you'll find many children complaining!

INGREDIENTS

23 cm (9 in) round cake
2 quantities buttercream
(see page 14)
710 g (1 lb 6 ¼ oz) white
sugarpaste (rolled fondant
icing)
50 g (2 oz) black sugarpaste
(rolled fondant icing)
525 g (1 lb 3 oz) green
sugarpaste (rolled fondant
icing)
25 g (1 oz) orange sugarpaste
(rolled fondant icing)
50 g (2 oz) flesh-coloured
sugarpaste (rolled fondant
icing)
25 g (1 oz) dark green
sugarpaste (rolled fondant
icing)
Green, brown and black food
colours
Dessicated (shredded) coconut

UTENSILS

30 cm (12 in) round cake
board
Carving knife
Small sharp knife
Palette knife (metal spatula)
Rolling pin
Cake smoothers
Drinking straw
Paintbrushes, one medium,
one fine
Small bowls x 2
Sieve (strainer)

fig 1

1 Cut and shape the cake into a misshapen rock shape (*fig 1*). (Use the pieces that you cut away from the sides to build up the height of the cake once it is on the cake board.)

2 Slice the cake and fill the centre with buttercream. Place it onto the cake board. Continue to spread the buttercream over the top and sides of the rock.

3 Take 700 g (1 lb 6 oz) white sugarpaste (rolled fondant icing) and the black sugarpaste and partially knead the two together to achieve a marbled effect.

4 Roll out the marbled grey sugarpaste. Place it over the cake. Smooth the sides with your hands and finish with cake smoothers. Trim away and keep the excess. Roll these bits into small round pebble shapes and put to one side for use later.

5 Make the dinosaur's back leg by rolling a 20 g (¾ oz) ball of green sugarpaste into a sausage (rope) about 10 cm (4 in) long (*fig 2*). Bend this into an 'L' shape and then make another bend at the end

of the foot for the toes. Making sure that the foot section rests on the ground, stick the leg against the rock using a little water.

6 Make the body using 450 g (1 lb) green sugarpaste. Knead and roll out the icing into a thick sausage about 20 cm (8 in) long. Continue to roll one end into a tapering tail and shape the other end into a head and neck.

7 Flatten the dinosaur slightly. (It should now measure about 44 cm (18 cm) from the end of tail to the tip of nose.) Then moisten the rock with a little water and wrap the dinosaur around it, by allowing the body to fall over the already positioned back leg.

8 Make a second back leg using 50 g (2 oz) green sugarpaste.

9 Make an arm by rolling 5 g (⅛ oz) of green sugarpaste into a sausage about 5 cm (2 in) long. Flatten one end and make three small cuts for fingers. Splay the fingers slightly and stick onto the body.

10 Stick a small almond shape of white sugarpaste onto the head to make an eye. Add a black circle and a small white flattened ball for a highlight. Finish the eye off with a thin green string of icing for an eyebrow.

11 Give the dinosaur scales by pressing a drinking straw held at a slight angle into the still soft icing and press the end of a paintbrush into the nose to make a nostril.

12 Stick little triangles of white sugarpaste along the edge of the mouth for teeth. The more teeth the better.

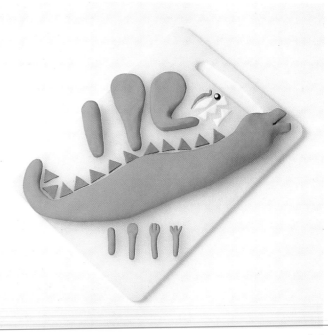

fig 2

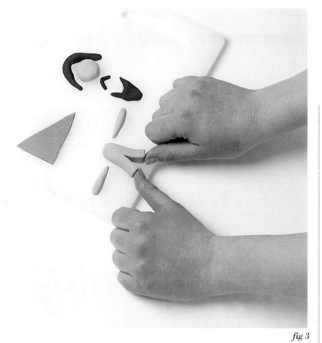

fig 3

about half way up and pull the icing apart slightly to make the legs. Bend the ends to make feet. Add a small ball for the head.

15 Place the man against the rock using a small amount of water to adhere him. Cut out a small, flat orange triangle and wrap this around his body.

16 Add two tiny arms, a beard and hair. Paint black splodges on his leopard skin and features on the face with black food colour.

17 Place some of the dessicated (shredded) coconut into a small bowl and mix with the green food colour. Repeat using more coconut and brown

food colour in a separate bowl. Moisten the cake board and sprinkle the coloured dessicated coconut around the board. Place the extra rocks that were made earlier in place.

18 To make the greenery on the rock, push the green sugarpaste through a sieve (strainer). Slice it off with a knife, moisten the rock and stick it into position over the top and side.

TIP: *If making the man looks too difficult, substitute a jelly animal or even a plastic model or doll instead.*

13 Roll out 20 g (¾ oz) of orange surgarpaste and cut out 16 small triangles. Stick these along the dinosaur's back with a little water.

14 To make the little man *(fig 3)*, roll 15 g (½ oz) flesh-coloured icing into a slightly tapered sausage shape. Make a cut from the wider end to

Toadstool

A lovely bold cake that should appeal to any child who believes in fairies and even those who don't. By covering the board, roof, window ledges and steps in white icing, this cake could easily be adapted into a magical snow-covered Christmas cake. The snail could have a Santa hat too.

1 Carve the 20 cm (8 in) cake into a rounded dome shape.

2 Now place the two smaller cakes on top of each other and carve into a slightly rounded base shape. Cut a thin strip off the top to ensure that the top is flat (*fig 1*).

fig 1

3 Place the stacked base cakes slightly towards the rear of the larger cake board. Slice the cakes and fill with buttercream. Reassemble the cakes and spread buttercream around the top and sides.

4 Knead and roll out 750 g (1 lb 10 oz) of white sugarpaste (rolled fondant icing) and use this to cover the base cakes. Lay the icing over the top of the two stacked base cakes and press it round. Neaten the sides with smoothers and trim away and keep any excess icing.

5 Spread a little buttercream onto the thin 20 cm (8 in) cake board and then place the round cake on top of it. Slice and fill the centre with buttercream and spread it over the top and sides. Roll out and cover the roof with the red sugarpaste. Smooth the icing and trim away any excess. Place the cake to one side for the moment.

6 Take the brown sugarpaste and partially knead a small ball of white icing into it to make a slight wood grain effect. Roll it out to a 3 mm (⅛ in) thickness and cut out an arched shape for the door. Stick this onto the front of the cake with a little water. Press the back of a knife vertically into the icing four times to leave the impression of wooden slats.

7 Roll out 50 g (2 oz) black sugarpaste to a 3 mm (⅛ in) thickness and cut out two smaller arch shapes for the windows. Stick one either side of the door with a little water.

8 Roll out 20 g (¾ oz) of white sugarpaste and cut four thin strips for the window frames about 5 mm (¼ in) wide. Stick two onto each window in the shape of a cross. Trim to fit.

9 Partially knead 275 g (10 oz) white sugarpaste together with 50 g (2 oz) of black to make a marbled stone effect. Make about seven misshapen balls of differing sizes for the pebbles and two flattened ovals for the path. Put to one side. Make two window ledges, two steps for the front door and a frame that sits around the edge of the window (*fig 2*). Keep a small amount of the grey sugarpaste to make the door hinges (see step 11). Stick the steps, ledges and frames into place.

fig 2

10 Knead and thinly roll out the green sugarpaste. Cut this into pointed strips of different lengths and stick these around the side of the house.

11 Finish off the door with a tiny yellow door knocker. This is made out of a small ring of yellow sugarpaste topped with a tiny flattened yellow ball.

The hinges are made out of two tiny strips of grey sugarpaste, one straight, the other one shaped into a small 'W' shape and placed on its side.

17 Now make the snail by partially kneading a little blue food colour into 25 g (1 oz) of white sugarpaste. Then roll it into a sausage approximately 15 cm (6 in) long. Roll it up and add a head made out of 10 g (¼ oz) black sugarpaste. Finally add its feelers made out of a tiny string of black sugarpaste bent into a small 'V' shape.

TIP: *If the chimney won't stay in place and keeps sliding off the cake, thread the sections onto a cocktail stick (toothpick) and insert into the cake. But please be careful to remove it when cutting if children are eating the cake.*

fig 3

12 Stick the three dowel rods into the base of the cake (*fig 3*) so that they rest on the cake board beneath. Make a small mark at the point at which they become level with the top of the cake. Pull them out and using a small hacksaw, trim them to size. Re-insert the rods back into the cake.

13 Smear about two tablespoons of royal icing over the top of the base cake and place the red roof cake into position. It's at this point that you find out why it is important to make the top of the base cakes as level as possible, otherwise the roof slides off while it's drying.

14 Make a small chimney out of 20 g (¾ oz) black sugarpaste. Roll half into a rounded shape with straight ends and the other half into a pointed triangular shape. Stick these onto the roof with a little water.

15 Thinly roll out 50 g (2 oz) of white sugarpaste. Using either circle cutters or the tip of a sharp knife, cut out about twelve spots of differing sizes. Stick these onto the roof with a little water.

16 For the grass, place the sugar into a small bowl and mix in a little green food colour.

Moisten the exposed cake board with a little water. Spoon the 'grass' over the board and position the pebbles and paving stones. Push the sugar into any awkward bits with a dry paintbrush.

Paddling pool

From the complete novice to the keen swimmer, this is the ideal cake for any water baby, especially if they are about to enter a swimming competition. If you really want to make the cake a memorable one, stir a little blue food colour into the cake mix before cooking to add an extra blue surprise when the cake is cut.

1 Level the cake if necessary and place upside down onto the cake board. Slice in half and fill the centre with buttercream. Then cover the top and sides with buttercream as well.

2 Cover the cake with the white sugarpaste (rolled fondant icing). Trim the edges and smooth the sides using smoothers. Keep the bits of excess white sugarpaste for the hat and bubbles later.

3 Now make the swimmer (*fig 1*). Mould 100 g (4 oz) of orange sugarpaste into a sausage about 18 cm (7 in) long. Moisten the ends and bend it round to form a doughnut shape. Make two arms out of 10 g (¼ oz) flesh-

fig 1

coloured sugarpaste by rolling out two small sausages (ropes) of about 5 cm (2 in) long. Flatten one end of each arm slightly and press this end over the top of the ring.

Roll 75 g (3 oz) of flesh-coloured sugarpaste into a ball to form the head. Lightly moisten the top of the rubber ring with a little water and carefully place the head on top of the arms.

Roll out 20 g (¾ oz) of white sugarpaste and cut out a semi-circle 9 cm (3 ½ in) wide to form the hat. Moisten the top of the head and fold the icing over the head. Cut a small

string of leftover icing and stick this under the head to make a strap. Press the tip of a No 3 piping nozzle (round tip) into one end of the strap to make a button.

Add two tiny flattened balls of white for eyes and a flesh-coloured ball for a nose. Paint in the eyeballs, eyelashes, eyebrows and mouth with black food colour and a fine paintbrush.

Stick small flattened balls of green icing onto the hat and a tiny black circle for a stopper onto the rubber ring.

4 Partially mix a small amount of blue food colour into the royal icing. Spread this around the top of the cake

with a small palette knife (metal spatula) (*fig 2*). Place the swimmer on top of the cake. Ease the icing into any awkward bits, such as under the arms, with a damp paintbrush.

fig 2

5 Knead and roll out about 375 g (13 oz) of blue sugarpaste to a thickness of 1 cm (½ in). Cut out a strip 55 cm x 7.5 cm (22 in x 3 in). Moisten the side of the cake. Roll the blue icing up like a bandage. Then, holding it upright, begin to unwind it around the cake starting from the back (*fig 3*). Press the ends together, applying a little water with a paintbrush if necessary. Add more royal icing if needed with a teaspoon and push it right to the edges of the pool.

Roll the remaining blue sugarpaste into a sausage about 60 cm (24 in) long. Moisten the top edge of the pool and lay it around the

edge. Press the blunt edge of a knife around the top to make a decorative pattern.

6 Wipe around the edge of the pool with a clean damp cloth to rid it of any dusty fingermarks.

7 Roll out the remaining orange sugarpaste and cut out ten simple fish shapes. Stick them around the pool.

fig 3

8 Attach tiny strips of green sugarpaste up the side of the pool. Moisten the exposed cake board and press the rest of the green sugarpaste around the base.

9 Give the fish tiny flattened balls of black sugarpaste for eyes and add a few tiny flattened balls of white sugarpaste near the fish to look like air bubbles.

10 Make two shark fins out of black sugarpaste triangles with the top bent back slightly. Place in the water behind the swimmer.

TIP: *If the recipient of the cake is male, omit the bathing cap and add a small tuft of suitably coloured hair instead.*

Christmas stocking

Just when everyone thinks that they've had all their surprises for the day, present this cake and wait for the gasps of admiration. If you have the time (usually in very short supply just before Christmas!) you could make small icing models for all the family and substitute them for the presents.

INGREDIENTS

15 cm (6 in) square fruit cake
900 g (2 lb) red sugarpaste
(rolled fondant icing)
275 g (10 oz) green sugarpaste
(rolled fondant icing)
500 g (1 lb 2 oz) white
sugarpaste (rolled fondant
icing)
3 tbsp brandy
3 tbsp apricot jam
725 g (1 lb 10 oz) marzipan
(almond paste)
26 edible gold balls
1 tsp red royal icing
(see page 15)
Icing (confectioners') sugar,
for rolling out
Water

UTENSILS

30 cm (12 in) gold-coloured
square cake board
Carving knife
Small sharp knife
Cocktail stick (toothpick)
Pastry brush
Rolling pin
Cake smoothers
Small holly cutter
Icing nozzle (tip)
Piping (decorating) bag fitted
with No 1 nozzle (round tip)
Small plastic bags for storing
icing

fig 1

1 Cut the cake in two so that one section measures 9 cm x 15 cm (3 ½ in x 6 in) and the other 7 cm x 15 cm (2 ½ in x 6 in). Place the thinner of the two strips at the base of the thicker one to produce the basic stocking shape *(fig 1)*. Cut small triangles away from the toe and heel of the stocking and also run a knife along the edges of the cake to make them rounded. Cut a slice about 2.5 cm (1 in) off the top of the cake to make the proportions look right and discard this piece.

2 Pierce the cake several times with a cocktail stick (toothpick) and drizzle the brandy over the cake. Allow the brandy to sink in, then place the cake onto the cake board.

3 Using a pastry brush, 'paint' the cake with warmed apricot jam.

4 Knead the marzipan (almond paste) on a surface dusted with icing (confectioners') sugar until it's nice and pliable. Roll it out into a rectangle approximately 5 mm (¼ in) thick and lift it over the cake. Ease it gently into position and trim away any excess marzipan. Run over the surface with cake smoothers.

5 Moisten the marzipan with a little water.

6 Knead and roll out 700 g (1 lb 8 oz) red sugarpaste (rolled fondant icing). Lay this carefully over the marzipan. Trim away the excess and keep this for modelling the presents later. Neaten the top and sides of the stocking with cake smoothers.

fig 2

7 For the presents, you will need 200 g (7 oz) of red sugarpaste, 220 g (8 oz) of green sugarpaste and 100 g (4 oz) of white *(fig 2)*. Make two 50 g (2 oz) red squares for presents, a green and white ball, using about 50 g (2 oz) of both green and white. Then make a completely green 50 g (2 oz) ball.

For the candy canes, roll out two 25 g (1 oz) sausages (ropes) of contrasting coloured icing. Twist the two sausages together and bend into a walking stick shape. Make three. Keep two back and pile the other one and the presents and balls up against the top of stocking, securing them with a little water.

8 Knead and roll 400 g (14 oz) white sugarpaste into a strip about 25 cm (10 in) long and about 13 cm (5 in) wide. Moisten the top of the stocking and lay the cuff into position so that it overlaps the presents slightly. Hold a piping nozzle (tip) at a slight angle and press it into the white to leave impressions in the still soft icing.

9 Slot the last two candy canes into position and secure with water.

10 Stick small flattened balls of white sugarpaste onto one of the red parcels to decorate it.

11 Thinly roll out 50 g (2 oz) green icing and cut out 26 holly leaves with a cutter.

fig 3

Stick these onto the cake in pairs and press the back of a knife into each one three times to make veins *(fig 3)*.

12 Attach two gold balls beneath each pair of leaves using the red royal icing in the piping (decorating) bag and two tiny balls of red icing beneath the leaves on the cuff.

TIP: *To take a lot of the hard work out of kneading marzipan (almond paste), heat it in a microwave for a few seconds. However, don't overdo it or the oil in the centre will get very hot and could give you a nasty burn.*

Christmas crackers

This novel way of decorating an ordinary square fruit cake should tempt even the most turkey-stuffed palate on Christmas afternoon. You could decorate the board with small gifts appropriate to your guests or arrange real crackers around them to make a stunning centrepiece for the Christmas table.

INGREDIENTS

18 cm (7 in) square fruit cake
150 g (5 oz) black sugarpaste
(rolled fondant icing)
400 g (14 oz) red sugarpaste
(rolled fondant icing)
400 g (14 oz) green sugarpaste
(rolled fondant icing)
4 tbsp brandy
3 tbsp apricot jam
1 kg (2 lb 4 oz) marzipan
(almond paste)
1 tbsp white royal icing (see
page 15)
Icing (confectioners') sugar,
for rolling out
Water

UTENSILS

30 cm (12 in) gold-coloured
square cake board
Carving knife
Small sharp knife
Cocktail stick (toothpick)
Pastry brush
Rolling pin
Cake smoothers
Clingfilm (plastic wrap)
Paintbrush
No 3 piping nozzle (round tip)
Piping (decorating) bag fitted
with No 1 nozzle (round tip)
2 m (2 yards 7 in) tartan
ribbon
Fish slice (pancake turner)

fig 1

1 Cut the cake into two 5 cm (2 in) strips. Use the remaining cake to extend the length of the first two strips (*fig 1*). Run a knife along the two long edges of each cracker to slightly round them.

2 Pierce both cakes a few times using a cocktail stick and pour the brandy over the holes.

3 Cover both crackers with a pastry brush dipped into warmed apricot jam.

4 Dust your work surface with a little icing (confectioners') sugar and knead 500 g (1 lb 2 oz) marzipan (almond paste) until

pliable. Smooth down the marzipan using your hands and a pair of cake smoothers and trim away any excess. Press a finger round the cracker to make a dent about 5 cm (2 in) from one end. Repeat at the other end. (This 'dent' is visible in *fig 2*.)

5 Repeat the above steps on the second cracker.

6 Measure the ends of the crackers and moisten with a little water. Roll out the black sugarpaste (rolled fondant icing). Cut out four circles slightly larger than the ends of the crackers. Stick one circle onto each end.

7 Moisten the ends of the cracker with water. Roll out 200 g (7 oz) red sugarpaste and cut out two strips about 20 cm x 7.5 cm (8 in x 3 in) Serrate one edge and wind around one end of the cracker (*fig 2*). Press the back of a knife into the icing a few times to make creases and tweak the jagged edges so that they stand out slightly. If they keep flopping, support them with a ball of scrunched up clingfilm (plastic wrap) until they dry.

fig 2

8 Roll out 200 g (7 oz) of green sugarpaste. Cut out a strip 20 cm x 13 cm (8 in x 5 in). Moisten the centre of the cracker and wind the strip around it. Take a No 3 piping nozzle and press a line of decorative circles along both edges of the strip.

9 Repeat the above procedures on the second cracker, except this time use green sugarpaste for the ends of the cracker and red for the central strip.

10 Pipe small loops along the edges of the central strips using a No 1 nozzle and white royal icing (*fig 3*).

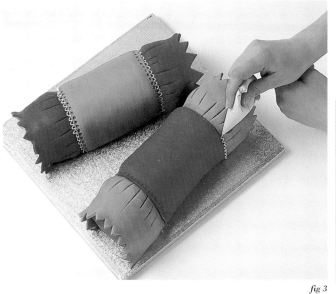

11 Pipe a line of small dots around the jagged edges of both crackers.

12 Lift and arrange both crackers on the board using a fish slice (pancake turner).

13 Cut two strips of tartan ribbon approximately 23 cm (9 in) long. Place one diagonally across the central strip of each cracker and secure with a little royal icing.

14 Finally, make two neat bows and stick on the top of each cracker with a little blob of royal icing.

TIP: *If you don't fancy piping around the centres of the crackers, drape some tinsel over the edges instead for a sparkling alternative look. Remove the tinsel before eating.*

fig 3

Extra Special Party Cakes

These cakes are all a bit special – perfect for important occasions when only an astounding cake will do. Once you have honed your skills on the easier cakes in the preceeding chapter, turn your hand to these. They are still easy-to-achieve, you just need to be brave and get stuck in! Choose from a magical Fairy-tale Castle, a sumptuous Chocolate Box, or delight friends and family at the festive table with the Christmas Santas cake.

Fairy-tale castle

Although this cake is a lot easier to make than it looks, you do have to allow drying time for the turrets (preferably overnight). Once you have mastered gelatin icing, a whole new world of standing models opens up.

■ INGREDIENTS

- 1 quantity gelatin icing (see page 15)
- Cornflour
- 18 cm (7 in) round sponge cake
- 1 quantity buttercream (see page 14)
- Icing sugar
- 700 g (1 lb 8 oz) white sugarpaste
- 10 g (¼ oz) brown sugarpaste
- 40 g (1¾ oz) black sugarpaste
- 1 quantity white royal icing (see page 15)
- 2 edible silver balls
- 25 mini marshmallows
- 6 ice cream cones
- Two 30 g (1 oz) bags white chocolate buttons or similar
- Green food colour (ideally gooseberry green but not essential)
- 1 sheet rice paper
- 70 g (2½ oz) green-coloured coconut (see page 14)

■ UTENSILS

- 6 cardboard tubes (5 kitchen roll inner tubes and one from a roll of tin foil are ideal. Please don't use toilet rolls!)
- Cling film
- Rolling pin
- Small sharp knife
- Water and paintbrush
- Carving knife
- 30 cm (12 in) square cake board
- Ruler
- 4 piping bags (minimum)
- Number 2 piping nozzle
- Scissors
- Small sieve

1 Begin by making the turrets. Cover all the cardboard tubes with cling film and dust lightly with cornflour. Make up the gelatin icing as shown on page 15 and place in a polythene bag. Dust the worksurface with cornflour. Pull off a lump of icing about 130 g (4¼ oz) and roll out no thicker than 3 mm (⅛ in). Cut out a rectangle about 14 cm x 16 cm (5½ in x 6 ½ in). Place the excess icing back in the bag.

Wrap the icing round one of the thicker tubes and secure the join with a little water *(fig 1)*. Place to dry (seam side down) on a spare cake board or similar. Make another four the same size and one shorter one using the thinner tube. The smaller turret should be about 8 cm (3 in) in length.

After about 4-6 hours of drying, the turrets should feel hard on the outside. Carefully slide them off their supports and stand them upright so the centres can dry out. Leave overnight.

2 Level the top of the cake and place it upside down in the middle of the board. Slice and fill the centre with buttercream. Spread a thin layer of buttercream over the top and sides.

3 Dust the worksurface with icing sugar. Roll out and cover the cake with 500 g (1 lb 2 oz) of white sugarpaste. Smooth the top and sides and trim any excess from the base. Press a clean ruler horizontally three or four times around the sides of the cake *(fig 2)*. Then use the back of a knife to make the vertical marks for the bricks.

4 When dry, place a long and short turret together on top of the cake. Ensure the seams are at the back and secure them using royal icing. To provide extra support, roll 30 g (1 oz) of white sugarpaste into a sausage about 28 cm (11 in) long. Paint a light line of water around the base of the two turrets and, starting from the back, press the sausage in place *(fig 3)*.

5 To make two doors, thinly roll out the brown sugarpaste and cut out two rounded, arched shapes. Press a few vertical lines into each one with the back of a knife. Stick the largest door on the front of the cake and the other on the front of the tallest turret. Make two steps in front of each door by sticking two small ovals of white sugarpaste

so that it can sit snugly against the taller turret (*fig 5*).

8 Neaten the base of each cone with a line of white chocolate buttons stuck on with dabs of royal icing.

9 Place the four remaining gelatin cylinders around the cake. Secure with royal icing and top each one with a cone and line of buttons as before.

10 To make the windows on the turrets, thinly roll out the black sugarpaste and cut out eight narrow rectangles. Keep the leftover icing. Cut one end of each rectangle into a point. Stick one on each turret and two either side of the front door.

Place a little white royal icing in a piping bag fitted with the number 2 icing nozzle. Pipe a neat line from the top to the bottom of a window (*fig 6*). Then pipe a line across the window. Repeat on all the rest. (Leave the windows bare if you find this too tricky.)

on top of each other (*fig 4*). Stick an edible silver ball on the front of each door with a little royal icing.

6 Stick about 25 mini marshmallows around the perimeter of the cake with royal icing. (If you cannot find mini marshmallows in the supermarket, cut up a sausage of sugarpaste instead.)

7 Take two of the ice cream cones. Break little pieces off the base if necessary to help them stand upright. Pipe a thin line of royal icing around the top edges of both turrets and then stick the cones carefully in place on top.

You may find that you have to break a little 'bite' shape out of one side of the cone that goes on top of the shorter turret

TIP

If the cake is for someone's birthday, make some extra rocks. Stick them at the front of the board to use as candle

11 To make the rocks, partially knead together 100 g (4 oz) of white sugarpaste and 10 g (¼ oz) of black. Pull off irregular lumps and stick these on the board around the cake using a little water.

12 Colour 45 ml (3 tbsp) of royal icing green. Place half into a piping bag fitted with the number 2 piping nozzle and pipe wiggly lines for the ivy stems all over the cake. Place the rest of the icing in a second bag and snip 3 mm (⅛ in) off the end of the bag. Press the end of the bag against a stem, squeeze lightly then pull the bag away. This should make a simple leaf shape. Continue all over the cake. Practise this first on a sheet of greaseproof paper if you are not very confident.

13 To make the flags, cut six small triangles out of the sheet of rice paper. Pipe a dot of royal icing on the top of one of the cones. Stick a small ball of sugarpaste on top and pipe another dot on top of that. Press one of the triangles into the sugarpaste (*fig 7*). Repeat on the other five cones.

14 Moisten the exposed cake board with a little water and sprinkle the coloured coconut around the base of the cake. To add snow, place a spoonful of icing sugar in a small sieve and sprinkle over the cake.

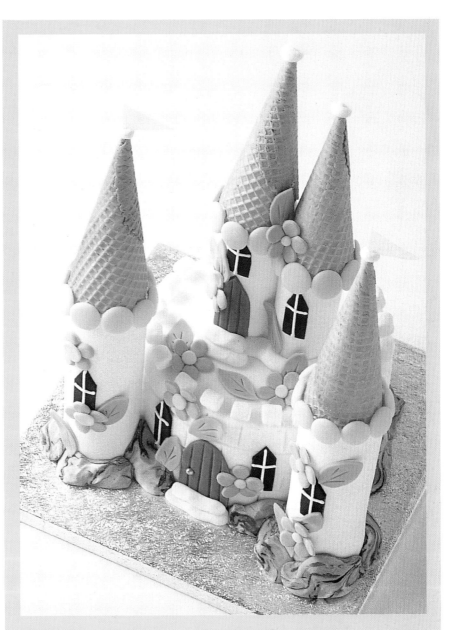

Decorating variation

In this simplified version there are only four turrets instead of six, which saves you time. Also, instead of piping leaves, I have used cut-out flowers and leaves which look just as good. You could also place little figures in front of the top turrets. Use the couple featured on the Bride and Groom cake on page 149 for instance and it turns into a stunning wedding cake with a difference.

Hot dog

How do you like yours? With or without mustard ... er... sorry, icing! Here's one mega bite-sized dog complete with all the trimmings that should satisfy a whole army of hungry party goers.

INGREDIENTS

- Icing sugar for rolling out
- 180 g (6¼ oz) dark blue sugarpaste
- Oblong sponge cake baked in loaf tin (see page 10)
- 1 quantity buttercream (see page 14)
- 800 g (1 lb 12 oz) light golden brown sugarpaste
- Assorted food colour pastes for painting sausage (see step 5)
- 100 g (3½ oz) white sugarpaste
- 15 ml (1 tbsp) yellow-coloured buttercream or royal icing
- 15 ml (1 tbsp) red-coloured buttercream or royal icing

UTENSILS

- Water and paint brush
- Rolling pin
- Small sharp knife
- Carving knife
- Palette or saucer
- 2 piping bags (see page 18)
- Scissors

1 Cover the cakeboard with blue sugarpaste as described on page 16. Trim and neaten the edges. Place the covered board to one side. Stand the cake the right way up and cut a groove lengthways out of the centre *(fig 1)*.

2 Round the corners slightly and cut away any rough, uneven bits of cake from the tops and sides. Slice and spread a layer of buttercream in the centre of the cake if you wish. Carefully reassemble the cake and spread buttercream over the top and sides and into the groove.

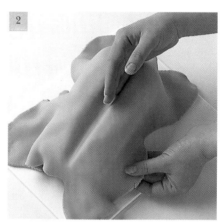

3 Still keeping the cake away from the covered board, knead 600 g (1 lb 5 oz) of the brown sugarpaste until pliable. Roll it out on a surface well dusted with icing sugar, then lift and place over the cake, allowing the sugarpaste to fall into the dip in the middle as much as possible. Starting from the middle of the cake to expel as much air as possible, smooth and ease the icing into position *(fig 2)*. Neaten the sides and trim away any excess from the base. Keep the left-over icing to add to the sausage later.

4 Carefully lift and place the cake on the covered board. Choose the side that looks best and press about six diagonal lines into that side using the back of a knife.

5 Roll the left-over brown sugarpaste into a thick sausage shape, then lay this across the dip. Press a few lines into the ends of the sausage with the back of a knife and to give it a luscious just-cooked look, paint the sausage using food colour. I found a mixture of watered-down dark brown, chestnut and autumn leaf food colour pastes worked well, but you could achieve the same effect by mixing brown with a touch of yellow, red or orange.

6 For the napkin, thinly roll out the white sugarpaste and cut two strips 28 cm x 8 cm (11 in x 3 in). Moisten the board and the base of the cake. Take one strip and lay it down one side of hot dog, allowing it to fall into folds. Repeat on the other side.

7 Make up two piping bags. Place the yellow-coloured royal icing or buttercream in one bag and the red in the other. Pipe a long squiggly line of yellow 'mustard' along the top of the sausage *(fig 3)*. Repeat using the red 'ketchup'.

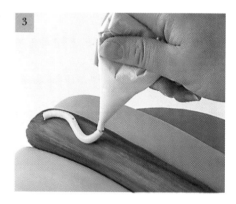

TIP

You may be able to find packs containing small tubes of red and yellow 'writing icing' in your local supermarket which could be used for the mustard and ketchup. Snip a little bit extra off the end of the tube to make the nozzle wider.

Handyman

Although this was designed with do-it-yourself fanatics in mind, this would make a good cake for someone who's just moved house and has all the joys of decorating ahead! Personalize the figure to resemble the recipient if you can.

■ INGREDIENTS

- 15 cm (6 in) square sponge cake
- 1 quantity buttercream (see page 14)
- Icing sugar for rolling out
- 500 g (1 lb 2 oz) white sugarpaste
- 90 g (3 oz) blue sugarpaste
- 20 g (¾ oz) flesh-coloured sugarpaste
- Black food colour paste
- 30 g (1 oz) black sugarpaste
- 10 g (¼ oz) grey sugarpaste
- 110 g (3¾ oz) dark brown sugarpaste

■ UTENSILS

- Carving knife
- 20 cm (8 in) square cake board
- Palette knife
- Small sharp knife
- Water and fine and medium paintbrushes
- Piping nozzle

1 Level the top of the cake, turn it upside down and place in the centre of the board. Slice the cake in half and fill the centre with buttercream. Reassemble the cake and spread a thin covering of buttercream around the top and sides.

2 Knead and roll out 400 g (14 oz) of white sugarpaste on a worksurface dusted with icing sugar. Carefully lay the icing over the cake. Smooth the icing into place and trim and neaten the base.

3 To construct the handyman himself, begin with the body. Roll 40 g (1¼ oz) of white sugarpaste into a cone (*fig 1*). Paint a little water in the middle of the cake and place his body in position. Next make his legs by rolling 40 g (1¼ oz) of blue sugarpaste into a sausage about 17 cm (7 in) long. Cut the sausage in half and bend the left leg slightly at the knee. Stick the legs in front of the body. For the arms, roll 20 g (¾ oz) of white sugarpaste into a thin sausage and cut it in half. Stick these either side of the handyman's body.

4 To make his head, use 10 g (¼ oz) of flesh-coloured sugarpaste and roll this into a ball. Slice a little icing off the top of his head to make a flat surface on which to attach the cap. Stick the head on top of the body. Flatten two tiny balls of white sugarpaste and stick these onto his face for his eyes. Add a tiny ball of flesh-coloured sugarpaste for his nose. Paint the pupils on the eyes and a smile on his face using black food colour and a fine paintbrush.

5 Partially mix a tiny amount of black sugarpaste with a little white for his hair. Scrunch and tear the icing into little bits and stick them to the sides of his head. Make a little cap by rolling 10 g (¼ oz) of white sugarpaste into a thick disc shape. Pinch and pull the icing on one side to form a peak. Stick this on his head. Finish off the head by sticking two tiny balls of flesh-coloured sugarpaste either side of the head for his ears. Add a little detail by making a small dent in each one with the end of a paintbrush.

6 Roll two 10 g (¼ oz) lumps of black sugarpaste into two oval shapes for his feet and stick one on the end of each leg.

7 To make the paint pot, roll 10 g (¼ oz) of grey sugarpaste into a stumpy cylindrical shape. Press an icing nozzle or something similar into the side to leave a semi-circular impression for the handle. Place the pot between his legs.

For the paintbrush, make two tiny oblongs of brown sugarpaste and one of black. Stick them together like an upside-down 'T' shape and press lines into the black one with a knife to make bristles. Place the brush just in front of the handyman's left arm. Use two small flattened balls of flesh-coloured sugarpaste for his hands and stick these as though he is holding the paint pot and brush.

8 To make the planks of wood, roll 100 g (3½ oz) of dark brown sugarpaste and 20 g (¾ oz) of white together into a sausage.

Fold the sausage in half and roll again. Keep rolling and folding to achieve a woodgrain effect. Roll out the icing and cut out strips of varying lengths (*fig 2*). Stick a few on and around the cake.

9 To make the rolls of wallpaper, partially knead 50 g (2 oz) of blue sugarpaste and 20 g (¾ oz) of white together to achieve a marbled effect. Carefully roll the sugarpaste out and cut out two strips. Roll one strip up completely and the other about halfway. Stick them onto the cake.

Finally, dab splodges of black food colour around the cake and on the character himself.

Wild animals

My nephew Jack helped with the colours of this cake. 'Potamusses are grey', he informed me gravely, but to balance the cake, they had to be brown. However Jack pointed out, 'That's why they're in the water — because they're all covered in mud!'

INGREDIENTS

- 20 cm (8 in) round sponge cake
- 1 quantity buttercream (see page 14)
- Icing sugar for rolling out
- 700 g (1 lb 8½ oz) white sugarpaste
- 150 g (5¼ oz) grey sugarpaste
- Black food colour
- 100 g (3½ oz) brown sugarpaste
- 20 g (½ oz) green sugarpaste
- Dark brown, gooseberry green and ice blue (or similar) food colour pastes
- 45 ml (3 tbsp) white royal icing (optional)
- 30 g (1 oz) black sugarpaste

UTENSILS

- Carving knife
- 25 cm (10 in) round cake board
- Rolling pin
- Small sharp knife
- Water and paintbrush
- Drinking straw
- Icing nozzle
- Large brush or pastry brush
- Piping bag
- Scissors

1 Shape the cake by cutting bits off the top to leave an irregular surface. Try to leave a flattish area towards the front of the cake for the 'lake'. Spread some of the cut-away pieces of cake with buttercream and build up a small hill behind the lake (*fig 1*).

2 Place the cake on the cake board and slice and fill the centre with buttercream. Reassemble the cake and spread a covering of buttercream over the sides and top. Keep any leftover buttercream if you are going to use this for the lake and greenery instead of royal icing. Sprinkle the worksurface with icing sugar and knead 500 g (1 lb 2 oz) of white sugarpaste until pliable. Roll out the sugarpaste, then lift and place it over the cake. Carefully smooth the icing into position.

3 To make life easier, construct the elephants, hippos and crocodile away from the cake and place in position later. For the elephants, first roll out 10 g (¼ oz) of grey sugarpaste to a thickness of about 1 cm (⅜ in) and cut out two discs. Make four small vertical cuts at quarterly intervals around the edge of each disc for the legs (*fig 2*). Roll two 40 g (1 ½ oz) lumps of grey sugarpaste into two balls for the bodies.

Press gently on the front of each ball to make a slope on which to rest the head. Stick one ball onto each set of legs, making sure that both the slope and one of the small cuts are facing forward.

4 To make the heads, roll two 20 g (¾ oz) lumps of grey sugarpaste into chunky tennis racquet shapes. Stick one onto each body. Add nostrils by pushing the end of a paintbrush twice into the end of each trunk. Also press a couple of lines across each trunk with the back of a knife. To make the ears, roll about 5 g (⅛ oz) of grey sugarpaste into a ball. Flatten the ball and cut in half. Moisten the sides of the elephant's head and stick the ears in position. Repeat for the other elephant.

To make a tail, roll a tiny ball of grey sugarpaste into a thin string and stick it onto the rear of the elephant. Finally, stick two tiny discs of white sugarpaste on each face for eyes. Paint in the pupils and eyebrows with black food colour.

5 To make the biggest hippo, roll 30 g (1 oz) of brown sugarpaste into a semi-circular shape for his body (*fig 3*). Add a head by

rolling 10 g (¼ oz) of brown sugarpaste into an oval. Squeeze the centre of the oval slightly and stick onto the body. Stick two tiny brown balls onto the sides of the head for ears and add detail to each one by making a small hollow with the end of a paintbrush. Paint two tiny dots of black food colour for the eyes. Make a smaller version for the baby.

To make the submerged hippo, simply roll 10 g (¼ oz) brown sugarpaste into an oval and flatten the base so it can stand upright. Add ears and eyes.

6 For the crocodile, roll 10 g (¼ oz) of green sugarpaste into a sausage about 6 cm (2½ in) long. Try to make the ends slightly thicker than the middle *(fig 3)*. Press a line around the base of the sausage to make a mouth and add scales by pressing a drinking straw held at an angle into the icing. Also poke two dents for nostrils using the end of a paintbrush.

7 To make his eye, stick a tiny flattened oval of white sugarpaste onto the side of the head and finish off with an eyebrow made from a tiny strip of green sugarpaste bent into an 'S' shape and stuck over the eye. Add a small dot of black food colour for the pupil.

   To make the tail, roll the remaining green sugarpaste into a long, tapering triangular shape and press a few scales into the sides, as on the head.

8 Using a fairly large paint- or pastry brush, paint the back of the cake using watered-down brown and green food colour *(fig 4)*. (I used dark brown and gooseberry green food colour pastes for this but anything similar will do.) Place the elephants into position on the 'grass' while it is still wet.

9 Partially mix a little blue food colour into about 30 ml (2 tbsp) of white royal icing or buttercream if you prefer a softer finish. Swirl this over the front section of the top of the cake and place the hippos and

crocodile sections into position.

10 To make a monkey, roll 10 g (¼ oz) of brown sugarpaste into a cone *(fig 5)*. Stick this against the side of the cake and add a brown sugarpaste ball on top for his head.

   For his features, make two tiny balls and an oval shape out of white sugarpaste. Flatten all three shapes and stick the two white discs on top of the head for his eyes and the oval just below for his muzzle. Press the edge of an icing nozzle or something

similar into the muzzle to make a smiling impression and paint three dots for the eyes and the nose with black food colour. Stick two tiny balls of brown sugarpaste either side of the head for his ears and make a small hollow into each one with the end of a paintbrush.

   For the arms, make two small sausages of brown sugarpaste and stick these in whatever position you wish. Make another monkey for the other side of the cake.

110

11 To make the rocks, take 170 g (6 oz) of white sugarpaste and 30 g (1 oz) of black. Partially knead the two lumps together *(fig 6)*. Pull off small irregular lumps and stick these around the base of the cake and a few on top.

12 Colour about 15 ml (1 tbsp) of royal icing or buttercream green. Place the coloured icing into a piping bag and secure the end. Snip about 3 mm (⅛ in) off the pointed end of the bag and pipe a few strands of foliage around the rocks on the sides and top of the cake *(fig 7)*.

TIP
If you're really short of time but still want to make a cake in this style, raid your local sweet shop or the confectionery counter at a large supermarket for jelly animal sweets. Either substitute these for the modelled animals or add to the animals in the scene.

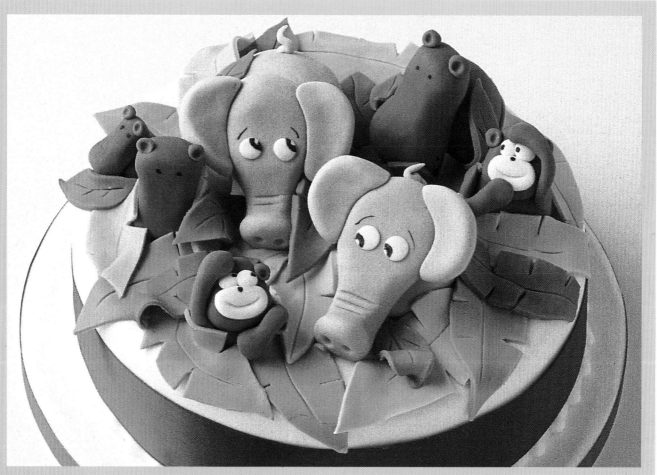

Decorating variation

In this simplified version, the basic cake was covered in the same way as the Christening cake on page 142. The animals were modelled as described above, then surrounded by simple jungle-type leaves made from several shades of green sugarpaste. Details for making these are given in the Sunbather cake on page 174.

Birthday fairy

Here's someone who should brighten up any girl's birthday. If you want to cheat, your local cake decorating shop should stock plastic figures made for inserting into cakes, although they may not have as much personality as this one!

1 Level the top of the cake and place upside-down in the centre of the cake board. Slice and fill the centre with a layer of buttercream and then spread a thin coating of buttercream over the top and sides of the cake.

2 Dust the worksurface with icing sugar. Knead and roll out 250 g (9 oz) of white sugarpaste. Carefully lift the icing over the cake. Smooth the top and sides and neaten the base.

3 Stick one candy stick into the top of the cake to provide internal support for the fairy and roll 50 g (2 oz) of white sugarpaste into an oval shape to form her body. Gently squeeze the centre to make a waist. Lightly moisten a small area on the top of the cake around the protruding candy stick and carefully slot the body into position *(fig 1)*.

4 Insert a second candy stick into the top of the body leaving about 3 cm (1¼ in) poking out.

Make a 10 g (¼ oz) ball of flesh-coloured sugarpaste for her head and slot this onto the candy stick. Paint her features using black food colour and a fine paintbrush. You can paint the head before putting it on her body but be careful not to squash the face when lifting it. Add a tiny dot of sugarpaste for a nose.

5 To make her hair, roll 5 g (⅛ oz) of yellow sugarpaste into a strip about 9 cm x 2 cm (3½ in x ¾ in) *(fig 2)*. Press lines down the length of the strip using the back of a knife. Stick the strip over her head and tweak the ends upwards to make them look like curls.

For the head-dress make six tiny balls of pink sugarpaste. Stick three in a line on the top of her head with a little water. Stick another two above these and a final one on top.

Finish off her hair by cutting a tiny leaf shape out of some leftover yellow sugarpaste. Press marks into it as you did for the other hair section, then stick this onto the front of her head.

6 Roll out 60 g (2 oz) of pink sugarpaste and cut out a strip approximately 46 cm x 4 cm (18 in x 1½ in). Making sure that the worksurface is well dusted with icing sugar so that the sugarpaste doesn't stick, roll the paintbrush backwards and forwards along a small section of the strip at a time and a wonderful frill will develop *(fig 3)*. Paint a line of water just above the base of the cake and, starting from the back of the fairy, carefully stick the frill into place. If it

breaks, simply cut off the straggly torn edge and continue with the rest of the frill.

Once you have gone all the way around, repeat the above procedure using about 50 g (1¾ oz) of white sugarpaste to make a white frill. Stick this above the pink so that it overlaps slightly.

Continue up the skirt, alternating pink and white frills right up to the fairy's waist. Each frill will be about 5 cm (2 in) shorter than the last. Try to keep all the joins at the back.

7   Make a ribbon to hide the joins by thinly rolling out 20 g (¾ oz) of pink sugarpaste. Cut out two thin strips for the tails of the ribbon *(fig 3)*. Cut a 'V' shape into the end of each one and stick them so that they fall down the back of the skirt.

Top with a 'bow' made of two tiny pink triangles and a small flattened ball of pink for the knot itself. As this detail is not visible from the front of the cake, you could always miss out this stage if you're a bit pushed for time.

8   Press and stick the remaining candy stick against the fairy's body using a little water. This will form the handle of the wand. Roll 10 g (¼ oz) of flesh-coloured sugarpaste into a sausage. Cut this in half for the arms. Flatten one end of each sausage slightly to make her hands, then carefully stick these against the side of the figure to look as though the hands are holding the fairy wand.

Roll out the leftover yellow sugarpaste and cut out a small star shape. Stick this onto the top of the wand with a little drop of water – not too much or the star will start to slide. You should also find that you are able to rest the star slightly against the fairy's body which will provide it with some additional support.

9   Make a curved row of 12 small dents on the top frill of the fairy's dress using the end of a paintbrush. Put a tiny dab of water in each hollow and then add an edible silver ball as decoration.

10 To make her wings, place the rice paper over the wing template shown on page 187. Trace over it using a pencil. To make the second wing, turn the rice paper over and trace over it the other way. Cut out both wings, cutting just inside the pencil outline to avoid grey edges on the wings.

Take a small lump of white sugarpaste and moisten it with a drop of water so that it becomes slightly tacky. Stick this onto the fairy's back and then carefully insert the two wings. Alternatively, you could stick them into position with a little dab of buttercream.

TIP
If you cannot find any candy sticks in your local sweet shop, you can use a strand of raw, dried spaghetti instead to provide support inside the body and to act as a handle for the wand. Do remember though, when cutting the cake, to remove the spaghetti first and not to serve it to your guests!

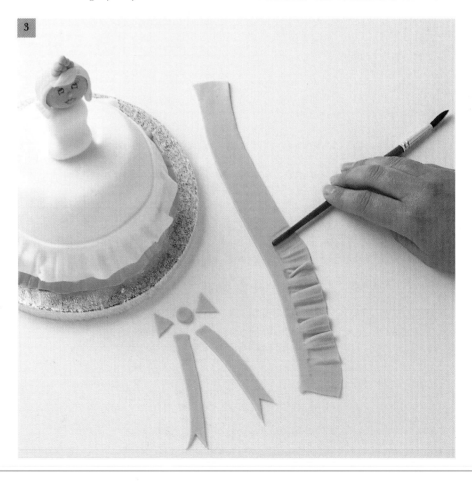

Christmas Santas

Ideal for anyone who loves the nuts and marzipan that abound around Christmas-time, this is an extremely easy cake to decorate. Try to use white marzipan rather than yellow as this takes the colours better.

1 Follow the fruit cake recipe for a 20 cm (8 in) round cake on page 11 to the point where you have spooned the mixture into the baking tin. Before placing it in the oven, arrange a selection of nuts over the top of the mixture. Use your favourite nuts or whatever you have in your store-cupboard and start from the outside of the cake and work in. I began with a circle of almonds, then a line of pecans. Next, I added a circle of hazelnuts, some nice big chunky brazil nuts and finally half a walnut in the centre.

Trim a piece of greaseproof paper to fit over the top of the tin and cut a small hole about 3 cm (1¼ in) out of the centre. Rest this over the cake before baking to stop the nuts browning too much during the cooking process. If you have a fan oven, use a sheet of greaseproof long enough to tuck under the baking tin, otherwise it will simply fly off as soon as you shut the door.

Bake as normal, removing the greaseproof about ten minutes before the end of the cooking time just to lightly brown and colour the nuts.

■ INGREDIENTS

- 20 cm (8 in) round fruit cake (see step 1 before baking.)
- Selection of nuts, such as almonds, pecans, hazelnut, walnuts, etc.
- 45 ml (3 tbsp) brandy (optional)
- 60 ml (4 tbsp) apricot jam
- Icing sugar for rolling out
- Red, paprika, dark brown and green food colour pastes
- 720 g (1 lb 9¼ oz) white (neutral) marzipan, divided and coloured as follows:
  240 g (8¼ oz) red
  150 g (5 oz) flesh colour (paprika)
  120 g (4 oz) dark brown
  30 g (1 oz) green
  Leave the remaining marzipan white (neutral)

■ UTENSILS

- Greaseproof paper
- 23 cm (9 in) round cake board
- Cocktail stick
- Sieve
- Pastry brush
- Rolling pin
- Small sharp knife
- Water and paintbrush

2 When the cake has cooled, turn it out of the tin and place onto a 23 cm (9 in) round cake board.

For an extra festive touch, pierce the cake a few times between the nuts with a cocktail stick (you can lift a few up if you wish) and carefully drizzle about 30 ml (2 tbsp) of brandy over the cake. Allow it to seep in and replace any nuts you might have moved.

Boil the apricot jam either in a saucepan or in a non-metallic dish in a microwave for about one minute. Sieve the jam to remove any lumps of fruit and mix in the last remaining tablespoon of brandy. (You may omit the brandy if you prefer.) Paint the mixture over the top and sides of the cake using a pastry brush to give it a wonderfully gleaming finish (*fig 1*).

3 To make the 12 figures, begin with the bodies. Sprinkle your worksurface with icing sugar. Take a 15 g (½ oz) piece of red-coloured marzipan and roll it into a flattish

7 To decorate a hat, take about 5 g (⅛ oz) of white marzipan. Pull off a tiny piece and roll it into a ball for the pom-pom. Stick in place. Roll the rest into a sausage and lay it around the brim of the hat so that it almost obscures all the face. Repeat on the rest of the hats.

8 Use 10 g (¼ oz) brown marzipan for each sack and shape into a cone. Stand each one on its fattest part, then pinch and pull the marzipan at the top to make a neck (fig 3). Press one between each Santa on the side of the cake.

9 To make the presents, roll out 30 g (1 oz) green marzipan to a thickness of about 1 cm (⅜ in). Cut out twelve tiny green squares. Using the back of a knife, make a criss-cross pattern on the front of each parcel. Place one in the top of each sack and bend the neck of the sack up slightly. Brush away any dusty icing sugar marks using a damp paintbrush.

TIP

If the marzipan is too hard for you to knead properly, soften it for just a few seconds on high in the microwave.

conical shape. Press and stick the body up against the side of the cake. You shouldn't need any water to keep it in place – the jam around the sides should be adequate to hold it.

Make another identical body and stick this directly opposite. Stick the third and fourth bodies halfway between the first two (fig 2). The cake should now be divided into quarters. Make and stick another two bodies between each of the four Santas already in position, leaving a small space between each one for his sack. Continue until all the bodies are evenly spaced around the side of the cake.

4 To make a head, roll a 10 g (¼ oz) ball of flesh-coloured marzipan into an oval shape (fig 3). Stick this on top of one of the bodies already in position. Repeat on the other eleven Santas.

5 For each hat, form 5 g (⅛ oz) of red marzipan into a small triangular shape. Tweak the end into a point and bend it over slightly. Place it on one of the heads. The tip of the hat should rest just on top of the cake. Repeat and make hats for all the other figures, ensuring that they all point in the same direction.

6 To make the beards, thinly roll out 10 g (¼ oz) of uncoloured (white) marzipan. Press lines into the marzipan using the

back of a knife and cut out a triangular shape. Stick this onto Santa's face so that the beard hangs over the front of the body. If it won't stay in place, use a little water.

Push the end of a paintbrush into the beard to leave behind a surprised, open-mouthed expression. Stick on a tiny ball of flesh-coloured marzipan for Santa's nose. Repeat on each Santa.

Weary windsurfer

This cake was made for a keen windsurfing friend. If you don't feel up to painting, make the pool from one solid colour or stick spots or other sugarpaste shapes around the sides.

■ INGREDIENTS

- Icing sugar for rolling out
- 300 g (10½ oz) white sugarpaste
- 15 cm (6 in) round cake
- ½ quantity buttercream (see page 14)
- 30 ml (2 tbsp) royal icing (optional)
- 60 g (2 oz) orange sugarpaste
- 50 g (1¾ oz) flesh-coloured sugarpaste
- Assorted food paste colours for painting, including black and brown
- 60 g (2 oz) dark blue sugarpaste
- 1 candy stick (sweet cigarette)
- 30 g (1 oz) green-coloured sugar (see page 14)

■ UTENSILS

- Rolling pin
- Small sharp knife
- Surfboard template (see page 187)
- Carving knife
- Palette knife
- Water
- Medium and fine paintbrushes
- Thin cardboard triangle for sail
- Clean damp cloth

1 Begin by making the surfboard. Roll out 40 g (1¾ oz) of white sugarpaste on a surface dusted with icing sugar and cut out a board shape, using the template if necessary. Place the board somewhere out of the way to harden slightly while you assemble the rest of the cake.

2 Level the top of the cake if necessary and turn it upside down. Slice and fill the middle of the cake with buttercream. Reassemble and place the cake in the centre of the cake board. Spread a thin layer of buttercream over the top and sides, saving some if using buttercream for the water.

3 Sprinkle the worksurface with icing sugar and roll out and cover the cake with the rest of the white sugarpaste. Smooth over the top and sides and trim away any excess from the base.

4 Begin constructing the windsurfer by building a life jacket. Shape the orange sugarpaste into a thick cone and press three vertical lines down the length of the

jacket using the back of a knife (*fig 1*). Stick this onto the cake. Roll 20 g (¾ oz) of flesh-coloured sugarpaste into a ball for his head and stick in position. Paint in the eyes using black food colour and a fine paintbrush and stick three tiny balls of flesh-coloured sugarpaste on the face for his ears and nose. To add detail, poke the end of a paintbrush into each ear to leave a little hollow.

5 Take about half a teaspoon of royal icing or buttercream and mix in a little brown food colour. (A nice touch here would be to colour the hair the same shade as the recipient's.) Using a knife, smear the hair on top of the head and pull it up slightly to give it a bit of texture.

Roll 5 g (⅛ oz) of flesh-coloured sugarpaste into a sausage for one of the arms. Flatten one end slightly to make a hand and stick the arm against the side of the body, bending it at the elbow so that the hand covers the mouth area.

6 For the water, partially mix a little blue food colour into about 30 ml (2 tbsp) of royal icing or buttercream. Spread around the windsurfer on top of the cake (*fig 2*).

7 Roll the dark blue sugarpaste into a sausage about 46 cm (18 in) long. Starting from the back of the cake, lay this around the top edge. Neaten and stick the join together. Place the surfboard in position so that the tip just rests on the edge of the pool. Make two flattish oval shapes from flesh-coloured sugarpaste for his feet and insert these into the water. Make the other arm, squashing one end slightly to make a hand and stick this in place with the palm just resting on the board.

8 Cut a triangle out of thin cardboard and stick this to the candy stick with a little royal icing or buttercream. Insert this into the top of the cake.

9 Paint a design on the sides of the pool. Start by painting the colours first and add the outlines in black food colour afterwards. If you do it the other way round, the black will bleed into the colour. If you make a mistake, wash over the area with fresh water and wipe away the mistake with a clean, damp cloth.

10 Moisten the exposed cake board with a little water and carefully spoon the coloured sugar around the base to cover the rest of the board.

Spotty dog

This chap just goes to prove that Man's best friend is his cake! If you're feeling adventurous, why not adapt him to look like the family pet. To make a hairy version, cover him with chocolate buttercream and 'rough it up' with a fork.

■ INGREDIENTS

- Icing sugar for rolling out
- 300 g (10½ oz) of green sugarpaste
- 1 pudding basin cake (see page 10)
- 1 quantity buttercream (see page 14)
- 810 g (1 lb 12 oz) white sugarpaste
- 300 g (10½ oz) black sugarpaste
- 20 g (¾ oz) red sugarpaste
- 40 g (1¼ oz) flesh-coloured sugarpaste
- Sweets for decoration

■ UTENSILS

- Water and paintbrush
- 30 cm (12 in) round cake board
- Rolling pin
- Carving knife
- Small sharp knife
- Fish slice
- Wooden spoon

1 Begin by covering the cake board. Lightly moisten the board with a little water and place to one side. Sprinkle the worksurface with icing sugar and begin to roll out the green sugarpaste. Carefully lift the icing and place it on the cake board. Continue to roll right to the edges of the cake board. Trim and neaten the edges and place the board to one side again.

2 On a spare cake board, cutting board or worksurface, check the cake will lie flat when it is turned upside down. Slice a little off the base if necessary. Cut the cake in half, and fill the middle with a layer of buttercream. Spread a thin coating of buttercream around the sides and top of the cake as well.

   Knead and roll out 300 g (10½ oz) of white sugarpaste. Lift and place the icing over the cake and carefully smooth it into position. Trim and neaten around the base. Lift the cake using a fish slice to help avoid getting fingerprints in the icing and place it towards the back of the covered cake board.

3 To make the dog's head, take 200 g (7 oz) of white sugarpaste and roll this into a ball. Flatten the ball slightly into a thick disc about 11 cm (4½ in) wide and stick this to the front of the cake.

4 To make the dog's eyes, thinly roll out about 20 g (¾ oz) of black sugarpaste. Cut out two discs about 4.5 cm (1¾ in) wide and two about 2.5 cm (1 in) in diameter.

   Wipe your hands (black sugarpaste has an annoying tendency to get everywhere!) and roll out about 10 g (¼ oz) of white sugarpaste. Cut out two discs each about 3 cm (1¼ in) wide and squash two tiny balls of white to make the tiny discs for the highlights. Assemble and stick the eyes in position on the face starting with the largest black disc first and alternating the colours.

5 For the tongue, use 20 g (¾ oz) of red sugarpaste. Roll this into a sort of flattish, carrot shape and bend it into a slight curve. Press a line down the centre using the back of a knife and stick it into position on the board, the pointed end just touching the base of the face.

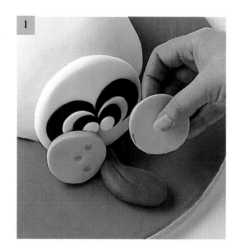

6 To make the dog's muzzle, divide the flesh-coloured sugarpaste in two and roll each half into a ball. Flatten each ball into a disc about 5 cm (2 in) in diameter. Stick the two circles in place and make three small dents in each using the end of a wooden spoon (*fig 1*).

   Finish off the face by sticking a small ball of black sugarpaste onto the muzzle for his nose.

7 To make the legs, divide 300 g (10½ oz) of white sugarpaste into four. Roll each quarter into a chunky carrot shape. Flatten each paw slightly and stick them on the board around the dog. Using the back of a knife, press three short lines into the front of each paw.

8 To make the ears, take 150 g (5 oz) of black sugarpaste. Divide it into two pieces and roll each half into the same sort of carrot shape as you did for the legs.

Use a rolling pin to flatten each half into an ear shape. Stick one either side of the head (*fig 2*).

9 Roll out 100 g (3½ oz) of black sugarpaste and cut out 'splodges' in a variety of shapes and sizes. Stick these all over the dog's back. Make a tail by rolling 10 g (¼ oz) of black sugarpaste into a tapering sausage shape. Bend it into a curl and stick in position.

10 Decorate the cake board with a selection of small sweets, securing them in place with little dabs of buttercream.

Football fan

Although the theme of this cake is football, it could be adapted to suit other sports too. Substitute a brown sugarpaste oval for the football and you have a rugby cake. Dress him in white with a bat and it becomes a cricket cake.

■ INGREDIENTS

- 15 cm (6 in) square sponge cake
- 1 quantity buttercream (see page 14)
- Icing sugar for rolling out
- 350 g (12 oz) green sugarpaste
- 300 g (10½ oz) white sugarpaste
- 150 g (5 oz) red sugarpaste
- 20 g (¾ oz) black sugarpaste
- 30 g (1 oz) flesh-coloured sugarpaste
- 40 g (1¼ oz) blue sugarpaste
- Black food colour
- 5 g (⅛ oz) brown sugarpaste
- 60 g (2 oz) green-coloured coconut (see page 14)

■ UTENSILS

- Carving knife
- 25 cm (10 in) square cake board
- Palette knife
- Cake smoother (optional)
- Small sharp knife
- Water
- Medium and fine paintbrushes

1 Slice a little off the top of the cake to level it if necessary. Turn it upside down and place towards the back of the board. Slice and fill the middle of the cake with buttercream, then reassemble and spread a thin covering of buttercream over the top and sides.

2 Dust the worksurface with a little icing sugar and knead all the green sugarpaste until pliable. Roll it out, then lift and place over the cake. Smooth over the top and sides, preferably with a cake smoother, as this irons out any lumps and bumps. Alternatively, simply smooth it as best you can with the flat of your hand. Trim away any excess from around the base.

3 Make the scarf by rolling out 250 g (8 oz) of the white sugarpaste and cutting it into a strip 30 cm x 10 cm (12 in x 4 in). Moisten the top of the cake and carefully lay the scarf over the top. Roll out and cut 150 g (5 oz) of red sugarpaste into about seven thin strips about 3 cm x 10 cm (1½ in x 4 in). Lay and stick the red stripes across the scarf. When you come to the ones at either end, cut a fringe into the strip before laying it into position on the board (*fig 1*).

4 Begin with the footballer's feet. Divide the black sugarpaste in two and roll each half into an oval. Stick these onto the board in front of the cake. Make two socks by rolling

1

10 g (¼ oz) of white sugarpaste into two balls. Flatten each ball slightly and press a few horizontal lines into each sock with the back of a knife. Stick these onto the boots (*fig 2*).

Make the footballer's legs by rolling 10 g (¼ oz) of flesh-coloured sugarpaste into a thin string. Cut this in half and stick into position.

5 For his shorts, take 10 g (¼ oz) of white sugarpaste and roll it into a boomerang shape (*fig 3*). Stick on top of the cake. Pull off and keep a little bit of the blue sugarpaste to make the sleeves later. Roll the rest into a cone for his body and stick

---

TIP

If the footballer loses his head or falls over, insert a small strand of dried spaghetti inside the body and slot the head on top for extra support.

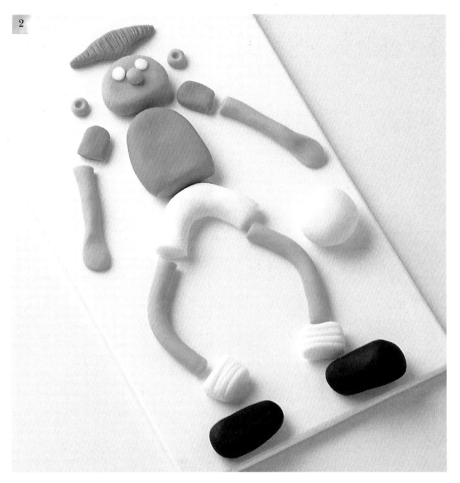

Paint in the pupils, eyebrows and mouth with black food colour. Finally, roll a little brown sugarpaste into a tiny strip and place on top of the head. Press some lines into the hair with the back of a knife.

9 Moisten the top of the cake and any exposed cake board with a little water and then sprinkle with the green-coloured coconut to look like the grass of a football pitch.

> **TIP**
>
> *If you know the home colours of the recipient's favourite football team, make the scarf and the footballer's kit in the appropriate shades.*

on top of the shorts (*fig 3*). Flatten the top of the cone slightly so the head has a level surface to sit on.

6 For the football, roll 20 g (¾ oz) of white sugarpaste into a ball. Stick this in place and paint a hexagonal design on the front with black food colour and a fine paintbrush. (If you don't want to paint, just press a few lines into the ball with the back of a knife or leave it plain.)

7 Roll 5 g (⅛ oz) of flesh-coloured sugarpaste into a thin sausage to make his arms. Cut in two and flatten one end of each half to make the hands. Stick these into position.

   Make two tiny shirt sleeves by rolling the leftover blue sugarpaste into an oval. Cut in half and stick one on the top of each arm.

8 To make the head, roll 10 g (¼ oz) of flesh-coloured sugarpaste into a ball. Stick on top of the body.

   Stick two tiny flattened discs of white sugarpaste onto the face for his eyes and three small balls of flesh-coloured sugarpaste in position for his ears and nose. Add some detail to the ears by making a small dent in them with the end of a paintbrush.

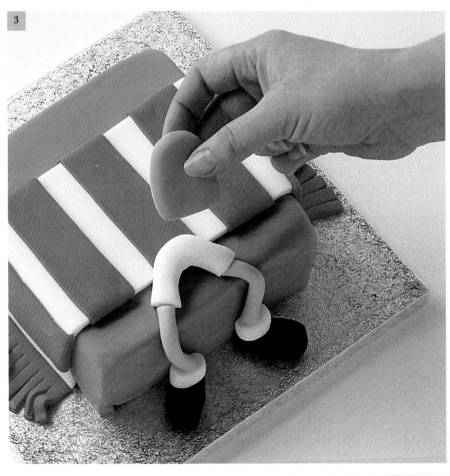

Make-up bag

This is for anyone who likes to experiment with the latest cosmetics. It is also very adaptable. Make a brown bag and fill with icing toys for a Christmas sack or pack with icing pencils and books for a 'Back to School' cake.

1 Begin by making up the little cosmetics themselves (*fig 1*) and, if possible, leave them overnight to harden. This will give them the strength to stand up and look even more realistic. If the recipient has a particular penchant for any specific brand of make-up or perfume, it might be fun to try to copy the bottles or packaging to give the cake a really personal touch.

Dust the worksurface with icing sugar. To make a basic eyeshadow palette, roll out about 20 g (¾ oz) of grey sugarpaste. Roll it fairly thickly and cut out a semi-circle. Roll out three small lumps of sugarpaste in various shades of brown and paprika and cut a different section of a smaller semi-circle out of each. Stick these onto the grey.

2 To make a duo eyeshadow, roll and cut about 10 g (¼ oz) of black sugarpaste into a rectangle. Cut two smaller rectangles out of two different shades of blue sugarpaste and stick these onto the black. Make an applicator wand by rolling a little light brown sugarpaste into a thin string and sticking a tiny oval of white or cream sugarpaste on either end.

3 To make a lipstick, roll about 10 g (¼ oz) of grey sugarpaste into a thick sausage. Slice a little off both ends to neaten them and press two lines across the icing using the back of a knife. Make another smaller sausage out of pink, red or whatever shade of sugarpaste you like and slice a small section to flatten one of the ends. Make a diagonal cut through the other end to make an authentic lipstick shape and stick the two sections together. Make another two or three of these.

To make a lip pencil, roll about 10 g (¼ oz) of red sugarpaste into a sausage about 9 cm (3 ½ in) long. Slice a little off both ends to neaten them. Roll a small piece of flesh-coloured sugarpaste into a tiny cone and slice a little off the pointed end. Make a tiny red point and stick all

three sections together. Make a couple of eye pencils in exactly the same way using blue and brown sugarpaste.

4 For the blusher brush, roll about 20 g (¾ oz) of light brown sugarpaste into a sausage. Slice off both ends to neaten them. Roll a little grey sugarpaste into a ball. Flatten the ball slightly and stick this against the brown. Press two lines into the grey with the back of a knife to add detail.

Roll out about 10 g (¼ oz) of black sugarpaste to a thickness of about 1 cm (⅜ in). Cut this into a triangular shape with a flat top and make bristles by pressing lines down the length of the shape with a knife. Stick the 'brush' in place on the handle.

INGREDIENTS

- Icing sugar for rolling out
- 60 g (2 oz) grey sugarpaste
- 30 g (1 oz) dark brown sugarpaste
- 20 g (¾ oz) flesh-coloured sugarpaste
- 60 g (2 oz) light brown sugarpaste
- 120 g (4¼ oz) black sugarpaste
- 20 g (¾ oz) dark blue sugarpaste
- 10 g (¼ oz) light blue sugarpaste
- 700 g (1 lb 9 oz) white sugarpaste
- 20 g (¾ oz) red sugarpaste
- 130 g (4¼ oz) pink sugarpaste
- 10 g (¼ oz) pale green sugarpaste
- 15 cm (6 in) round sponge cake
- ½ quantity buttercream (see page 14)

UTENSILS

- Rolling pin
- Small sharp knife
- Water and paintbrush
- Carving knife
- Palette knife
- 23 cm (9 in) round cake board
- Ruler

1

5 Make a simple pot of cream by rolling about 60 g (2 oz) of white sugarpaste into a round cylindrical shape with a flat base and top. Roll 20 g (¾ oz) of pink sugarpaste into a thick disc and stick this on top of the pot. Press a few vertical lines around the edge of the lid. Make another smaller pot out of two shades of brown sugarpaste to sit on the board.

6 To make a tube, roll about 20 g (¾ oz) of white sugarpaste into a slightly tapering rectangular shape. Make a small flowerpot shape out of a little white sugarpaste and stick this onto the end of the tube for a lid. Press lines down the length of the lid using the back of a knife.

7 For the mascara wand, simply roll about 10 g (¼ oz) of pale green sugarpaste into a sausage. Neaten both ends and press two lines into the icing about a third of the way along the top of the shape. Make any additional cosmetics and place all the components to one side whilst you deal with the cake.

8 Slice and fill the middle of the cake with buttercream. Reassemble the cake and place it in the centre of the board. Spread a thin covering of buttercream over the top and sides.

   Roll out 100 g (3½ oz) of black sugarpaste and cut out a 15 cm (6 in) disc and place on top of the cake. You could use your baking tin as a template for this but accuracy is not vitally important here as most of it will be hidden. The reason for the black is simply to help seal in the cake beneath and to give the illusion that the bag is full, should you have any gaps between your components. Place the pink and white pot and the white tube of cream on top of the black.

9 Take 300 g (10½ oz) of white sugarpaste and 100 g (3½ oz) of pink. Partially knead

TIP

For a really quick cake with no modelling, simply fill the top of the cake with sweets or biscuits instead.

the two colours together to achieve a light marbled effect. Roll the icing out fairly thickly and cut out a strip about 46 cm x 15 cm (18 in x 6 in). Using the edge of a clean ruler, gently press a criss-cross pattern across the strip to give a quilted effect (*fig 2*).

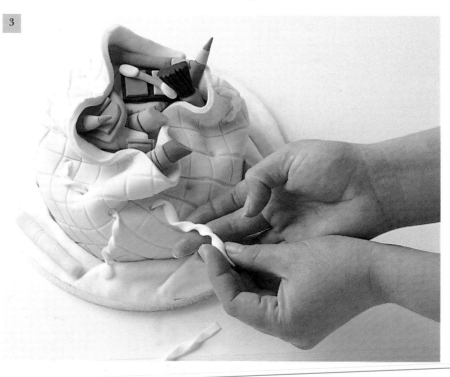

10 Carefully wind the strip up loosely like a bandage and, holding it vertically, start at the back and unwind it around the side of the cake (see page 130). Neaten the join and base. If it looks a bit flat in places, insert a few lumps of sugarpaste to pad out the top of the bag slightly. Using the end of a paintbrush, make a line of circular dents around the side of the bag. Carefully place the cosmetics into the top of the bag and secure with a little water.

11 Moisten the exposed cake board. Thinly roll out 250 g (9 oz) of white sugarpaste into a long strip. Lay the strip around the base of the cake allowing it to fall into folds like fabric. Press down the icing at the edges of the board and trim away any excess. Place any leftover cosmetics around the board.

12 Thinly roll out 20 g (¾ oz) of white sugarpaste and cut into small thin strips. Take one strip and twist it (*fig 3*). Hang it between two of the holes around the side of the cake and secure the ends with a little water. Repeat using alternate holes to look like a cord threaded through the icing. When you come to the final two at the front of the cake, allow them to hang down. Finish off each one with a tiny ball of white sugarpaste.

Lovebirds

Here's a novel idea for an engagement cake without a pink sugar heart in sight! It would also make a loving gift for Valentine's day. This is an extremely easy cake to put together as the chocolate sticks hide a multitude of sins!

■ INGREDIENTS

- Icing sugar for rolling out
- 120 g (4 oz) pale blue sugarpaste
- 10 g (¼ oz) white sugarpaste
- Black food colour
- 1 pudding bowl cake (see page 10)
- ½ quantity chocolate buttercream (see page 14)
- Two 120 g (4 oz) boxes of chocolate sticks (flavour of your choice!)
- 60 g (2 oz) dark blue sugarpaste
- 30 g (1 oz) green sugarpaste

■ UTENSILS

- Water
- Fine and medium paintbrushes
- Rolling pin
- Piping nozzle
- Small sharp knife
- Carving knife
- 20 cm (8 in) round cake board
- Palette knife
- Template for tail (see page 187)
- Garrett frill or jam tart cutter

1

1 Roll two 60 g (2 oz) lumps of pale blue sugarpaste into two conical shapes for the birds' bodies. Check that the bases are flat enough for them to stand upright. Make two 30 g (1 oz) balls of pale blue sugarpaste for the heads (*fig 1*). Stick a head onto each body with a little water.

2 To make the eyes, thinly roll out about 10 g (¼ oz) of white sugarpaste. Cut out four small circles using a piping nozzle and stick two on each head. Paint pupils and eyelashes using black food colour. Make two tiny yellow sugarpaste triangles for the beaks. Press a line using the back of a knife into the sides of each beak and stick one on each bird. Make a tiny pale blue triangle and press a few lines into the front of it. Stick it on top of the male bird's head. Put the birds to one side.

3 Level the top of the cake if necessary and slice and fill the centre with buttercream. Reassemble the cake and dab a little buttercream in the centre of the cake board to help hold the cake in place. Stand the cake, widest part up, and spread a thick layer of buttercream all over the sides and top.

4 Place the two birds into position on top of the cake and begin to build up the nest. Do this by pressing the chocolate sticks, one at a time, around the sides of the nest (*fig 2*) and over the top edge.

2

5 Roll out 30 g (1 oz) of the dark blue sugarpaste and cut out a tail using the template on page 109 if necessary. Re-knead the leftover icing and cut out a second tail. Place the two tails in position, one behind each bird.

6 To make the birds' wings, roll out another 30 g (1 oz) of dark blue sugarpaste and using either a garrett frill or a jam tart cutter, cut out a frilly circle. Re-knead the sugarpaste and cut out a second circle of the same size. Cut both circles in half. Carefully stick two wings onto each of the birds, overlapping them slightly at the front as though they are holding hands (sorry – wings!) (*fig 3*).

7 Roll out the green sugarpaste and cut out some simple leaves. Press a couple of veins into each leaf using the back of a knife and stick the leaves around the board and against the cake with a little water.

3

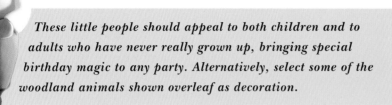

Woodland creatures

These little people should appeal to both children and to adults who have never really grown up, bringing special birthday magic to any party. Alternatively, select some of the woodland animals shown overleaf as decoration.

INGREDIENTS

- 18 cm (7 in) round sponge cake
- 1 quantity buttercream (see page 14)
- Icing sugar for rolling out
- 800 g (1 lb 12 oz) white marzipan
- Dark brown food colour paste
- 200 g (7 oz) white sugarpaste
- 50 g (2 oz) flesh-coloured sugarpaste
- 100 g (4 oz) mint green sugarpaste
- 50 g (2 oz) gooseberry green sugarpaste
- 50 g (2 oz) red sugarpaste
- 20 g (¾ oz) black sugarpaste
- 10 g (¼ oz) grey sugarpaste
- Black food colour paste
- 75 g (3 oz) dark brown sugar

UTENSILS

- 28 cm (11 in) round cake board
- Carving knife
- Palette knife
- Rolling pin
- 18 cm (7 in) round cake board or plate
- Small sharp knife
- Water
- Paintbrush

1 Level the top of the cake and turn it upside down. Slice the cake in two and fill the centre with buttercream. Place on the board and spread more buttercream around the sides and top.

2 Knead and roll out 300 g (11 oz) of the white marzipan. Place either an 18 cm (7 in) round cake board or plate on top to act as a template and cut round it using a sharp knife. Place the marzipan disc on top of the cake.

3 Roll out the remaining marzipan and cut a strip measuring approximately 58 cm x 8 cm (23 in x 3 in). Carefully roll up the strip like a bandage then unwind it around the side of the cake (*fig 1*).

4 Press irregular vertical lines around the sides of the cake using the back of a knife.

> **TIP**
>
> *Use the leaves as camouflage and position them to hide any mistakes or unsightly marks!*

Use a paintbrush to paint the bark with a wash of watered-down brown food colour (*fig 2*). Finally, paint a few 'age' rings on top of the tree stump with brown food colour and a fine paintbrush.

5 To make the troll, roll out 30 g (1 oz) of white sugarpaste into a cone (*fig 3*) to form the basis for his body. Stick this in position on top of the tree stump.

6 For the troll's legs, roll 20 g (¾ oz) of mint green sugarpaste into a sausage and cut this in half. Stick the two halves to the base of the body.

7 To make the arms, roll 10 g (¼ oz) of white sugarpaste into a sausage and cut in half, as for the legs. Stick one arm either side of the body.

3

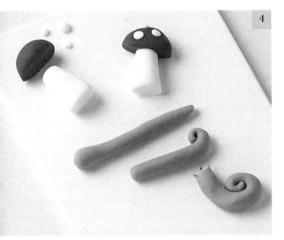

4

white sugarpaste into a cone *(fig 4)*. Make another three cones and stick them in position around the base of the cake. Divide 20 g (1 oz) of the red sugarpaste into two and roll into little balls. Cut each ball in half and stick one on top of each toadstool base. Decorate each one with a few tiny flattened discs of white sugarpaste.

12 To make the snail, roll 10 g (¼ oz) of grey sugarpaste into a small sausage. Paint a line of water along the top. Roll it up, leaving about 2 cm (¾ in) protruding for the head *(fig 4)*.

Pinch two tiny 'feelers' out of the top of the head and paint three dots of black food colour on the face for the eyes and mouth. Place the snail at the foot of the tree stump and secure with a little water.

13 For the leaves, take the two remaining shades of green coloured sugarpaste and roll each one out flat. Cut out some very basic leaf shapes using the tip of a knife.

TIP

If your marzipan is difficult to handle, soften it for a few seconds on high power in a microwave.

food colour on the face for his eyes.

10 Repeat steps 5-9 given above for the remaining trolls, although you can omit making legs for the one shown on the right of the cake as his lower body is strategically hidden by some of the leaves!

11 For each toadstool, roll out 10 g (¼ oz) of

5

8 Stick a small ball of flesh-coloured sugarpaste on top of the body for the troll's head. For the hat, roll 10 g (¼ oz) of red sugarpaste into a pointed triangular shape and stick on top of the head, tweaking the end out at an angle. Make three tiny balls of flesh-coloured sugarpaste. Use one for his nose and the other two as hands. Make two tiny flesh-coloured triangles for ears. Stick these in place and add a little detail by pressing the end of a paintbrush lightly into each ear.

9 To complete the troll, make two small ovals of black sugarpaste and stick one onto the end of each leg. Paint two tiny dots of black

Press a simple vein pattern into each leaf using the back of the knife *(fig 5)*. Arrange around the scene.

14 Lightly moisten the exposed cake board and carefully spoon the dark brown sugar around the bottom of the cake board to look like earth.

TIP

Instead of sugar, you could substitute green-coloured desiccated coconut as grass. Together with quick-to-make details like the little snail, the area around the cake contributes to the overall 'tableau' resulting in a totally professional finish.

Decorating variation

In this alternative version, I have used rabbits instead of figures. Instructions for making these appear on page 21 and the effect is just as charming as the original. Add some sugar eggs for an Easter theme. If your creativity is really flowing, you could also add mice, squirrels or other small creatures. You could also devise a Christmas or winter scene. Spread a layer of royal icing over the top of the tree stump and the group to look like snow and add beards and white trims to the hats of the figures.

Santa and his teddies

I do like cakes that tell a story. It means that people actually have to take some time to look at them to work out what's going on. Here, Santa and his helper are putting the finishing touches to some teddies ready for the big night.

1 Although I have used a traditional fruit cake base here, you could substitute sponge if you prefer. Just omit the brandy, jam and marzipan and use buttercream instead. To shape the cake, cut irregular lumps out of the cake and place these pieces around the cake to create the snow drifts *(fig 1)*. (You could leave the cake intact if you prefer.)

If you wish, pierce the cake a few times with a cocktail stick and drizzle the brandy over the top. Place the cake on the board and 'paint' with boiled apricot jam, applied with a pastry brush.

2 Dust the worksurface with icing sugar and knead the marzipan until pliable. (If it is difficult to knead, heat it for a few seconds in a microwave on full power.) Roll it out and cover the cake.

3 Lightly moisten the whole of the cake and the exposed cake board with a little water. Roll out 400 g (14 oz) of white sugarpaste. Lay this over the cake and board. Smooth the icing over the cake and board, starting from the centre to try to prevent air bubbles from forming in the hollows. Trim and neaten the edges.

If you do get an air bubble, prick it gently with the cocktail stick and press out. Hide the little hole left by the cocktail stick under a figure or snowball later.

4 To make Santa, roll 40 g (1¼ oz) of red sugarpaste into a cone *(fig 2)*. Stick this in the middle of the cake. Roll 10 g (¼ oz) of flesh-coloured sugarpaste into a ball for his head and stick on the body.

To make his beard, roll out about 5 g (⅛ oz) of white sugarpaste and cut out a triangular shape. Press lines into the beard with the back of a knife and stick onto the face. Stick a tiny ball of flesh-coloured sugarpaste just above the beard for his nose and two either side of the head for his ears. Push the end of a paintbrush into each ear to add detail.

For the hat, roll 5 g (⅛ oz) of red sugarpaste into a triangle. Stick on top of the head and bend the end over slightly. Roll 5 g (⅛ oz) of white sugarpaste into a thin sausage and lay this around the base of the hat. Stick a small ball of white on the end of the hat for a pom-pom. Paint two dots of black food colour for his eyes.

5 Next, roll 10 g (¼ oz) of black sugarpaste into a sausage about 7.5 cm (3 in) long for his boots. Cut this in half and bend up the end of each to make an 'L' shape. Stick in position, making sure that you leave enough room for the teddy later. Press a few lines into the sole of each boot with the back of a knife. Roll 10 g (¼ oz) of white sugarpaste into a sausage about 17 cm

INGREDIENTS

- 15 cm (6 in) square fruit cake
- 45 ml (3 tbsp) brandy (optional)
- 45 ml (3 tbsp) boiled apricot jam
- Icing sugar for rolling out
- 500 g (1 lb 2 oz) marzipan
- 450 g (1 lb) white sugarpaste
- 50 g (2 oz) red sugarpaste
- 30 g (1 oz) flesh-coloured sugarpaste
- Black food colour
- 30 g (1 oz) golden brown sugarpaste
- 30 g (1 oz) green sugarpaste

UTENSILS

- Carving knife
- Cocktail stick
- 20 cm (8 in) square cake board
- Pastry brush
- Rolling pin
- Small sharp knife
- Water
- Medium and fine paintbrushes
- Drinking straw

1

an upside-down, semi-circular impression. Paint the pupils on these teddies as though they are looking to the right.

On the finished teddies add ears, and pupils looking to the left. Hold and press the drinking straw the other way up to give them smiling expressions.

8   To make the elf's body, roll 10 g (¼ oz) of green sugarpaste into a ball (*fig 3*). Stick towards the front of the cake. Roll 5 g (⅛ oz) of flesh-coloured sugarpaste into a ball for his head and stick on the body.

Top the head with a small triangle of green and tweak the end into position.

Make eyes in the same way as for the teddies and paint a smiling mouth using black food colour. Make two tiny pointed ears and a nose and stick in position on the head.

To make the legs, roll 5 g (⅛ oz) of green sugarpaste into a sausage. Cut in half and stick in position. Make a smaller sausage for the arms and stick these in place too. Make two tiny flesh-coloured hands and make and place a teddy's ear in one. Stick in place.

Make two smaller versions of Santa's boots out of 5 g (⅛ oz) of black sugarpaste and stick on the ends of the legs. Finally, roll any leftover bits of white sugarpaste into balls and stick around the cake to look like snowballs.

(7 in) long. Lay this neatly around the base of the figure.

6   Make the first teddy. Roll 10 g (¼ oz) of the brown sugarpaste into a cone (*fig 3*). Stick this in front of Santa. Roll 5 g (⅛ oz) of brown sugarpaste into a ball for his head. Stick this on top of the body. Make two small sausage shapes for his legs and bend up the end of each one to make a foot. Stick one either side of the body. Stick two smaller sausage shapes in place for his arms.

Make two tiny flattened white sugarpaste discs for his eyes and one black one for a nose and stick in position. Paint in the pupils with black food colour. Stick a small ball of brown on top of the head for an ear and add detail with the end of a paintbrush.

Roll 5 g (⅛ oz) of red sugarpaste into a sausage. Cut this in half to make Santa's arms and stick these in position on his body. Make two tiny flesh-coloured oval shapes for his hands and stick these on the ends of the arms.

7   Make another five teddies in the same way (you will probably find it easier to make these away from the cake and to stick them in position when they are finished). On the three unfinished teddies, omit the ears and give each a glum-looking mouth by pressing a drinking straw held at an angle to leave

TIP

If you are very short of time, just make the one teddy that Santa is in the process of finishing off – the cake will look just as charming and will take you far less time. You could also leave out Santa's helper if you wish.

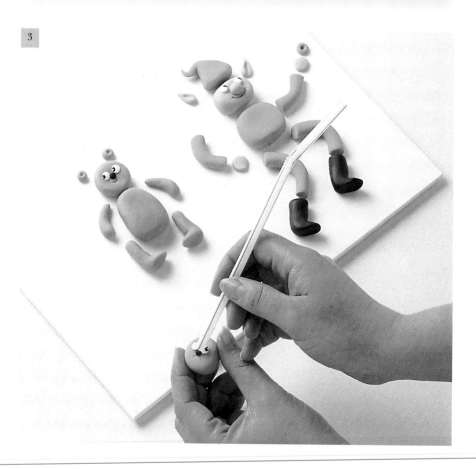

Comfy chair

Unless they have a hobby, men can be difficult subjects to make cakes for. This is a neat solution, ideal for a birthday or Father's Day. If it's children that harangue him rather than a cat, substitute a child climbing over the back instead.

1 Cover the board with white sugarpaste as on page 16. Trim away the excess and place the board to one side *(fig 1)*.

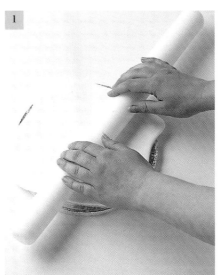

2 Cut the cake into shape by slicing off about one third. Place the smaller, cutaway piece flat side down on the remaining section of cake to form the basic seat shape *(fig 2)*. If there is not much seat area, slice a thin section away from the back of the chair. 'Glue' the two sections of seat together with buttercream. Spread a layer of buttercream over the outside of the cake.

3 Knead and roll out 300 g (10½ oz) of pale blue sugarpaste. Carefully lift up the icing and place over the cake. To prevent air being trapped, start from the central seat area and smooth the icing into position. You may find that the icing gathers into folds at the back of the chair. These can usually be eased out by gently lifting and fanning the icing out slightly. Trim and neaten the base.

4 Carefully lift and place the cake towards the back of the covered cake board. If you're worried about getting fingerprints in the icing, use a fish slice to lift it.

5 Roll out about 50 g (2 oz) of the pale blue sugarpaste. Cut out a strip about 46 cm x 3 cm (18 in x 1¼ in). Ideally the strip should be slightly wavy down one of the longest sides. This is not essential but it does make for a better frill. Making sure you have plenty of icing sugar on the worksurface to prevent the frill sticking, roll a paintbrush or cocktail stick backwards and forwards over the wavy edge of the strip *(fig 3)*. Paint a line of water around the side of the cake, about 3 cm (1¼ in) up from the base. Stick the frill around the cake. Neaten the join by pushing the end of a paintbrush along the top of the strip to leave a circular pattern.

6 To make the cushions, roll out about 60 g (2 oz) of white sugarpaste fairly thickly. Cut out three squares about 6 cm (2½ in) square. Tweak the ends slightly and using the end of a drinking straw, poke four small circles into each one to look like buttons *(fig 4)*. Stick the cushions onto the back of the chair.

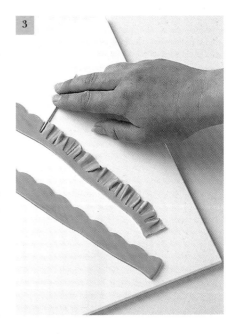

7 To make the man himself, begin with his legs. Roll 80 g (2¾ oz) of grey sugarpaste into a long sausage. Cut the sausage in half and stick it onto the chair. Roll two 10 g (¼ oz) lumps of black sugarpaste into oval shapes for his feet and stick one on the end of each leg.

Decorating variation

A comfy chair is not just for people to snooze in — in fact, once you have made the basic shape you could sit virtually anything on it. The cat in this variation looks especially at home! Make a potato like those in the flowerpot cake (page 160), decorate it with eyes and a mouth, sit it on the seat and you have a cheeky couch-potato cake. A chair cake is an extremely useful shape to add to your repertoire because it provides an easy way to put full-length, upright figures onto a cake without having to fiddle about with awkward supports inside them.

10 To make the newspaper, cut a flat rectangle out of 10 g (¼ oz) of white sugarpaste. Fold the icing in half, then half again. Paint squiggles onto the newspaper with black food colour to resemble the print and stick the paper onto the man's lap.

11 To make the cat, roll about 5 g (⅛ oz) of brown sugarpaste into a tapering sausage shape for his body. Pinch a couple of small ears out of the thicker end.

Stick two tiny strings of brown sugarpaste onto the back of the chair for his paws and stick the body on top. Roll another tiny piece of sugarpaste into a string for his tail. Paint on the cat's features and stripes neatly with some black food colour.

as I did, that the head flops backwards, simply prop it up with a small triangle of white sugarpaste which will just look like another cushion. Push the end of a paintbrush into the lower part of the head and pull it down slightly to give him an open-mouthed expression.

Stick a small ball of sugarpaste on the front of the face for his nose and two at the sides for his ears. Add a little detail to the ears by making a small hollow with the end of a paintbrush. Either paint in the eyes with black food colour or press two semi-circular impressions into the face using the drinking straw held at an angle.

Add two flattened balls of flesh-coloured sugarpaste for his hands.

8 Make his body by rolling 50 g (2 oz) of green sugarpaste into a conical shape and stick this on top of the legs (*fig 5*). Roll out a thin strip of the same colour green and press vertical lines into the strip using the back of your knife. Lay this around the base of his jumper. Make a polo neck by sticking a small but thick disc of green sugarpaste on top of the jumper and again press a few vertical lines around the edge.

For his arms, roll 20 g (¾ oz) of the green sugarpaste into a sausage. Cut it in half and arrange and stick the arms in whatever position you wish.

9 To make the man's head, roll 20 g (¾ oz) of flesh-coloured sugarpaste into a ball (*fig 6*). Stick this onto the neck. If you find,

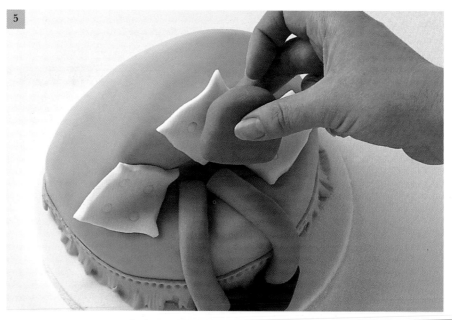

Piggy bank

Here's a cake to appeal to anyone with an interest in money, from the youngest saver to the most hard-bitten of accountants. To make the pig more dramatic, paint a pattern on his back using food colours or stick on sugarpaste shapes.

1. Cover the cake board with green sugarpaste as explained on page 16.
   Trim and neaten the edges, then place the covered board to one side.

2. Slice and fill the centre of the cake with buttercream. Reassemble the cake and spread a layer of buttercream over the top and sides. Roll out and cover the cake with 250 g (8¾ oz) of pink sugarpaste. Trim and neaten the base, then place the cake towards the rear of the covered cake board.

3. Make a simple floral pattern on the pig's back by pressing something circular (such as an icing nozzle or small circle cutter) into the icing while it is still pliable, then surrounding it with smaller circles made from a drinking straw (*fig 1*).

4. To make his face (*fig 2*), thinly roll out 10 g (¼ oz) of white sugarpaste. Cut out two discs about 2.5 cm (1 in) in diameter. Stick these to the front of the pig. Roll out the black sugarpaste and cut out two smaller discs and a small rectangle for the money slot. Stick the circles onto his eyes and the slot in the middle of his back. Finish off each eye with a tiny flattened ball of white sugarpaste as a highlight.

5. For his snout, roll and shape 40 g (1¾ oz) of pink sugarpaste into a thick disc about 6.5 cm (2½ in) in diameter. Stick this to the front of his face. Don't use too much water

to do this or the snout will start to slide. Using the end of a wooden spoon, press two nostrils into the snout. Make a mouth either by pressing something circular into the icing (such as a cutter) or by using the back of a knife to make a curved line. Make two small cuts at each end of the mouth.

6. Make a tail by rolling about 5 g (⅛ oz) of pink sugarpaste into a tapering sausage shape. Bend it into a curly tail shape and stick to the back of the pig.

7. To make the pig's ears, roll out 40 g (1¾ oz) of pink sugarpaste to a thickness of about 5 mm (¼ in). Cut out an ear shape, using the template if necessary. Scrunch up the leftover icing and cut out a second ear. Stick the ears to the sides of the head, allowing them to fold over slightly at the top (*fig 3*).

8. Cut one of the chocolate coins in half and press it into the money slot. A drop of water should be enough to hold it in place but you could use a dab of royal icing if you prefer. Arrange the rest of the coins around the board.

INGREDIENTS

- Icing sugar for rolling out
- 200 g (7 oz) green sugarpaste
- Cake baked in a pudding basin (see page 10)
- ½ quantity buttercream (see page 14)
- 340 g (12 oz) pink sugarpaste
- 10 g (¼ oz) white sugarpaste
- 20 g (¾ oz) black sugarpaste
- About 200 g (7 oz), or 4 small bags, of chocolate coins
- 15 ml (1 tbsp) royal icing (optional)

UTENSILS

- 25 cm (10 in) round cake board
- Water and paintbrush
- Rolling pin
- Small sharp knife
- Icing nozzle
- Drinking straw
- Wooden spoon
- Large circle cutter (optional)

TIP

If you don't have any royal icing readily available for sticking the coins, use leftover buttercream instead. It will hold them in place just as well, but may be a little greasy when unwrapping the coins.

Christening cake

If you're worried about piping directly onto the top of this cake, two methods of writing in icing are also shown. Read the instructions in step 1 first and see which one suits you best.

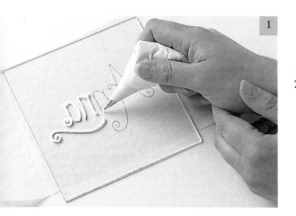

1 If you feel confident enough to pipe the baby's name directly on to the top of the cake without following a guide, go straight to step 2. If you're not, then one of these two solutions might help.

(**a**) Do this after you have covered the cake with sugarpaste. Write the baby's name on a piece of greaseproof paper. Place the paper, right way up, on the top of the cake and using either a cocktail stick, dressmaking pin or scriber (this is a sugarcraft tool especially designed for the job), trace over the lettering. Lift off the greaseproof paper and a scratched impression of the name should be left behind on the sugarpaste.

Place about 15 ml (1 tbsp) royal icing into a piping bag fitted with a number 2 piping nozzle and secure the end. Pipe over the lettering.

This method works best on a sugarpasted cake that has been allowed to harden overnight, otherwise it is very easy to dent the cake accidentally when leaning on it.

(**b**) Prepare this before you cover the cake with sugarpaste.

Write the baby's name on greaseproof paper. Turn the greaseproof over so that the writing is still visible but now reads back to front. Place a small piece of perspex over the greaseproof. Pipe over the name with royal icing on to the perspex *(fig 1)*.

Put to one side, leave to dry and go on to step 2.

2 Level the top of the cake. Turn it upside down and place on the cake board. Slice and fill the centre with buttercream. Reassemble the cake and buttercream the sides and top.

Dust the worksurface with a little icing sugar and knead and roll out 500 g (1 lb 2 oz) of yellow sugarpaste. Place this over the cake and carefully smooth it into position. Run over the surface with a cake smoother, if you have one, to iron out any bumps. Alternatively, use the flat of your hand. Trim away any excess sugarpaste from the base.

Lightly moisten the exposed cake board with a little water. Roll out 200 g (7 oz) of yellow sugarpaste and cut out a strip approximately 61 cm (24 in) long and 3 cm (1¼ in) wide. Carefully roll up the sugarpaste strip, then unwind it to cover the cake board (see page 16). If you find this too time-consuming, you can leave the base uncovered.

3 If using the second method of writing,

■ INGREDIENTS

- Royal icing (see page 15)
- 20 cm (8 in) round sponge cake
- 1 quantity buttercream (see page 14)
- Icing sugar for rolling out
- 700 g (1 lb 9 oz) yellow sugarpaste
- 100 g (3½ oz) flesh-coloured sugarpaste
- 50 g (2 oz) light brown sugarpaste
- 50 g (2 oz) darker brown sugarpaste
- 35 g (1¼ oz) pale blue sugarpaste
- 15 g (½ oz) white sugarpaste
- Black food colour
- 20 small sweets

■ UTENSILS

- Greaseproof paper
- Pencil
- Eraser
- Sheet of clear perspex (about 20 cm x 13 cm/ 8 in x 5 in) (optional)
- Pin or scriber (optional)
- Piping bags (see page 18 for details)
- Scissors
- Number 2 or 3 piping nozzles
- Clean damp cloth
- Carving knife
- 25 cm (10 in) round cake board
- Rolling pin
- Cake smoother (optional)
- Small sharp knife
- Water
- Medium and fine paintbrushes
- Cocktail stick
- 150 cm (60 in) white ribbon

3

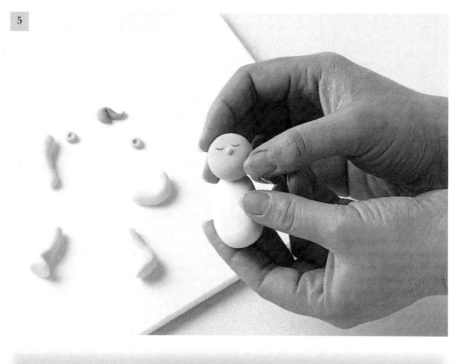

5

board. Starting from the back of the cake, hold the piping bag at a slight angle. Squeeze out a little icing, then release the pressure and pull slightly. Keep the tip of the nozzle in the icing all the time. Squeeze out a little more icing, release the pressure and pull (*fig 3*). Repeat all the way round the base of the cake.

You may wish to practise this technique on your worksurface first if you are not too confident of your piping skills. Alternatively, pipe a simple line of dots or stick sweets on the cake instead.

5 All the babies, dressed or undressed, are composed of the same six basic shapes (*fig 4*). To make the baby's body, roll 20 g (¾ oz) of flesh-coloured sugarpaste into a conical shape. Make the head by rolling 5 g (⅛ oz) of flesh-coloured sugarpaste into a small ball. Stick in place with a little water (*fig 5*).

Make the baby's legs by rolling approximately 10 g (¼ oz) of flesh-coloured sugarpaste into a sausage. Cut this in two,

gently touch the royal icing on the perspex to check that it has dried. If it still feels soft, then place a bit of cling film over the top of the cake to stop the sugarpaste surface from hardening too much before the royal icing is ready. (The sugarpaste has to be soft enough to take an impression.) When the piping feels hard to the touch, turn the perspex over and press the lettering into the top of the cake (*fig 2*). Carefully pull it away. The baby's name should now be visible as an impression. Pipe over the name with white royal icing, using a number 2 nozzle.

4 When the name is on the top of the cake, pipe a 'snail trail' around the base of the cake to hide the join between cake and

4

TIP

To avoid damaging the sugarpasted cake, you may find it easier to make the models of the babies away from the cake and then stick them in position once they are finished.

then gently bend the end of each one to form a foot. Stick these in whatever position you wish.

For the arms, take about 5 g (⅛ oz) of sugarpaste and roll into a sausage. Cut in two and flatten one end of each half to make a hand. Stick these against the body. Thinly roll out a little white sugarpaste and cut out a tiny triangle. Stick this on as a nappy.

Paint the facial details with black food colour and a fine paintbrush, and stick two tiny dots of icing either side of the head for the ears and one in the middle of the face for a nose. To make a frilly mop hat, simply cut out a thin disc of white sugarpaste and roll a cocktail stick around the edge to frill it *(fig 6)*. Stick onto the back of the head and roll a tiny bit of yellow sugarpaste into a curl and stick onto the forehead.

6 Make as many or as few babies as you want (or you have time for), altering the positions of the hands and feet and giving each one an individual expression and different hair colour.

Use the same shapes for the baby in the romper suit, but use coloured sugarpaste for the arms, legs and body to look like the clothing.

7 To complete the cake, stick small sweets around the top and the board and tie a bow around the sides as the perfect finishing touch.

Decorating variation

As you can see, this cake works just as well in a different colour. If you prefer something paler, leave the base of the cake white and colour the piping instead. If you find it difficult to tie a bow, leave it off and add a couple more babies and sweets to fill the space instead.

Twitcher

There's a type of person who at the mere rumour of a lesser-spotted-swamp gurgler near Congleton will miss appointments, cross continents and sit for hours in freezing conditions just to catch the merest sight. Weird, but it makes for a good cake!

INGREDIENTS

- 1 pudding basin cake (see page 10)
- 1 quantity buttercream (see page 14)
- Icing sugar for rolling out
- 260 g (9 oz) black sugarpaste
- 20 g (¾ oz) pale blue sugarpaste
- 10 g (¼ oz) flesh-coloured sugarpaste
- 50 g (2 oz) brown sugarpaste
- 10 g (¼ oz) white sugarpaste
- Black food colour
- 150 g (5 oz) dark green sugarpaste
- 150 g (5 oz) mid-green sugarpaste
- 150 g (5 oz) pale green sugarpaste
- Brown food colour
- 10 g (¼ oz) pale brown sugarpaste
- 10 g (¼ oz) very dark brown sugarpaste
- 20 g (¾ oz) yellow sugarpaste
- 30 g (1 oz) golden brown sugarpaste
- 30 g (1 oz) green-coloured desiccated coconut (see page 14)
- 30 g (1 oz) brown-coloured desiccated coconut

UTENSILS

- Carving knife
- 25 cm (10 in) round cake board
- Palette knife
- Rolling pin
- Water
- Medium and fine paintbrushes
- Small sharp knife
- Piping nozzle

1 Turn the cake upside down so that the widest part sits on the board. If it wobbles, cut a slice from the base so that it sits securely. Split it in half and fill the centre with buttercream and reassemble. Position the cake to the left of the board and then spread a layer of buttercream over the sides and top.

2 Dust the worksurface with icing sugar. Knead 250 g (9 oz) of black sugarpaste until it is pliable. Roll it out and place over the cake. Smooth it into position, and trim and neaten the base.

3 To make the twitcher, begin with his binoculars. Roll 5 g (⅛ oz) of black sugarpaste into a small sausage. Cut this in half and stick the two halves side by side, pointing outwards, on the front of the cake. If they start to droop at all, stick a little ledge of black sugarpaste underneath them to provide extra support.

Next, roll 20 g (¾ oz) of pale blue sugarpaste into a sausage. Cut this in half and bend each half slightly into a curved boomerang shape. Stick these pieces onto the cake with the flat, cut ends up against the binoculars.

4 To make the twitcher's head, roll a 5 g (⅛ oz) lump of flesh-coloured sugarpaste into a semi-circular shape. Stick this just above the binoculars.

Next, make two tiny flattened ovals of flesh-coloured sugarpaste for his hands and stick these on top of the binoculars. Thinly roll out a little brown sugarpaste. Cut out and fringe a tiny rectangle. Stick this on top of his head *(fig 2)*.

To make his ears, stick two tiny balls of flesh-coloured sugarpaste either side of his head and push the end of a paintbrush into each ear to add detail.

Thinly roll out a little white sugarpaste and cut out two tiny discs (a piping nozzle is useful for doing this). Stick the white circles to the ends of the binoculars and paint a small picture of a bird with black food colour (you can miss this stage out if you wish).

5 Roll out a small piece of each of the green sugarpastes and cut out some basic leaf

2

Cut out a diamond shape for his beak. Bend it in half and stick onto the face. Stick two tiny flattened balls of white sugarpaste onto his face for his eyes and paint in pupils and eyebrows with black food colour.

Roll out and cut two longish triangles for his wings and stick these either side of his body in an outraged, hands-on-hips position. Carefully place the bird on top of the cake.

9 Moisten the cake board with a little water and carefully spoon the coloured coconut around the base of the cake to look like grass and earth.

TIP
If the person you are making this cake for 'twitches' for something else, substitute flowers or butterflies or a train for the bird.

shapes. Press a simple vein pattern into each one using the back of a knife. Starting from the base, stick the leaves around the sides of the cake, alternating the different shades and allowing them to overlap until the entire cake has been covered *(fig 3)*.

6 To make the tree stump, mould 40 g (1 ¾ oz) of brown sugarpaste into a rounded stump shape with a flat base and top *(fig 1)*. Holding the back of a knife vertically, press irregular lines around the sides of the stump. Paint a wash of watered-down brown food colour around the stump to pick out the bark.

Cut out a thin disc of pale brown sugarpaste and stick on top of the stump. Paint a few age rings on the top with brown food colour.

Roll some little bits of leftover green sugarpaste into thin strings and stick these up against the sides of the stump. Place it in position on the board and secure with a little water.

7 To make the smaller bird, roll about 5 g (⅛ oz) of very dark brown sugarpaste into a tapering sausage shape *(fig 1)*. Bend the head end up slightly and flatten and pull the tail into a point.

Add two tiny flattened balls of white sugarpaste for his eyes and a tiny triangle of yellow for a beak. Stick two tiny dark brown triangles either side of the body for wings. Paint the pupils on the eyes with black food colour.

8 For the large bird, use 30 g (1 oz) of golden brown sugarpaste. Mould this into a rounded cone. Bend the smaller end over to make a head *(fig 1)*.

Roll out a little yellow sugarpaste and cut out a rectangle for the tail. Cut a triangle out of one end and stick it against the back of the bird.

3

Bride and Groom

A special feature of this cake is that as the models are on a thin cake board, they can be lifted off and kept as mementoes. If you prefer a rich fruit cake instead of sponge, cover with a layer of marzipan first.

1 Level the top of the cake, spread with buttercream and cover both the cake and board with 700 g (1 lb 9 oz) of cream-coloured sugarpaste as described in step 2 of the christening cake on page 142. Place the cake to one side.

Bend the collar forwards slightly.

2 Cover the thin 15 cm (6 in) round cake board with 60 g (2 oz) of cream-coloured sugarpaste as described on page 16. Trim and neaten the edges. Place this to one side too.

3 On a spare board or worksurface, make the groom. Roll 80 g (2¾ oz) of grey sugarpaste into a chunky conical shape about 7 cm (2¼ in) tall. Check that the base is flat so that it stands upright. To add extra internal support, insert a strand of dried spaghetti into the body, leaving about 4 cm (1½ in) protruding out of the top (fig 1).

4 Roll 15 g (½ oz) of flesh-coloured sugarpaste into an oval shape (fig 2). Stick onto the body (use a little water as well), leaving about 1 cm (⅜ in) of spaghetti still protruding.

Make his shirt by rolling out about 10 g (¼ oz) of white sugarpaste and cutting out a rectangle, using the template if necessary. Make a little cut in the centre of the top edge. Stick this to the front of the body, allowing the collar to just overlap the face.

5 To make the cravat, roll a tiny piece of pink sugarpaste into a thin string. Stick this just under the collar. Roll out a little more pink and cut into a thin, tapering rectangular shape. Press lines down the length of the strip using the back of a knife. Stick this in place on the front of the shirt (fig 3).

6 Roll out a tiny strip of brown sugarpaste.

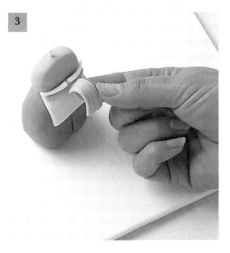

Cut out a thinnish rectangle and press lines down its length. Moisten the top of the head and lay this across for his hair. Stick three tiny balls of flesh-coloured sugarpaste

on the head for his ears and nose and push the end of a paintbrush into each ear to add detail. Paint his features with black food colour.

To make the hat, roll out 10 g (¼ oz) of grey sugarpaste. Cut out a circle about 3.5 cm (1½ in) in diameter and stick onto the head. Re-knead the rest of the grey and mould into a rounded shape with a flat base and top. Stick onto the head and bend up the sides of the brim.

7 To make the jacket, roll out 20 g (¾ oz) of the black sugarpaste. Cut out a jacket shape, using the template if necessary. Make a cut for the tails and wrap and stick the jacket around the groom's body (any gaps in the tummy area will be hidden by his arm at a later stage). Place the groom to one side.

- 20 cm (8 in) round sponge cake
- 1 quantity buttercream (see page 14)
- Icing sugar for rolling out
- 800 g (1 lb 12 oz) cream-coloured sugarpaste
- 90 g (3 oz) grey sugarpaste
- 2 strands raw dried spaghetti
- 30 g (1 oz) flesh-coloured sugarpaste
- 150 g (5 oz) white sugarpaste
- 10 g (¼ oz) pink sugarpaste
- 5 g (⅛ oz) brown sugarpaste
- Black and gooseberry green food colour pastes
- 30 g (1 oz) black sugarpaste
- 5 g (⅛ oz) yellow sugarpaste
- 90 g (3 oz) green sugarpaste
- ½ quantity royal icing (see page 15)

UTENSILS

- Carving knife
- 25 cm (10 in) round cake board
- Rolling pin
- Cake smoother (optional)
- Small sharp knife
- 15 cm (6 in) round thin cake board
- Water
- Fine and medium paintbrushes
- Templates for shirt, jacket and veil (see page 187)
- 2 piping bags (see page 18)
- 150 cm (60 in) ivory ribbon

some on the bride's front to make a bouquet. Intersperse the flowers with tiny bits of green sugarpaste. Push little hollows in each flower with the end of a paintbrush.

11 Stick the bride and groom next to each other on the covered board and then make the groom's arms. Roll 10 g (¼ oz) of black sugarpaste into a sausage. Cut it in two. Bend one half into a right-angle and stick on the front of the groom. Position and stick the other one so that it looks as though the groom has his arm around the bride (fig 6).

   Add two flattened balls of flesh-coloured sugarpaste for the hands.

8 Make the bride's skirt by rolling 50 g (2 oz) of white sugarpaste into a pointed conical shape. Stick a 5 g (⅛ oz) oval of white sugarpaste on top (fig 1). Insert a strand of dried spaghetti as you did for the groom. Roll 5 g (⅛ oz) of flesh-coloured sugarpaste into a ball for her head (fig 4) and stick it to the body. Paint her features with black food colour and a fine brush and stick a tiny piece of flesh-coloured sugarpaste on the front of her face for a nose. Roll a little flesh-coloured icing into a thin sausage for her arms. Stick this onto the front of the body in a 'U' shape.

9 To make the hair, roll a little yellow sugarpaste into a thin strip about 6 cm

(2½ in) long. Press lines into it with a knife, then lay and stick it over the bride's head (fig 5). Tweak the ends up into a curl. Make a tiny yellow rectangle for a fringe. Press lines into this also and stick on her forehead.

10 To make her veil, roll out 15 g (½ oz) of white sugarpaste. Cut out a veil, using the template if necessary. Moisten the bride's head and back and stick it in place.

   Stick a line of tiny pink sugarpaste balls along the edge of the veil and one on the groom's jacket as a buttonhole. Also stick

12 To make a rose, use about 10 g (¼ oz) of white or cream sugarpaste. Roll the icing into a thin strip. Paint a line of water down one side and roll up the icing (fig 7). Tweak the petals into position and slice a little away from the base so the rose can stand up. Make a total of at least eight roses in this way.

13 To make a bud, roll about 5 g (⅛ oz) of sugarpaste into a sausage with two pointed ends. Press a line down the top and bend it into an 'S' shape.

14 For the leaves, roll out a little of the green sugarpaste and cut out a few very basic leaf shapes. Press a simple vein pattern into each one with the back of a knife and stick the roses, leaves and buds around the bride and groom. Add little swirls of green food colour and dots of royal icing, too, if you like.

Little monster

Not only is this a quick cake to make but it's a useful one because you can use odd bits of coloured sugarpaste to cover the monster. This cake was designed as a child's cake, but I know quite a few grown-up monsters it would suit too!

1 Place the cake upside down with the widest part forming the base and cut irregular lumps and bumps out of the cake *(fig 1)*. Slice and fill the middle of the cake with a layer of buttercream. Reassemble the cake and place it on the board. 'Glue' the cut-out lumps around the sides and top of the cake with buttercream. Spread a layer of buttercream over the top and sides.

2 Roll out 300 g (10½ oz) of the multi-coloured sugarpaste *(fig 2)* and use this to cover the cake. Smooth it into position over the cake, taking care to press out any air trapped in the hollows. Trim, neaten and cut the excess from the base. Add the effect of scales by pressing something circular, such as a cutter or a piping nozzle held at an angle, into the icing.

3 To make his eyes, take two 25 g (¾ oz) lumps of white sugarpaste. Roll them both into ball shapes then flatten slightly. Stick them to the front of his face.

Roll out 10 g (¼ oz) of black sugarpaste and cut out two flat discs (your piping nozzle will come in useful again to do this). Stick the discs onto the eyes. Flatten two tiny balls of white sugarpaste and stick these onto the black for highlights. Finish off each eye by painting a few ghoulish blood vessels with red food colour and a fine paintbrush *(fig 3)*.

4 To make his whiskers, cut liquorice or strawberry bootlace into twelve shortish sections of between 5 cm and 9 cm (2 in and 3½ in). Poke three holes above and below each eye using a cocktail stick and insert a length of bootlace into each one.

5 For his ears, take 100 g (4 oz) of the multi-coloured sugarpaste. Divide it in two and mould each half into a slightly misshapen triangular shape. Stick the ears to the sides of the head.

6 Roll 10 g (¼ oz) of the multi-coloured sugarpaste into a round ball and stick onto the front of the face to make the monster's nose.

7 To make the mouth, thinly roll out 20 g (¾ oz) of black sugarpaste and cut out a wonky smiling shape. Stick this onto the face. Roll out 10 g (¼ oz) of white sugarpaste and cut out three rectangles of slightly different sizes. Stick these onto the mouth to give the monster a gap-toothed smile.

8 To make the hands, roll 20 g (¾ oz) of white sugarpaste into a ball then flatten it slightly. Cut the resulting disc in half. Make three partial cuts into each semi-circle and then splay the cuts out to make the fingers. Stick one hand on either side of the body.

9 To make the feet, take 20 g (¾ oz) of white

INGREDIENTS

* 1 pudding bowl cake (see page 10)
* 1 quantity buttercream (see page 14)
* Icing sugar for rolling out
* 400 g (14 oz) multi-coloured mixture of various coloured sugarpastes (eg green, white, orange, blue, yellow and red)
* 110 g (4 oz) white sugarpaste
* 30 g (1 oz) black sugarpaste
* Red food colour
* Liquorice or strawberry bootlace
* 100 g (3½ oz) coloured sugar or 'Hundreds and Thousands'

UTENSILS

* Carving knife
* 25 cm (10 in) round cake board
* Rolling pin
* Small sharp knife
* Piping nozzle
* Water
* Medium and fine paintbrushes
* Cocktail stick

sugarpaste. Roll it into a flattish circle the same as for the hands and cut it in half. Stick the two semi-circles against the monster's body. Press some lines into each foot using the back of a knife.

10 Lightly moisten the exposed cake board with a little water and sprinkle with coloured sugar or 'hundreds and thousands'.

Sports car

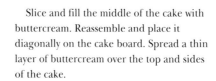

This will suit anyone with a passion for fast cars and will disappear off the tea table speedily too! It's also very versatile – see how the basic shape can be adapted into an aeroplane (page 157). The rocks double up as candle holders.

see how the basic shape can be adapted into an aeroplane (page 157).

1 Stand the cake up with the thinnest part at the bottom. Cut two triangular pieces away from the sides to form the bonnet. Cut a slope into the top of the bonnet too. Level the remaining top section of the cake where the driver will eventually sit and round all the top edges slightly to form the basic shape *(fig 1)*.

Slice and fill the middle of the cake with buttercream. Reassemble and place it diagonally on the cake board. Spread a thin layer of buttercream over the top and sides of the cake.

2 Dust the worksurface with icing sugar and knead and roll out the green sugarpaste. Carefully lift this over the cake and gently smooth into position. Trim and neaten the base.

3 To make the driver, first roll 100 g (3½ oz) of flesh-coloured sugarpaste into a flattish oval shape *(fig 2)*. Stick this with a little water towards the back of the car.

Roll 70 g (2½ oz) of brown sugarpaste into a ball then flatten the base to make a semi-circular shape for the driver's helmet. Stick this on top of his head. Roll out about another 10 g (¼ oz) of brown sugarpaste and cut out a thin, flat semi-circle. Stick this to the front of the helmet to form the brim *(fig 3)*.

INGREDIENTS

- Cake baked in loaf tin (see page 10 for details)
- 1 quantity buttercream (see page 14)
- Icing sugar for rolling out
- 250 g (9 oz) green sugarpaste
- 130 g (4½ oz) flesh-coloured sugarpaste
- 110 g (3¾ oz) brown sugarpaste
- 120 g (4 oz) white sugarpaste
- 150 g (5 oz) black sugarpaste
- 40 g (1½ oz) grey sugarpaste
- 40 g (1½ oz) cream sugarpaste
- Black and green food colour pastes
- 60 g (2 oz) desiccated coconut

UTENSILS

- Carving knife
- Palette knife
- 25 cm (10 in) square cake board
- Rolling pin
- Small sharp knife
- Water and paintbrush
- Circle cutters or similar
- 2 small bowls

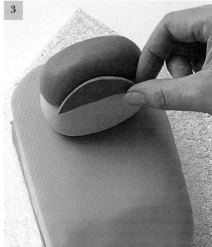

4 For the eyes, roll out 10 g (¼ oz) of white sugarpaste to a thickness of 5 mm (¼ in) and cut out two discs about 2 cm (¾ in) in diameter. If you don't have a circle cutter this size and can't find a lid or anything else to use as a cutter, simply divide the icing into two, roll each half into a ball, then squash each ball down to the right size. Finish off the eyes by sticking two tiny flattened balls of black sugarpaste onto the

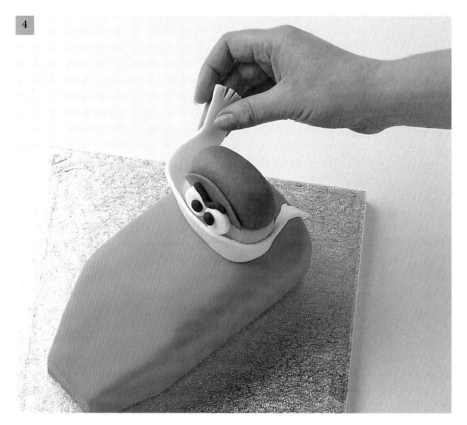

4

white for his pupils and a small sausage of black over the top for his eyebrows.

5   To make the scarf, roll out the cream sugarpaste. Cut into a strip about 28 cm x 2.5 cm (11 in x 1 in). Cut a fringe into both ends and paint a line of water around the driver's neck. Lay the scarf into position (*fig 4*). Tweak the ends up slightly into a jaunty, 'blowing in the wind' angle.

6   Roll a pea-sized ball of flesh-coloured sugarpaste and stick onto the driver's face

for his nose. Knead and shape about 10 g (¼ oz) of grey sugarpaste into a thickish semi-circle for the steering wheel. Stick this in front of the driver.

Roll 20 g (¾ oz) of black sugarpaste into a sausage about 25 cm (10 in) long. Starting from the back, lay and stick this on top of the car, around the driver (*fig 5*).

7   To make the driver's arms, roll about 15 g (½ oz) of brown sugarpaste into a sausage about 10 cm (4 in) long. Cut it in half. Make two partial cuts in the centre of each

arm at the elbow and bend each one into a right-angle. Stick an arm on each side of the body.

Finish off the arms by sticking on a pair of hands made from small flattened circles of flesh-coloured sugarpaste. Arrange the hands so that they hold onto the steering wheel.

8   To make the ear flaps for the helmet, roll out approximately 15 g (½ oz) of brown sugarpaste. Cut out two small oval shapes. If you find cutting out an oval using the tip of your knife too fiddly, cut out a circle instead using a small lid or circle cutter, then gently pull it into shape. Another method is to cut out a rectangle, slice off the corners and gently smooth the edges into an oval.

When you have made your oval shapes, stick one either side of the helmet for the flaps (*fig 6*). Next, cut two tiny strips for his helmet straps and stick one on either flap.

6

5

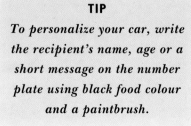

TIP
To personalize your car, write the recipient's name, age or a short message on the number plate using black food colour and a paintbrush.

9 To make the wheels, roll out about 125 g (4¼ oz) of black sugarpaste to a thickness of about 5 mm (¼ in). Cut out two discs about 6 cm (2¼ in) in diameter. Scrunch up the leftover icing. Re-roll it and cut out another two discs. Stick the wheels into position *(fig 7)*.

Roll out about 10 g (¼ oz) of white sugarpaste and cut out four smaller and much thinner discs. If you haven't got anything suitable to cut out a circle with, simply divide the sugarpaste into four. Roll each quarter into a ball and flatten to the required size. These circles form the centres of the wheels. Stick them neatly into position.

10 For the bumpers, roll 30 g (1 oz) of grey sugarpaste out to a thickness of about 5 mm (¼ in). Cut out two strips. The first should measure about 8 cm (3 in) long by 2 cm (¾ in) wide. Stick this around the front of the car. The back bumper should measure about 15 cm x 2 cm (6 in x ¾ in). Stick this into place too.

11 To make the headlights, take another 10 g (¼ oz) of grey sugarpaste and roll this into an egg shape. Cut it in half and stick both halves to the front of the bonnet. Thinly roll out about 20 g (¾ oz) of white sugarpaste and cut out two small discs. Stick one disc onto the front of each headlight.

Also cut out two small rectangles for the number plates and stick them to the front and back of the car.

12 Place 20 g (¾ oz) of the desiccated coconut in one of the bowls and colour it green by mixing in a little green food colour paste. Colour the rest grey in another bowl with a little black food paste.

Decorating variation

To adapt the car into an aeroplane, the same basic body shape was covered with grey sugarpaste. The wings and tail were made out of grey-coloured gelatin icing (see page 15) and allowed to harden overnight. (Turn the components over after about 4-5 hours to allow the undersides to dry out as well.) They were attached to the body of the plane with royal icing and supported by balls of scrunched up clingfilm placed underneath the wings while drying in position. Add a propeller to the front of the plane. Decorate the nose of the plane and the wings with circles of coloured sugarpaste. The cake board was covered in pale blue sugarpaste and decorated with white cut-out clouds and birds painted in black food colour.

Lightly moisten the exposed cake board with a few drops of water. Carefully spoon the grey coconut immediately around the car then spoon the green over the edges. To make things easier and quicker, you could colour all the coconut just one shade if you prefer.

13 Finally, to make the rocks, partially knead about 80 g (2¾ oz) of white sugarpaste and about 20 g (¾ oz) of black together for a marbled effect. Pull off irregular sized lumps and stick these along the side of the road. These rocks can also be used as candle holders.

157

Chocolate box

A wonderful cake suitable for all sorts of occasions – birthdays, Valentine's day, Mother's day, anniversaries or any chocoholic type of day (and you don't need much of an excuse for those!).

■ INGREDIENTS

- 15 cm (6 in) round sponge cake
- ½ quantity buttercream (see page 14)
- Icing sugar for rolling out
- 100 g (3 oz) black sugarpaste
- 300 g (10 oz) pink sugarpaste
- 30 g (1 oz) bag white chocolate buttons
- 227 g (½ lb) box milk chocolates
- 200 g (7 oz) white sugarpaste

■ UTENSILS

- Carving knife
- 23 cm (9 in) round cake board
- Rolling pin
- 15 cm (6 in) round thin cake board
- Small sharp knife
- Ruler
- Heart-shaped cutter
- Drinking straw
- Water and paintbrush
- 70 cm (30 in) ribbon

1 Level the cake if necessary then turn it upside down and place onto the cake board. Slice and fill the centre with buttercream and spread a thin layer of buttercream around the top and sides.

2 Knead and roll out all the black sugarpaste on a work surface dusted with icing sugar. Using the thin 15 cm (6 in) cake board as a template, cut out a black disc and lay this on top of the cake. Clean your hands, rolling pin and worksurface to avoid getting black sooty smudges everywhere.

3 Measure the height of the cake. Sprinkle the worksurface with icing sugar and roll out 200 g (7 oz) of pink sugarpaste so that you can cut out a strip about 46 cm (18 in) long and about 1 cm (½ in) wider than the depth of your cake (this cake measured about 9 cm/3½ in). Roll the icing up like a bandage, making sure it is not too tight or you will have problems unwinding it. Dust with more icing sugar if it seems to be sticking and then unwind it around the side of the cake (fig 1).

   If the icing won't stick, it probably means the previous buttercream covering around the sides has dried out so simply spread another thin layer to provide better adhesion. Neaten and trim away any excess from the base and the join.

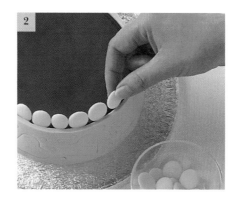

4 Using a heart-shaped cutter and a drinking straw, press a pattern around the side of the box.

5 Carefully paint a light line of water around the inside edge of the black disc. Neatly press a line of white chocolate buttons vertically into the black icing, allowing them to rest against the pink sugarpaste (fig 2).

6 Arrange the chocolates in the top of the box, securing them in position with dabs of buttercream. Unfortunately, this arrangement uses up most of a 227 g (½ lb) box of milk chocolates, leaving only a couple left over for the cook. Stick one of these on top of the chocolates to support the lid and sample the leftovers – all for purely professional taste testing purposes, of course!

7 Moisten the top and sides of the thin cake board with a little water, roll out and cover with 100 g (3 oz) of pink sugarpaste. Trim and neaten the edges and press the heart cutter and drinking straw into the icing to echo the pattern around the sides. Place the lid to one side temporarily whilst you cover the base to avoid it from getting damaged.

8 Moisten the exposed cake board with a little water. Knead and roll 200 g (7 oz) of white sugarpaste into a strip. Roll it up, then unwind it around the board allowing it to fall into folds like fabric as you go (see page 17). Press the icing down neatly at the edges of the board and trim away any excess.

9 Place a small dab of buttercream on top of the highest chocolate. Place the lid in position on top.

10 Make a bow out of the ribbon and attach this to the cake with a little more buttercream.

TIP

For a completely edible box (if you have time), you could make the lid out of pink-coloured gelatin icing as shown on page 15 and decorate this with an icing bow.

Gardener's delight

A novel cake for budding gardeners. It could be decorated with flowers instead if you prefer – see page 149 for effective but extremely fast roses. If you're not keen on marzipan, this cake looks just as effective made up in sugarpaste.

■ INGREDIENTS

- Flowerpot-shaped cake (see step 1)
- 1 quantity buttercream (see page 14)
- Icing sugar for rolling out
- 920 g (2 lb) white marzipan
- Paprika, red, green, dark brown, black, orange and yellow food colour pastes
- 60 g (2 oz) dark brown sugar

■ UTENSILS

- 23 cm (9 in) round cake board
- Carving knife
- Palette knife
- Rolling pin
- Tape measure
- Water and paintbrush
- Small sharp knife

1 The easiest way to make a cake of this shape is to bake the cake itself in a new 15 cm (6 in) terracotta plant pot. Simply wash the pot out, grease and line it with greaseproof paper. Use the same amounts given on page 10 for a 15 cm (6 in) square cake. Level the top of the cake and turn upside down so the widest part sits on the board. Slice and fill the centre with buttercream and spread extra buttercream around the top and sides.

2 Colour 550 g (1 lb 4 oz) marzipan terracotta using paprika food colour paste. If you can't obtain paprika colour, use a mixture of red, yellow and a hint of brown. Roll out 400 g (14 oz) on a worksurface dusted with icing sugar and cover the cake. Smooth over the top and sides and trim any excess from the base.

3 Re-knead the excess into the rest of the terracotta-coloured marzipan. Roll it out and cut out a strip about 46 cm x 4 cm (18 in x 1½ in). Paint a line of water around the base of the cake. Wind up the marzipan strip like a bandage. Then, starting from the back, unwind it around the base of the cake so it resembles the lip of a real flowerpot (fig 1). Neaten the join.

4 To make the tomatoes, colour 50 g (1¾ oz) marzipan red. Roll into two balls and make a dent in the top of each one with the end of a paintbrush. Roll out about 5 g (⅛ oz) green-coloured marzipan and cut out two rough star shapes. Stick one on the top of each tomato with a little water (fig 2).

5 For the potatoes, roll 120 g (4 oz) of white marzipan into two misshapen oval shapes. Leave them like this for the moment as they are easier to paint once in position.

6 For the carrots, colour 60 g (2 oz) of marzipan orange. Divide into three and roll into carrot shapes. Press a few lines across the top using the back of a knife. Roll out 5 g (⅛ oz) of green marzipan and cut out three irregular rectangles. Make cuts down almost the whole length of each shape and fringe. Stick one on each carrot.

7 For the peas, simply colour about 10 g (¼ oz) of marzipan a pale green colour and roll into small balls.

8 For the pepper, colour 80 g (2¾ oz) of marzipan yellow and roll into a conical shape. Press small grooves into the sides and top and finish with some green marzipan bent into a stalk.

9 Arrange the vegetables around the base of the flowerpot, securing them with a little

water. Make sure the join on the lip of the flowerpot is hidden at the back. Moisten the exposed cake board with a little water and spoon the dark brown sugar around the board to look like soil.

10 Paint the potatoes with a wash of watered-down brown food colour. Finish with tiny dots of black food colour and also paint a black circle on the top of the cake to look like the hole in the top of the flowerpot.

11 Roll out 40 g (1½ oz) of green marzipan and cut out some leaves. Press a few veins in each one using the back of a knife and stick these around the flowerpot.

Cheeky rabbits

On this design the cake and board are covered all in one go. If you don't feel comfortable doing it this way, cover the cake first and then the board separately. Hide any tears under rocks and rabbits later.

INGREDIENTS

- 20 cm (8 in) round sponge cake
- 1 quantity buttercream (see page 14)
- Icing sugar for rolling out
- 600 g (1 lb 5 oz) mid-green sugarpaste
- 20 g (¾ oz) black sugarpaste
- 200 g (7 oz) grey sugarpaste
- 70 g (2½ oz) white sugarpaste
- 10 g (¼ oz) flesh-coloured sugarpaste
- 40 g (1¾ oz) pink sugarpaste
- 30 g (1 oz) orange sugarpaste
- 10 g (¼ oz) dark green sugarpaste

UTENSILS

- Carving knife
- 25 cm (10 in) round cake board
- Palette knife
- Water and paintbrush
- Rolling pin
- Small sharp knife
- Wooden spoon
- Five-petal flower cutter (optional)
- Piping nozzle

1   Carve the cake into an irregular shape by cutting out lumps and bumps (*fig 1*). Place some of the cut-out pieces on top of the cake to increase its height and some around the edges. 'Glue' all the cut out pieces in place with dabs of buttercream, then slice and fill the middle of the cake with more buttercream. Spread a thin covering of buttercream over the outside of the cake as well.

2   Dust the worksurface with icing sugar and knead the mid-green sugarpaste until pliable. Lightly moisten the exposed cake board with a little water. Roll out the sugarpaste, then lift and place it over both the cake and the board. Starting from the middle of the cake and trying to expel any trapped air, smooth the icing into position. Trim and neaten the edges around the board.

3   To make the rabbit popping out of the burrow, first roll out about 10 g (¼ oz) of the black sugarpaste and cut out a flat disc about 5 cm (2 in) in diameter. Stick this on top of the cake with a little water.

Roll 5 g (⅛ oz) of grey sugarpaste into a sausage, cut this in two and flatten both halves to make the paws. Stick these onto the edge of the burrow.

To make the head, roll 50 g (2 oz) of grey sugarpaste into a cone. Flatten the cone slightly, making sure it can still stand upright. Make a cut from the tip of the cone to about one-third of the way down the centre of the head. Pull the two sections apart slightly to make his ears and add detail by pressing a paintbrush lightly into each one (*fig 2*). Stick the head onto the paws.

4   Roll out about 10 g (¼ oz) of white sugarpaste. Cut out a tiny rectangle for rabbits teeth and two small round discs for

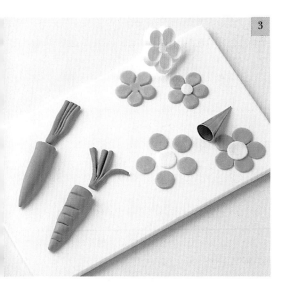

Make arms for the sitting up rabbit by rolling 5 g (⅛ oz) of grey sugarpaste into a thin sausage. Cut it in half and stick the two paws as though they are holding the carrot. Roll out the dark green sugarpaste and cut into small, thin strips. Fringe each strip and stick one on the end of each carrot.

8   To make the rocks, partially knead together 20 g (¾ oz) of grey sugarpaste and 40 g (1 ¾ oz) of white. Pull off small lumps and mould into irregular rock-like shapes. Dot

these around the cake.

9   For the flowers, roll out a little pink sugarpaste. If using the flower cutter, cut out a flower shape or if using a piping nozzle, cut out five pink circles and arrange them in a circle. Place the flower on the cake and top with a small central circle of white sugarpaste. Make about six flowers in this way and position them around the cake.

his eyes (*fig 2*) – a small piping nozzle is useful for cutting out these. Make a small cut in the middle of the rectangle and stick both the teeth and the eyes in position. Make two tiny balls of black sugarpaste and flatten them. Stick these onto the eyes for his pupils.

Roll out 5 g (⅛ oz) of flesh-coloured sugarpaste and cut out two slightly larger circles for his muzzle. Stick these over the teeth. Finish off the rabbit's face with a tiny, flattened ball of pink sugarpaste for a nose.

5   To make the seated rabbit, roll 50 g (2 oz) of grey sugarpaste into a flattish circle for the body. Stick this against the cake. Roll out about 5 g (⅛ oz) of white sugarpaste and cut out a small circle. Stick this to his tummy.

Make another head as before and stick this onto the body. If the head starts to fall backwards, support it from behind with a bit of grey sugarpaste, and tell anyone who spots it that it's a rock and is supposed to be there!

6   For his feet, roll two 10 g (¼ oz) lumps of grey sugarpaste into oval shapes then flatten them both slightly. Stick them onto the front of the body and make three dents into the end of each one using the end of a wooden spoon or paintbrush. Cut out and stick a small white disc onto each foot too.

7   To make the carrots, divide the orange sugarpaste into six and roll each bit into a carrot shape. Using the back of a knife, press a few lines into the top of each one (*fig 3*). Take a 'bite' out of one using a piping nozzle. Stick the bitten carrot onto the front of the rabbit and the rest around the board.

TIP

This cake also introduces a five-petal flower cutter that, amongst other things, can be used to produce these marvellous bold cartoon-type flowers. These cutters are available from specialist cake shops but if you don't wish to buy one, an alternative method using a piping nozzle is also shown.
If you want to cut down on the modelling, have both bunnies popping out of burrows.

Horse and rider

If making this cake for someone who owns a horse, try to copy the markings and hair colour of the characters involved. To make a male rider, simply shorten the hair. You can substitute buttercream for the royal icing if you wish.

1 Level the top of the cake, if necessary, turn upside down and place in the middle of the cake board. Slice and fill the centre of the cake with a layer of buttercream. Reassemble the cake and then spread a thin covering of buttercream around the sides and top.

2 Dust the worksurface with icing sugar and knead and roll out 300 g (10½ oz) of white sugarpaste. Carefully lift the icing and place it over the cake. Smooth it into position and trim and neaten the base. Place the cake to one side while you make the horse.

3 Begin with the body. Roll 50 g (2 oz) of golden brown sugarpaste into a tapering cone shape. Lie this on its side *(fig 1)*. Make the head out of 20 g (¾ oz) of golden brown sugarpaste. Pull off two tiny bits and keep for the ears. Roll the rest into an oval shape. Lightly squeeze the centre to make one rounded end bigger than the other. This bigger end will form the horse's nose. Stick the head onto the body and make dents for nostrils using the end of a paintbrush.

4 Make a saddle out of 5 g (⅛ oz) of dark brown sugarpaste. First cut out and stick a tiny, thin strip across the horse's back. Roll the rest of the dark brown into an oval shape, then flatten it slightly. Stick this onto the girth.

5 To make the forelegs, roll 10 g (¼ oz) of the golden-brown icing into a sausage. Cut this in two and bend each leg in half. Stick these against the body.
   To make the hind legs, roll 20 g (½ oz) of golden brown sugarpaste into a sausage approximately 10 cm (4 in) long. Again, divide the sausage in two and bend both halves. As you stick them against the sides of the horse, slightly flatten the top section of the leg.
   Make two tiny triangular ears out of the

leftover icing and stick these onto the head. Press a paintbrush into each ear to add some detail. Carefully position the horse on top of the cake and secure in place with a little water.

6 To make the rider's head, take 10 g (¼ oz) of flesh-coloured sugarpaste. Pull off a tiny piece for a nose and roll the rest into a ball. Stick the nose into position and paint eyes and a disgruntled mouth using black food colour.

7 Partially mix a little blue food colour into 30 ml (2 tbsp) of royal icing and smear this on the top of the cake in a sort of kidney shape. Place the rider's head in the water.

INGREDIENTS

- 15 cm (6 in) round sponge cake
- ½ quantity buttercream (see page 14)
- Icing sugar for rolling out
- 400 g (14 oz) white sugarpaste
- 100 g (3½ oz) golden brown sugarpaste
- 20 g (¾ oz) dark brown sugarpaste
- 10 g (¼ oz) flesh-coloured sugarpaste
- white royal icing (optional) (see page 15)
- Black, blue, yellow (melon) and gooseberry-green food colour pastes
- 30 g (1 oz) black sugarpaste

UTENSILS

- Carving knife
- 20 cm (8 in) round cake board
- Palette knife
- Rolling pin
- Small sharp knife
- Water and paintbrush
- 3 piping bags (see page 18)
- Scissors

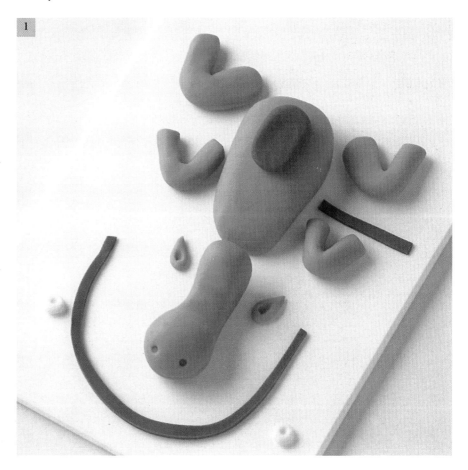

2

Make her hair by rolling out a little dark brown sugarpaste and cutting it into a rectangle. Press lines down the length of the rectangle with the back of a knife. Moisten the top of the rider's head and lay the hair in position *(fig 2)*.

Make a riding hat by rolling 5 g (⅛ oz) of black sugarpaste into a round lump, then flatten the base so that it will sit on her head. Pinch a peak into the front of the hat and stick in position.

8 Partially knead 20 g (¾ oz) of black sugarpaste into 100 g (3½ oz) of white. Pull off little lumps and stick around the edge of the pond and the base of the cake to look like rocks.

Paint some watered-down green food colour around the horse and pond (gooseberry food colour paste is the ideal shade for this).

9 Mix a tiny bit of yellow food colour into 15 ml (1 tbsp) of royal icing to turn it cream. Place the icing in a piping bag and

snip about 2 mm (⅛ in) off the end. Pipe the horse's mane and tail using a squiggly motion *(fig 3)*.

10 Colour 30 ml (2 tbsp) of royal icing light green and place into a piping bag. Do the same with some darker green royal icing. Snip the ends off both piping bags and pipe wiggly lines of greenery up the sides of the cake.

11 Finally, to finish off the horse, roll out a little dark brown sugarpaste. Cut out a long, thin strip for the horse's reins and lay this over the nose and around the back of the horse. Stick a tiny ball of white sugarpaste either side of the mouth and push a small hole in each one using the end of a paintbrush.

TIP
If you have problems making piping bags, your local cake decorating equipment shop should stock ready-made ones. Alternatively, you can buy tubes of 'writing' icing which could also be used to make the mane and tail.

Golfing star

A fun way of incorporating a person's favourite sport into a design is to base the cake itself on a piece of equipment such as a golf bag or a tennis racquet, then make a small model of the recipient dressed in the appropriate outfit.

INGREDIENTS

- Icing sugar for rolling out
- 300 g (10½ oz) green sugarpaste
- 15 cm (6 in) square cake
- 1 quantity buttercream (see page 14)
- 360 g (12½ oz) white sugarpaste
- 50 g (2 oz) grey sugarpaste
- 70 g (2¼ oz) dark brown sugarpaste
- 90 g (3¼ oz) red sugarpaste
- 50 g (2 oz) light brown sugarpaste
- 40 g (1½ oz) yellow sugarpaste
- 80 g (2¾ oz) blue sugarpaste
- 30 g (1 oz) flesh-coloured sugarpaste
- 10 g (¼ oz) black sugarpaste

UTENSILS

- 30 cm (12 in) round cake board
- Water
- Paintbrush
- Rolling pin
- Small sharp knife
- Cake smoother (optional)
- Carving knife
- Fish slice (optional)
- Palette knife
- Piping nozzle

1 Moisten the cake board with a little water. Sprinkle some icing sugar onto the worksurface and knead the green sugarpaste until it becomes pliable. Begin to roll it out into a thick, flattish disk, then lift and place the sugarpaste on the cake board. Continue to roll the icing up to and over the edges of the board. Trim and neaten the edges.

If you possess one, run a cake smoother over the surface of the board to iron out any lumps and bumps. Alternatively, use the flat of your hand and strategically position the cake, figure and golf clubs over the worst bits later! Place the covered board to one side.

2 Cut the cake into shape by slicing about 5 cm (2 in) off one side. Place this against one of the now shorter sides to increase the length of the bag. Now cut the cake into a more recognisable bag shape by making two diagonal cuts at the top of the bag to give it a tapering neck and also cut a slope into the neck of the bag (*fig 1*). Round all the corners slightly.

3 Slice and fill the middle of the cake with a layer of buttercream, then spread a thin covering of buttercream over the top and sides. Wipe away any crumbs from the worksurface and dust with icing sugar.

Knead and roll out 300 g (10½ oz) of white sugarpaste. Lift and place over the cake. Smooth the icing into position and trim away any excess from the base. Carefully lift the cake and place on the covered cake board. (You may find using a fish slice to lift the cake helps to prevent fingerprints on the icing.)

4 Roll and shape about 20 g (¾ oz) of grey sugarpaste into a sort of tennis racquet shape. Bend the large, rounded end over to one side to make a golf club and stick onto the board at the neck of the bag.

To make the wooden club, roll 40 g (1½ oz) of brown sugarpaste into a more rounded club shape. Stick a small flat oval of grey sugarpaste onto the top of the club and stick into position. Press a few lines into the top of the first club using the back of a knife (*fig 2*).

3

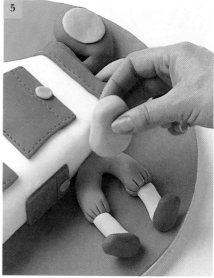

5

5   Roll out 20 g (¾ oz) of red sugarpaste and cut out a strip about 2.5 cm x 13 cm (1 in x 5 in). Make a series of small cuts along the two longer sides using just the tip of your knife to look like stitching. Lightly moisten the back of the strip with a little water and lay this over the base of the golf clubs and the neck of the bag (*fig 3*).

6   Roll out a further 70 g (2½ oz) of red sugarpaste and cut out four rectangles of varying sizes. Stick two on the front of the bag and two on the sides. Press the back of a knife across each one to leave a line looking like a flap. Using the tip of your

knife again, 'stitch' around each pocket (*fig 4*). Finish off each pocket with a button made from a small flattened ball of grey sugarpaste.

7   To make the golfer himself, begin with his legs. Roll about 40 g (1½ oz) of light brown sugarpaste into a sausage about 13 cm (5 in) long. Slightly bend the sausage into a 'U' shape and press a few lines into both ends to look like folds in the fabric. Stick this on the board towards the neck of the bag. Roll 20 g (¾ oz) of yellow sugarpaste into a sausage and cut in half. Stick one onto the end of each leg for his socks. Roll two 10 g (¼ oz) lumps of dark brown sugarpaste into two oval

shapes for his feet and stick one on the end of each sock.
    Make a body by rolling about 40 g (1¾ oz) of blue sugarpaste into a cone and stick this on top of the legs (*fig 5*).

8   To make the arms, roll 20 g (¾ oz) of blue sugarpaste into a sausage and cut in half. Stick one arm either side of the body, allowing them to rest on the legs and the side of the golf bag itself. Slightly flatten a small ball of blue sugarpaste to make a thickish disk for the golfer's polo neck (*fig 6*). Stick this on top of the body.

9   Make a head by rolling 10 g (¼ oz) of flesh-coloured sugarpaste into a ball. Stick this onto the neck. Give him a smiling mouth by pressing a piping nozzle or something similar into the lower part of the face and pulling it slightly downwards. His eyes are made by sticking two small disks of white sugarpaste onto his face.

4

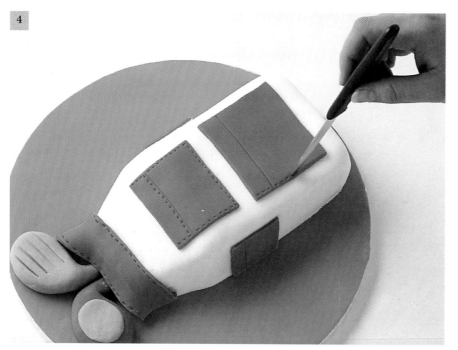

TIP
Personalize the figure by colouring the hair and eyes the same colour as the recipient's. Add any distinguishing features too, such as glasses, a beard or long hair.

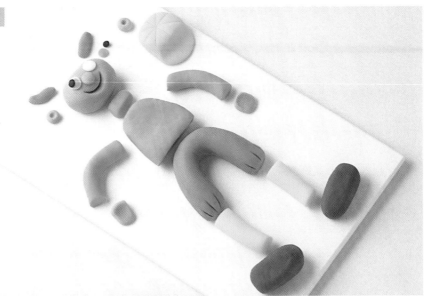

Stick two smaller disks of blue onto the white and top with two even smaller discs of black sugarpaste. Stick a tiny ball of flesh-coloured sugarpaste onto the face for his nose and two on either side of the head for his ears. Press the end of a paintbrush into each ear to leave a small hollow. Stick a small oval of flesh-coloured sugarpaste onto the end of each arm for his hands.

10 Make hair by sticking a couple of tiny bits of light brown sugarpaste to the top of the head. To make the cap, roll 10 g (¼ oz) of yellow sugarpaste into a flattish oval shape. Tweak the front into a peak and press lines across the top in a sort of star shape. Top with a tiny ball of yellow sugarpaste and stick on the top of the head. Decorate the front of the jumper and both socks with small, contrasting squares of blue and yellow sugarpaste.

11 To make the strap, thinly roll out 50 g (2 oz) white sugarpaste and cut out a strip about 30 cm x 2.5 cm (12 in x 1 in). 'Stitch' along the edges of the strap in the same way as you did for the pockets, then lay the strap over the top of the bag (*fig 7*). Use a little water to secure the handle in place.

12 Finally, finish the board with two tiny golf clubs made by rolling about 5 g (⅛ oz) of black sugarpaste into a thin string for the handles. Cut this in half and stick onto the board. Make two tiny golf club heads out of a little brown and grey sugarpaste.

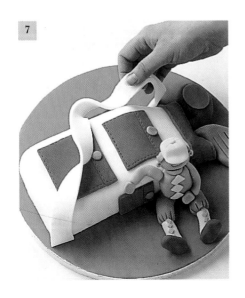

Decorating variation

Another easy sports theme is a sports cap cake. The cake itself was baked in an ovenproof pudding bowl which automatically gave it an authentic rounded shape. It was covered with sugarpaste and a semi-circle of blue sugarpaste was placed on the board to look like its peak. It could be decorated with models from virtually any sport or you could paint a badge or emblem to stick on the front using food colour.

Teddy bear

It is possible to buy a ready-coloured sugarpaste from cake decorating shops that is aptly called 'Teddy Bear Brown'. If you can't get hold of this, use brown sugarpaste mixed with a little yellow and red for a similar colour.

■ INGREDIENTS

- 15 cm (6 in) round sponge cake
- ½ quantity buttercream (see page 14)
- Icing sugar for rolling out
- 900 g (2 lb) golden brown sugarpaste
- 2 candy sticks or strands of dried spaghetti
- 10 g (¼ oz) white sugarpaste
- 40 g (1¾ oz) black sugarpaste
- Black food colour

■ UTENSILS

- Carving knife
- 20 cm (8 in) round cake board
- Rolling pin
- Small sharp knife
- Water and paintbrush
- Wooden spoon
- 1 m (39 in) ribbon

1 Cut the cake to shape by lying it flat on its base and slicing off about a third of the cake. This section is then placed on top of the remaining cake so that it looks a bit like an 'L' shape from the side.

2 Stick the two sections together with a little buttercream and, if you wish, slice the base cake through the middle and spread a layer of buttercream there as well. Then place the cake towards the rear of the cake board and spread a thin covering of buttercream over the entire cake.

3 Dust the worksurface with icing sugar and knead 300 g (10½ oz) of the golden brown sugarpaste until pliable. Roll the icing out, then lift and place it over the cake. Starting with the tummy area, to stop air bubbles getting trapped there, smooth the icing into position over the cake. You may find that the sugarpaste falls into folds at the back. By gently lifting and pulling the icing you should be able to smooth these out. Trim and neaten the base.

4 To provide support for the head, insert two candy sticks into the top of the body leaving about half the stick protruding *(fig 1)*. If you can't get hold of candy sticks (or sweet cigarettes, as they used to be called), use some shortened strands of raw, dried spaghetti instead. Lightly moisten the area around the candy sticks with water to help keep the head in position, but don't use too much or the head will slide about.

5 Make the head by rolling 300 g (10½ oz) of sugarpaste into a ball. Flatten the ball to make a thick disc and slot the head into position onto the candy sticks.

6 Roll another 90 g (3 oz) of golden brown sugarpaste into an oval for the muzzle. Stick this to the lower part of the face.

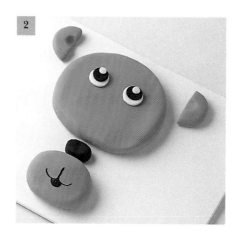

7 To make the ears, roll 30 g (1 oz) of golden brown sugarpaste into a ball. Flatten the ball into an oval and cut in half. To add detail, press a rounded hollow into each ear using a wooden spoon handle *(fig 2)* and stick one either side of the head with a little water.

8 To make the eyes, thinly roll out the white sugarpaste. Cut out two discs and keep the leftover white icing. Stick the circles just above the muzzle. Roll out 10 g (¼ oz) of black sugarpaste and cut out two smaller black discs. Stick these onto the white. Flatten two tiny balls of white sugarpaste. Stick these onto the black as highlights. Finish the face by rolling 10 g (¼ oz) of black sugarpaste into an oval for his nose. Stick this onto the muzzle. Paint a mouth using black food colour.

9 To make the legs, roll two 100 g (3½ oz) lumps of golden brown sugarpaste into

chunky carrot shapes. Bend the end of each leg up slightly into an 'L' shape to make a foot and stick the legs into place. Cut two round discs out of the remaining black sugarpaste and stretch them into ovals. Stick one on the pad of each foot.

10 For the paws, roll two 50 g (2 oz) lumps of golden brown sugarpaste into two flattish carrot shapes. Rest the hand sections on the teddy's tummy *(fig 3)*. Using the back of a knife, press a few lines into each paw.

11 For the final finishing touch, tie a ribbon around his neck.

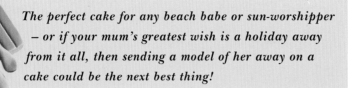

Sunbather

The perfect cake for any beach babe or sun-worshipper – or if your mum's greatest wish is a holiday away from it all, then sending a model of her away on a cake could be the next best thing!

■ INGREDIENTS

- 20 cm (8 in) round sponge cake
- 1 quantity buttercream (see page 14)
- Icing sugar for rolling out
- 500 g (1 lb 2 oz) white sugarpaste
- Blue food colour
- 150 g (5¼ oz) pink sugarpaste
- 30 g (1 oz) dark blue sugarpaste
- 40 g (1¼ oz) flesh-coloured sugarpaste
- 10 g (¼ oz) yellow sugarpaste
- 30 g (1 oz) brown sugarpaste
- 30 g (1 oz) green sugarpaste
- 15 ml (1 tbsp) white royal icing (optional)
- 50 g (2 oz) light golden brown sugar

■ UTENSILS

- 25 cm (10 in) round cake board
- Carving knife
- Small sharp knife
- Rolling pin
- Water and paintbrush
- Piping bag
- No. 3 nozzle

1 Level the top of the cake if necessary. Turn the cake upside down; slice and fill the centre with buttercream. Place on the centre of the cake board and spread a thin layer of buttercream on the top and sides.

2 Dust the worksurface with icing sugar and knead 500 g (1 lb 2 oz) of white sugarpaste until pliable. Partially knead in a little blue food colour for a marbled effect. Roll out, then cover the cake. Smooth the top and sides and trim any excess from the base.

3 For the air-bed, roll out the pink sugarpaste and cut out a rectangle 7 cm x 15 cm (2¾ in x 6 in). Using the back of a knife, press one line horizontally to mark the headrest, then press another five lines vertically down the length of the bed (*fig 1*). Lightly moisten the top of the cake with a little water and place the bed in position.

4 For the figure, take 30 g (1 oz) of dark blue sugarpaste and mould this into a conical shape. Pinch the middle to make a waist (*fig 1*) and stick on top of the air-bed.

5 For the head, roll a ball from 10 g (¼ oz) flesh-coloured sugarpaste. Take another 10 g (¼ oz) of flesh-coloured icing and roll this into a sausage for her arms. Divide this into two and flatten one end of each sausage slightly for the hands. Using 20 g (½ oz) of flesh-coloured icing for the legs, roll into a sausage, divide into two and flatten and shape the ends into feet. Stick the arms, legs and head into position.

6 Roll a small ball of brown sugarpaste out flat and cut out a thin strip for the hair. Press lines along the length of the strip with the back of a knife. For the sun hat, thinly roll out 10 g (¼ oz) of yellow sugarpaste and cut out a 5 cm (2 in) circle. Stick this over the face. Re-knead the leftover yellow and cut out a slightly thicker circle about 3 cm (1 in) in diameter. Stick this on top of the brim. Decorate with a few balls of pink icing.

7 For the palm trees, thinly roll out the brown sugarpaste and cut out about 14 small, curved tree trunks (*fig 2*). Press a few horizontal lines into each with the back of a knife and stick these to the sides of the cake. For the leaves, roll out the green sugarpaste and cut out about 28 basic leaf shapes. Make a few tiny cuts in each leaf. Bend each leaf slightly so that the cuts separate and stick a couple to each trunk.

8 For the waves, place 15 ml (1 tbsp) of royal icing into a piping bag fitted with a number 3 nozzle. Pipe a few lines around the air-bed. Using a damp paintbrush, pull the icing back from the air-bed (*fig 3*). Buttercream can be used as a softer, but

yellower alternative. Stroke into place with a dry brush.

9 Finally, moisten the exposed cake board and spoon brown sugar around the base.

TIP

If you don't want to make up a full quantity of royal icing just for the waves, buy a tube of ready-made icing from the supermarket which comes with its own set of nozzles.

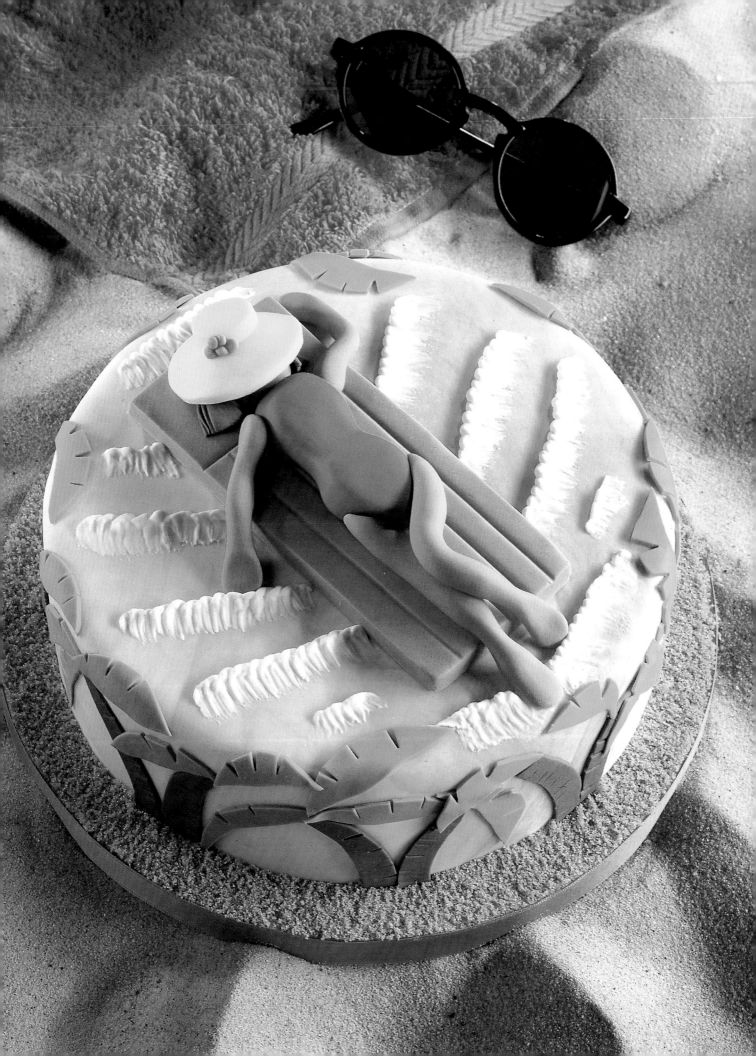

Party animal

Here's a party animal who's almost completely partied out! If you're sure that they won't take offence, change the hair colour to match that of the recipient and substitute their favourite tipple for the beer can.

■ INGREDIENTS

- 1 pudding bowl cake (see page 10)
- 1 quantity buttercream (see page 14)
- Icing sugar for rolling out
- 320 g (11 oz) white sugarpaste
- 300 g (10½ oz) pale blue sugarpaste
- 90 g (3 oz) black sugarpaste
- 300 g (10½ oz) flesh-coloured sugarpaste
- 5 g (⅛ oz) dark blue sugarpaste
- 10 g (¼ oz) yellow sugarpaste
- 40 g (1¾ oz) green sugarpaste
- 10 g (¼ oz) grey sugarpaste

■ UTENSILS

- Carving knife and small sharp knife
- 30 cm (12 in) round cake board
- Rolling pin and wooden spoon
- Water and paintbrush
- Piping nozzle

1 Check that the cake will sit flat on the cake board when it is turned upside down. If the cake rose slightly unevenly in the oven, you may need to slice a little away from the top. Place the cake towards the back of the board, rounded side uppermost, and slice and fill the centre with buttercream. Reassemble the cake and spread a layer of buttercream over the outside.

2 Dust the worksurface with icing sugar. Knead 100 g (3½ oz) of white sugarpaste until it becomes pliable. Roll it out, then place it so that it covers just over half of the cake. Smooth and trim the base.

3 Roll out 100 g (3½ oz) of the pale blue sugarpaste. Lift and position this so that it overlaps the white. Smooth it into position, and again trim and neaten the base.

4 For the legs, roll 200 g (7 oz) of blue sugarpaste into a thick sausage about 20 cm (8 in) long. Cut it in half. Moisten the board and place the legs into position.

5 Using 200 g (7 oz) of white sugarpaste, make the arms in the same way as the legs. Stick them in position, pointing them forwards towards the front of the board.

6 For the feet, divide a 60 g (2 oz) ball of black sugarpaste in two and roll each half into a chunky oval shape. Stick one to the end of each foot with water, positioning them in a pigeon-toed fashion (fig 1). To add detail, press the back of a knife into the sole of each foot a few times.

7 For the hands, take 50 g (1 ¾ oz) of flesh-coloured sugarpaste and roll into a thick oval shape. Cut the oval in half and using the back of a knife, press four lines into the rounded ends to make fingers. Stick the hands in place. His right one should be flat on the board and his left one on its side and curved, to hold the beer can!

8 To make his face, roll 200 g (7 oz) of flesh-coloured sugarpaste into a ball. Flatten the ball into a rounded disc about 11 cm (41 in) in diameter. Moisten the side of the cake and the board in front of the cake with water and lay the disc into position.

9 Make his smile by drawing a line with the back of a knife. For his eyes, roll out 10 g (¼ oz) of white sugarpaste and cut out two small circles 2.5 cm (1 in) in diameter. Stick these on the face. Roll out 5 g (⅛ oz) of black sugarpaste and cut out two smaller discs. Stick the black circles onto the white (fig 2). Complete by sticking on a flattened ball of white sugarpaste as a highlight.

10 For the eyelids, roll out 10 g (¼ oz) of flesh-coloured sugarpaste and cut a circle about 4.5 cm (1¾ in) in diameter. Cut the circle in two and stick one half over each eye to create a droopy-eyed expression.

11 Take a 20 g (¾ oz) ball of flesh-coloured sugarpaste and slightly flatten it. Stick it in the middle of the face to make his nose.

12 For his hair, roll 20 g (¾ oz) of black sugarpaste into a long thin strip. Press the back of a knife along the length of the strip, then moisten the top of the head with water and lay the strip in place.

13 For the ears, roll 20 g (¾ oz) of flesh-coloured sugarpaste into a ball. Flatten it and push the end of a wooden spoon into the centre to leave a hollow. Cut the circle in half and stick both ears onto the head.

14 For the hat, roll the dark blue sugarpaste into a triangle. Stick this at an angle on top of his head. Roll the yellow sugarpaste into thin strings and stick to the hat.

15 To make the can, roll the green sugarpaste into a sausage. Flatten both ends. Cut out two flat discs from grey sugarpaste the same size as the beer can. Sandwich the green between the two grey discs and stick a small triangle of black sugarpaste onto the top of the can. Place in position.

Deep sea fishing

Here's one to hook a hungry fisherman! If you prefer a softer sea, substitute buttercream for the royal icing, but use unsalted butter as this produces a whiter buttercream which takes the colour better. You could also personalize the fisherman if you wish.

1 Turn the cake upside down and carefully carve the front of the cake into a rounded shape. Slice the cake and fill the centre with buttercream. Place the cake in position on the cake board and spread a thin layer of buttercream around the top and sides.

2 Dust the worksurface with a little icing sugar and roll out 350 g (12 oz) of grey sugarpaste. Lift this over the cake and ease it into place, using cake smoothers if you possess them to achieve an extra smooth finish on the sugarpaste. Alternatively, use the palms of your hands.

    Trim and neaten the base, keeping the excess sugarpaste for making the tail. Using the back of your knife, press a curved line into the front of the whale to make a sneaky, smiley mouth *(fig 1)*.

3 To make the eyes, roll out about 5 g (⅛ oz) of white sugarpaste. Using a circle cutter or

a lid of some sort, cut out two flat discs about 2.5 cm (1 in) wide. (If you cannot find a cutter of the right size, simply squash two small balls of white sugarpaste instead.) Stick one either side of the face with a little water.

    Roll out a small lump of black sugarpaste and cut out two smaller discs (a piping nozzle makes an ideal cutter for these). Stick the black discs onto the white. Flatten two tiny balls of white sugarpaste and stick these onto the black discs to look like highlights.

    Finally, to finish the eyes, roll out 10 g (¼ oz) of grey sugarpaste and cut out a disc approximately 4.5 cm (1¾ in) wide. Cut this in half and stick one half over each eye *(fig 2)*.

4 Make the rocks by partially kneading together 150 g (5 oz) of white sugarpaste and 40 g (1¾ oz) of black sugarpaste (refer to the Wild Animals cake on page 108 for

to the Wild Animals cake on page 108 for

INGREDIENTS

- 1 pudding basin cake (see page 10)
- 1 quantity buttercream (see page 14)
- Icing sugar for rolling out
- 400 g (14 oz) grey sugarpaste
- 180 g (6 oz) white sugarpaste
- 50 g (2 oz) black sugarpaste
- 10 g (¼ oz) green sugarpaste
- 10 g (¼ oz) flesh-coloured sugarpaste
- Black and blue food colours
- 10 g (¼ oz) yellow sugarpaste
- ½ quantity royal icing (see page 15)

UTENSILS

- Carving knife
- 25 cm (10 in) square cake board
- Rolling pin
- Cake smoothers (optional)
- Small sharp knife
- Circle cutters or similar for cutting out eyes
- Water, and fine and medium paintbrushes
- Drinking straw
- White cotton thread
- Cocktail stick
- Small bowl and palette knife
- Piping bag, if making waves

more details if you're unsure how to do this). Pull off lumps of various sizes and mould these into rock shapes. Make sure that the largest, which the fisherman will sit on, has a flattish top so that he doesn't fall off! Place the rocks to one side.

5 To avoid any accidents, make the fisherman on his rock away from the board. Roll 5 g (⅛ oz) of black sugarpaste into a sausage. Cut it in half for his legs and bend the end of each leg up to make a foot *(fig 3)*. Stick both the feet onto the largest rock. Roll 5 g (⅛ oz) of green sugarpaste into an oval for his body. Stick this above the legs.

TIP
Remember to remove the thread and cocktail stick when cutting the cake, especially if there are children around.

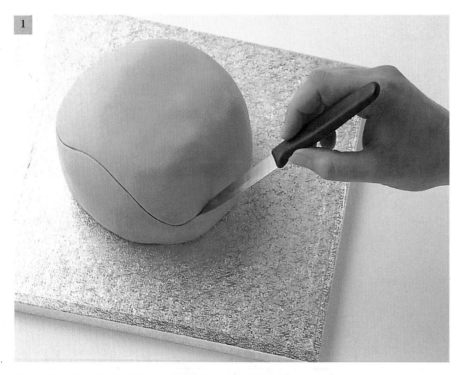

1

2

Roll a tiny bit of green into a sausage and cut this in half for his arms. Stick one either side of the body so that they almost meet on his tummy.

6 Make a tiny flesh-coloured ball for his head and stick on top of the body. Holding a drinking straw at a slight angle, press this into the lower part of his face to leave behind a smiling impression. Paint two tiny dots for his eyes and two little lines for his eyebrows using black food colour and a fine paintbrush.

Stick a tiny ball of flesh-coloured icing onto his face for his nose and two either side of the head for his ears. Gently push the end of a paintbrush into each ear to add some definition.

Finally, place a final ball of flesh-coloured sugarpaste between the arms for his hands.

7 To make his hat, roll about 5 g (⅛ oz) of yellow sugarpaste into a ball. Pinch around the base, to fan out the icing into a brim. Flatten the top and stick it onto his head. Tie a short length of thread onto a cocktail stick and insert this through his hands into the rock.

8 Make a whale of a tail by rolling about 30 g (1 oz) of grey sugarpaste into an oval

shape. Pinch a 'waist' into the middle of the oval and flatten one of the ends. You should now have a shape that looks a bit like a violin. Make a cut down the centre of the flat end and splay the two halves. Cut a small slice off the other end if necessary to make sure it can stand up.

9 Place the royal icing or buttercream into a small bowl and partially mix in a little blue food colour. Spread this around the cake board with a palette knife, roughing it up as you go.

Place the rocks, fisherman and tail in the 'sea'. Add some waves if desired (see the Sunbather cake on page 174 for details on how to do this). If using buttercream for the sea, gently 'stroke' the waves into shape with a dry paintbrush rather than a damp one.

10 Finally, to make the seagulls, simply roll a small lump of white sugarpaste into a tapering sausage shape, then bend this into a 'Z' shape. Add a tiny triangle of yellow for a beak and two dots of black food colour for eyes. Stick one on a rock and one in the sea. If you've got the time, inclination and the sugarpaste, you could make a whole flock and stick some onto the whale's back too.

TIP

For a quicker cake, place jelly fish sweets around the whale.

Cookery book

By changing the pictures featured on the open pages of this book to ones of the recipient's favourite hobby, this cake could easily be adapted to suit anyone and any pastime.

1   Lightly moisten the cake board with a little water and place temporarily to one side. Dust the worksurface with icing sugar and partially knead 10 g (¼ oz) of black sugarpaste and 40 g (1¾ oz) of grey sugarpaste into 200 g (7 oz) of white. Stop kneading before the point at which it all turns a solid grey colour (if it does, simply re-knead some more white and black sugarpaste into it).

Roll out the sugarpaste and a marbled effect should develop. Lift and place the icing on top of the cake board. Continue to roll until the board is completely covered. Neaten the edges and place the board to one side.

2   Cut the cake to shape on a separate cutting board or worksurface, slicing about 2.5 cm (1 in) off one edge of the cake. Place this cut-off strip against one of the shorter sides of the rectangle to increase the width of the book *(fig 1)*. Carefully cut a shallow triangle out of the centre of the book as shown to form the spine and discard (or eat!) this piece.

3   Cover the sides and top of the cake with buttercream. Knead and roll out 500 g (1 lb 2 oz) of white sugarpaste and use this to cover the cake. Smooth over the top and sides, starting from the centre of the book to expel any air trapped in the spine. To represent the pages, press horizontal lines

■ INGREDIENTS

- Icing sugar for rolling out
- 20 g (½ oz) black sugarpaste
- 850 g (1 lb 14 oz) white sugarpaste
- 40 g (1¾ oz) grey sugarpaste
- 20 cm (8 in) square sponge cake
- 1 quantity buttercream (see page 14)
- Assorted food colour pastes e.g. red, blue, yellow, green, brown, black etc
- 80 g (2¾ oz) blue sugarpaste
- 20 g (½ oz) red sugarpaste
- 35 g (1¼ oz) light brown sugarpaste
- Assorted sweets, cherries, mini cakes, etc, for decoration

■ UTENSILS

- 30 cm (12 in) round cake board
- Water and assorted paintbrushes
- Rolling pin
- Small sharp knife
- Carving knife
- Ruler
- Palette or saucer
- Clean damp cloth
- Templates for book spine arches if necessary (see page 187)
- Sieve

around the sides using the back of a knife.

4   Knead and thinly roll out 150 g (5 oz) of white sugarpaste. Measure the top of the cake and cut out two thin sheets of sugarpaste to make the top two pages of the book. Lay and stick these in place and turn the top right corner of the right hand page back slightly *(fig 2)*.

5   Paint your design on top of the cake. To do this, use the food colours like watercolours. You may want to plan out your design on a piece of paper first. Put a dab of colour onto a palette or saucer and dilute it slightly with a little water.

If you are right-handed, start by painting the design on the left page first. This stops your hand smudging the painted areas as you work across the book. If you are left-handed, you may find it easier to start from the right. Paint the solid areas of colour first *(fig 3)*. Then paint in the outlines using black food colour and a fine brush

TIP

If you feel happier wielding a piping bag than a paintbrush, you could pipe a message onto the cake instead of painting on it.

afterwards. If you try to do the outlines first, you may find that the black bleeds into the colours.

If you make a mistake, simply wash over the error using a clean paintbrush and fresh water and wipe it away with a clean, damp cloth.

6   To 'write', simply paint black squiggles across the page, leaving a few indentations to look like paragraphs. Also vary the length of the lines to give the page a more authentic feel. Of course if you're feeling very ambitious you could actually write a message instead.

7   Paint a wash of light brown food colour around the sides of the book to pick out the pages. Do this by mixing some water into a little brown food colour and applying it with a large paintbrush or pastry brush.

8   To make the spine of the book, thinly roll out about 20 g (¾ oz) of blue sugarpaste. Cut out two small arched shapes using the templates if necessary. Stick one on either

side of the book on top of the wash you have just applied. The flat edge of the arch should just rest on the cake board. Roll out about 10 g (¼ oz) of black sugarpaste and cut out two smaller arches. Stick one neatly on the top of each blue arch.

Paint a line of water around the edge of the book on the cake board itself. Roll 60 g (2 oz) of blue sugarpaste into a thin string and lay this around the cake to look like the book cover.

9   To make the book mark, thinly roll out about 20 g (¾ oz) of red sugarpaste. Cut a strip about 25 cm x 2 cm (10 in x ¾ in). Cut a small triangle out of one end of the strip. Paint a line of water down the centre of the book and lay the book mark carefully in position.

10   Decorate the board using anything you want, such as glacé cherries, small sweets, mini muffins, jelly shapes, raisins and mini paper cake cases.

To make a wooden spoon, roll 20 g (¾ oz) of light brown sugarpaste into an

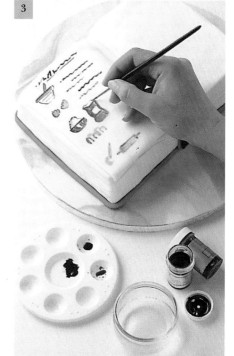

oval then press a hollow into the centre. Make a handle by rolling another 15 g (½ oz) of brown sugarpaste into a sausage about 12 cm (4¾ in) long and press two small dents into the end of the handle using the back of your knife.

11   Finally, to give the whole design an authentic 'messy cook' look, place a little icing sugar into a sieve and sprinkle carefully over the cake.

TEMPLATES

HORRIBLE CHILD page 34
enlarge templates by 145%

TEDDY CAKE page 28
enlarge templates by 125%

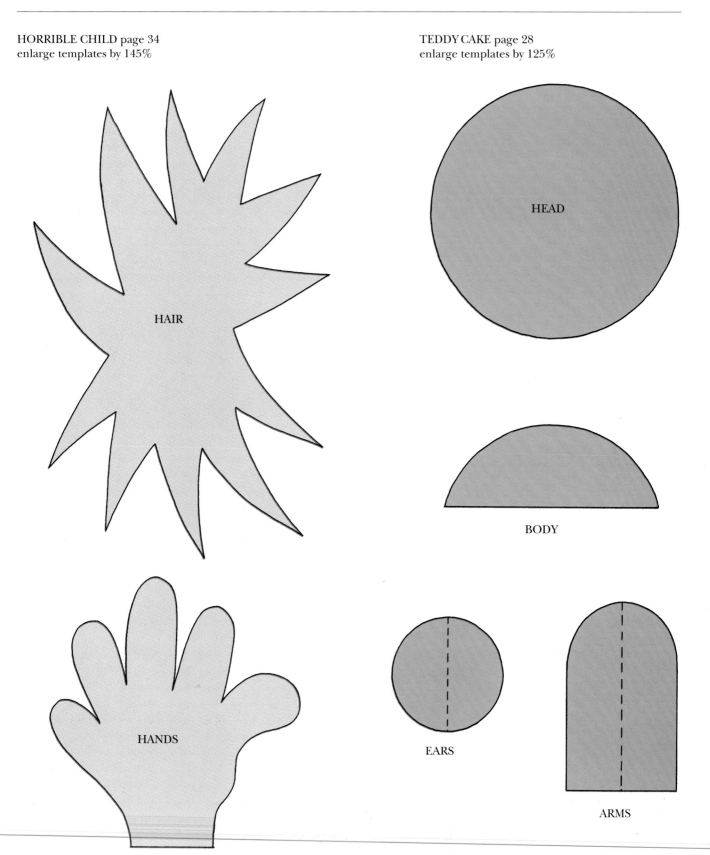

HAIR

HEAD

BODY

HANDS

EARS

ARMS

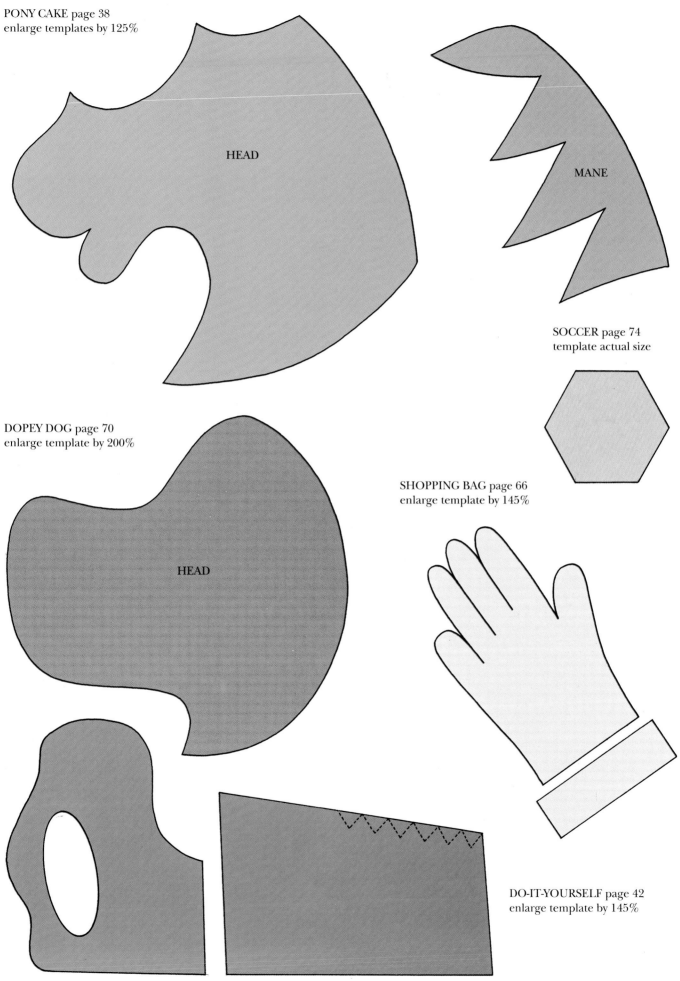

PONY CAKE page 38
enlarge templates by 125%

HEAD

MANE

SOCCER page 74
template actual size

DOPEY DOG page 70
enlarge template by 200%

HEAD

SHOPPING BAG page 66
enlarge template by 145%

DO-IT-YOURSELF page 42
enlarge template by 145%

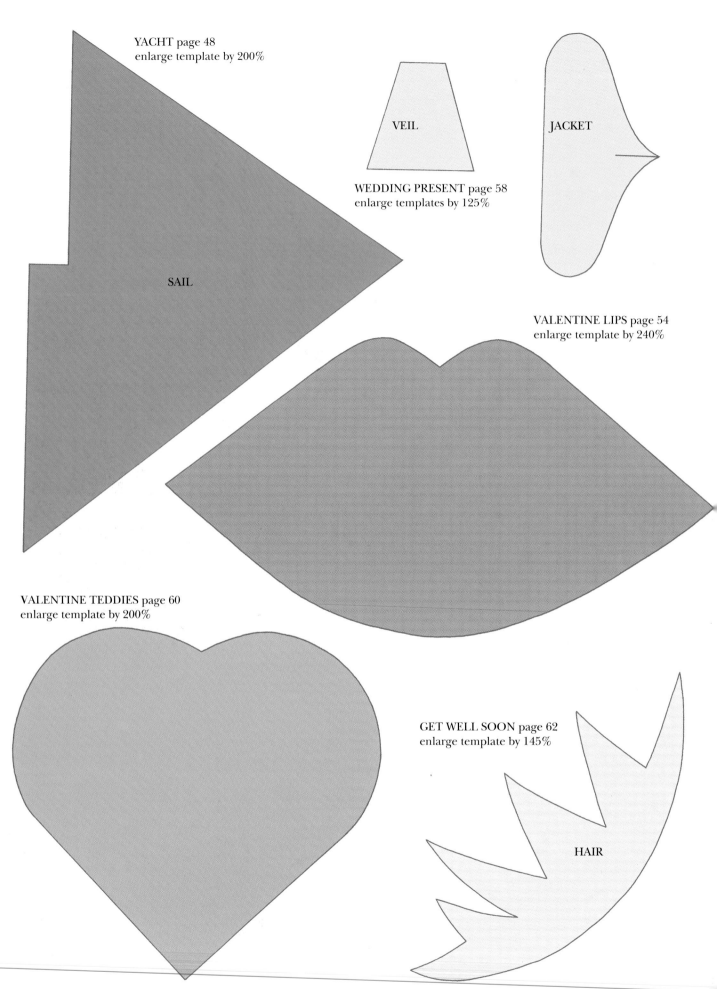

YACHT page 48
enlarge template by 200%

VEIL

JACKET

WEDDING PRESENT page 58
enlarge templates by 125%

SAIL

VALENTINE LIPS page 54
enlarge template by 240%

VALENTINE TEDDIES page 60
enlarge template by 200%

GET WELL SOON page 62
enlarge template by 145%

HAIR

All templates on this page are at actual size

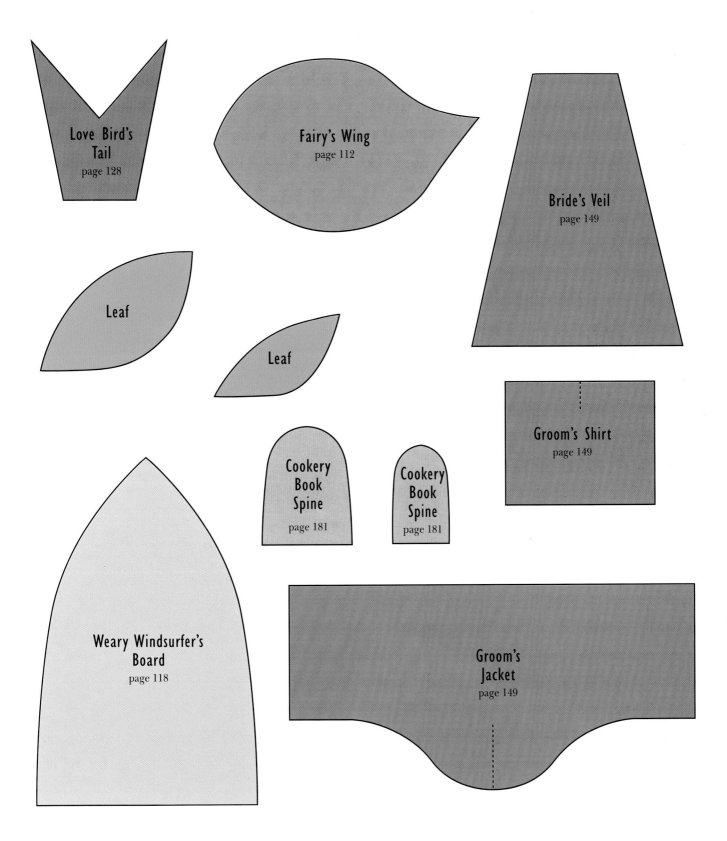

Love Bird's
Tail
page 128

Fairy's Wing
page 112

Bride's Veil
page 149

Leaf

Leaf

Groom's Shirt
page 149

Cookery
Book
Spine
page 181

Cookery
Book
Spine
page 181

Weary Windsurfer's
Board
page 118

Groom's
Jacket
page 149

Suppliers

UNITED KINGDOM

The British Sugarcraft
Guild
Wellington House
Messeter Place
London SE9 5DP
Tel: (020) 8859 6943

The Cake Makers Depot
57 The Tything
Worcester
WR1 1JT
Tel: 01905 25468

Confectionery Supplies
29-31 Lower Cathedral
Road
Cardiff
CF1 8LU
Tel: 01222 372161
Also outlets in Bristol,
Hereford and Swansea

Culpitt Ltd
Jubilee Industrial Estate
Ashington
NE63 8UQ
Tel: 01670 814545
Website: www.culpitt.com
Freephone enquiry line:
0845 601 0574
Distributor of cake
decorations, telephone for
your nearest retail outlet

Jane Asher Party Cakes
22-24 Cale Street
London SW3 3QU
Tel: (020) 7584 6177
Fax: (020) 7584 6179
Website:
www.jane-asher.co.uk
Range of equipment for
sale, cake tins and wedding
stands for hire

Kit Box
1 Fernlea Gardens
Easton in Gordano
Bristol BS20 0JF
Tel/Fax: (01275) 374557
Cutters, tools
and templates

London Sugarart Centre
12 Selkirk Road
London SW17 0ES
Tel: (020) 8767 8558
Fax: (020) 8767 9939
Everything for the cake
decorator - cake tins, cake
decorating equipment
and accessories

Orchard Products
51 Hallyburton Road
Hove
East Sussex BN3 7GP
Tel: 0800 9158 226
Fax: (01273) 412512
Fine quality sugarcraft
cutters and tools

Pipe Dreams
2 Bell Lane
Eton Wick
Windsor
Berkshire SL4 6JP
Tel: (01753) 865682
Tools, accessories, cake
stands and tins

Renshaw Scott Ltd
229 Crown Street
Liverpool
L8 7RF
Tel: (0151) 706 8200
Websites:
www.renshawscott.co.uk
or www.supercook.co.uk
Manufacturers and
distributors of cake
decorations and baking
supplies, including the
Supercook brand

Special Occasions
39 High Street
Kirkaldy
Fife, Scotland
KY1 1LB
Tel: (01592) 267 635
Large selection of
equipment

Squire's Kitchen
International School
of Cake Decorating
and Sugarcraft
Squire's House
3 Waverley Lane
Farnham
Surrey
GU9 8BB
Tel: (01252) 734309
Fax: (01252) 714714
Website:
www.squires-group.co.uk
Courses in cake
decoration and sugarcraft
Online shop for specialist
sugarcraft products:
www.squires-shop.co.uk

SOUTH AFRICA

The Baking Tin
52 Belvedere Road
Claremont
7700
Cape Town
Tel: (021) 671 6434

South Bakels
55 Section Street
Paarden Eiland
7420
Cape Town
Tel: (021) 511 1381

Confectionery
Extravaganza
Shop 48, Flora Centre
Ontdekkers Road

Florida, Roodepoort
1724
Johannesburg
Tel: (011) 672 4766

South Bakels
235 Main Road
Martindale
2092
Johannesburg
Tel: (011) 673 2100

Chefs and Ices
Shop 3, Lower Level
Sandton City
Sandton
2196
Johannesburg
Tel: (011) 783 3201

Party's, Crafts and
Cake Decor
Shop 4, East Rand Mall
Rietfontein Road
Boksburg
1459
Johannesburg
Tel: (011) 823 1988

Chocolate Den
Glen Dower Shopping
Centre
99 Linksfield Road
Glen Dower
Edenvale
1609
Johannesburg
Tel: (011) 453 8167

The Baking Tin
Shop 108, Glenwood
Village
Cnr Hunt & Moore Road
Glenwood
4001
Durban
Tel: (031) 202 2224

Jem Cutters
128 Crompton Street
Pinetown
3610
Durban
Tel: (031) 701 1431
Fax: (031) 701 0559

Bubbles Plastic
11 Cobalt Street
Border Industries
Rustenburg
0299
Tel: (014) 538 0236
Fax: (014) 538 0250

South Bakels
125 Pat Mullin Street
Bloemfontein
9301
Tel: (051) 435 7224

The Baking Tin
Rochel Road
Perridgevale
6001
Port Elizabeth
Tel: (041) 363 0271

South Bakels
41 Patterson Road
North End
6001
Port Elizabeth
Tel: (041) 484 2878

AUSTRALIA

NSW

Cake Art Supplies
Kiora Mall
Shop 26 Kiora Rd
MIRANDA
NSW 2228
Tel: (02) 9540 3483

Hollywood Cake
Decorations
52 Beach St
KOGARAH
NSW 2217
Tel: (02) 9587 1533

SA

The Cake Decorating
Centre
36 Timwilliam St
GOODWOOD
SA 5034
Tel: (08) 8271 1171

VIC

Susie Q
Shop 4/372, Keilor Rd
NIDDRIE
VIC 3042
Tel:(03) 9379 2275

QLD

Cake and Icing Centre
651 Samford Rd
MITCHELTON
QLD 4053
Tel: (07) 3355 3443

WA

Petersen's Cake
Decorations
370 Cnr South St and
Stockdale Rd
OCONNOR
WA 6163
Tel: (08) 9337 9636

TAS

Gum Nut Cake and Craft
Supplies
SORELL
TAS 7172
Tel: (03) 6265 1463

NEW ZEALAND

Auckland

Chocolate Boutique
5 Mokoia Road
Birkenhead
Tel: (09) 419 2450

Decor Cakes Ltd
435 Great South Road
Otahuhu
Tel: (09) 276 6676

Golden Bridge
Marketing Ltd
8 Te Kea Place
Albany
Tel: (09) 415 8777

Innovations Specialty
Cookware
52 Mokoia Road
Birkenhead
Tel: (09) 480 8885

Milly's Kitchen Shop
273 Ponsonby Road
Ponsonby
Tel: (09) 376 1550

Regina Special Cake
Designs
419 Dominion Road
Mt Eden
Tel: (09) 638 6363

Spotlight
(branches throughout New
Zealand)
19 Link Drive
Glenfield
Tel: (09) 444 0220
www.spotlightonline.co.nz

Sugarcrafts NZ Ltd
99 Queens Road
Panmure
Tel: (09) 527 6060

Wellington

Starline Distributors Ltd
28 Jessie Street
Wellington
Tel: (04) 385 7424

Christchurch

Hitchon International Ltd
220 Antiqua Street
Christchurch
Tel: (03) 365 3843

Icing Specialists
Equipment
Shop 6, Church Corner
Mall
Riccarton
Tel: (03) 348 6828

Index

Reprinted in 2012
First published in 2003 by
New Holland Publishers (UK) Ltd
London • Cape Town • Sydney • Auckland
www.newhollandpublishers.com

Garfield House, 86-88 Edgware Road, London W2 2EA, United Kingdom
Wembley Square, Solan Street, Gardens, Cape Town 8000, South Africa
Level 1, Unit 4, 14 Aquatic Drive, Frenchs Forest, NSW 2086, Australia
218 Lake Road, Northcote, Auckland, New Zealand

ISBN 978 1 84330 474 6

Production: Hazel Kirkman
Co-ordinating Editor: Emily Preece-Morrison
Cover Design: Glyn Bridgewater
Editors: Gillian Haslam and Caroline Plaisted
Designers: Paul Cooper and Helen Gibson
Photographer: Edward Allwright
Managing Editor: Coral Walker
Editorial Direction: Rosemary Wilkinson

Reproduction by Hirt & Carter Cape (Pty) Ltd
Printed and bound by Times Offset (M) Sdn Bhd.

ACKNOWLEDGEMENTS

The author and publishers would like to thank Renshaw Scott Ltd for supplying sugarpaste, Cake Art Ltd for equipment,
Divertimenti for the loan of the kitchen equipment and the Carlton Food Network News.

Carol Deacon would also like to thank Tory Brettell, Kath Christensen, Sandy Dale, Nicola Gill, Sally Hodgson, Chris Jones
and Claire Stickland for their unwavering support during various cake crises over the years; Richard Shelton for the use of
his kitchen; and Richard Dale and Anna Hodgson for inspiring the Windsurfer and Christening cakes respectively.

Important: In the recipes, use either metric or imperial measurements, but never a
combination of the two, as exact conversions are not always possible. Every effort has been
made to present clear and accurate instructions. Therefore, the author and publishers can
accept no liability for any injury, illness or damage which may inadvertently be caused to the
user whilst following these instructions.